Grandmaster Chess

Glenn Flear

CADOGAN CHESS
LONDON, NEW YORK

CADOGAN BOOKS DISTRIBUTION

UK/EUROPE/AUSTRALASIA/ASIA/AFRICA
Distribution: Grantham Book Services Ltd, Isaac Newton Way,
Alma Park Industrial Estate, Grantham, Lincs NG31 9SD
Tel: (01476) 67421 Fax: (01476) 590223

USA/CANADA/LATIN AMERICA/JAPAN
Distribution: Paramount Distribution Center, Front and Brown
Streets, Riverside, New Jersey 08075, USA
Tel: (609) 461 6500 Fax: (609) 764 9122

First published 1995 by Cadogan Books plc, London House,
Parkgate Road, London SW11 4NQ

Copyright © 1995 Glenn Flear

British Library Cataloguing in Publication Data
A CIP catalogue record for this book is available from the British
Library.

ISBN 1 85744 100 1

Cover photographs by Mark Huba
Cover design by Brian Robins
Typesetting by B. B. Enterprises
Printed in Great Britain by BPC Wheatons Ltd, Exeter

A CADOGAN CHESS BOOK
Chief Advisor: Garry Kasparov
Editor: Andrew Kinsman
Russian Series Editor: Ken Neat

For a complete catalogue of CADOGAN CHESS books please write
to: Cadogan Books plc, London House, Parkgate Road,
London SW11 4NQ. Tel: (0171) 738 1961 Fax: (0171) 924 5491

Contents

Introduction

This book is a look at modern grandmaster chess, a world of exciting and exotic places (although not always!), weird and wonderful characters, and of course some terrific games of chess. I have detailed the main happenings of 1994 and picked out those games that shaped the chess year, and I hope the reader finds my selection of games and events both representative and enjoyable. However, it is merely a selection of the thousands of games and hundreds of tournaments that make up professional chess in the 1990s, and I hope that the result is both informative and a useful source of reference.

In recent years there has a been tremendous expansion in chess literature; there are now dozens of teaching manuals and huge theoretical tomes on every popular opening. Such books are necessary but I personally found in my youth that the most enjoyable books to read were games collections, or those covering tournaments and matches. Nowadays these are somewhat out of fashion and this collection of the best games by the best players introduces this type of book in a modern setting.

One possible criticism of my approach is that magazines already tell the story of the recent past. This is true, but each periodical gears its coverage to its readership, such as over-emphasis on domestic tournaments, and I am frequently dissatisfied with the quality of their annotations. I have tried to be objective in annotating games and in covering controversial events, so if the reader objects to something that I have written then I apologize in advance.

Glenn Flear
January 1995

1 A Brief Summary of 1993

A look at 1994 naturally needs a beginning and where better to start than 1993!

The FIDE World Championship cycle is currently a three-year affair, and 1993 was the year in which the Zonals and Interzonals took place. Boris Gelfand won the Biel Interzonal outright and Paul van der Sterren was the shock qualifier. The top ten (including Viswanathan Anand who scraped in at the death) joined Jan Timman and Artur Yusupov (semi-finalists from the previous cycle) in the first round of the FIDE Candidates matches in January (see Chapter 3).

Meanwhile the previous cycle was continuing; Nigel Short edged out Timman 7½-5½ and then national adulation turned to shock and confusion as Garry Kasparov and Short broke away from FIDE to form the Professional Chess Association (PCA). Throughout the year there was much speculation, rumour and bad feeling but the result of it all was the establishment of a parallel World Championship cycle.

Kasparov beat Short 12½-7½ after an explosive start, followed by a rather tame end to the match, to become the first PCA World Champion. Karpov and Timman filled the void created by FIDE's disqualification of the rebels and Karpov won equally convincingly by a score of 12½-8½.

We now had two world champions; FIDE's Karpov, for the second time(!), as a result of the holder relinquishing the crown, and the PCA's Kasparov, still widely recognized as the strongest player.

There was little general support for the rebels' action but FIDE chose to drop them from the international rating list, a move seen by many as petty. At first, the PCA was almost universally viewed with suspicion but when their own 'alternative' cycle (see Chapter 2) got off the ground in December most top players participated. Further, with the announcement that a series of PCA-run quickplay events (well sponsored by Intel) would take place in 1994 (see Chapter 4) and the introduction of a PCA rating list, the rebels had to be taken seriously.

Kasparov had overall a good year in 1993, winning Linares (the world's strongest tournament) with 1st Kasparov on 10 points, 2nd=

Anand and Karpov on 8½, but Linares 1994 (see Chapter 5) was to be a different story.

The Women's World Championship final was a very one-sided affair; Xie Jun demolishing Nana Ioseliani 8½-2½. There would certainly have been more media interest if Zsuzsa Polgar had been playing, but she had squandered a seemingly invincible lead in the Candidates final allowing a fortunate Nana Ioseliani to win the play-off. Judit, her younger sister, made further progress in 1994, including the best ever result by a woman (see Chapter 5). Developments in women's chess are otherwise covered in Chapter 7.

In 1993, the Junior World Champion was Mladinovic, from 'the rest of Yugoslavia', and the Girls' Champion Churtsidse of Georgia; both came from war-weary lands. It's hard to explain how the former Soviet republic of only five and a half million people can produce so many of the world's leading female players.

Team chess (see Chapter 9) can be a lucrative source of income for the top echelon, especially in Germany where the 'Bundesliga' is well established. France has also developed team chess to the extent that Kasparov and Karpov both participated in the league in 1993. Lyon-Oyannax, the European Champions of 1993, were 'French', although the entire team of six (Lautier, Anand, Shirov, Dorfman, Vaiser and Sharif) could manage only one French parent between them!

The most important team event of 1993 was the World Team Championships, held as always in Lucerne, Switzerland. The USA surprisingly clinched first, ahead of the Ukraine with Russia only third, but nations such as the USA and Israel have gradually been strengthened by the arrival of several ex-Soviet grandmasters, indeed Larry Christiansen was the only 'home-grown' American.

The last major development of the year was the PCA Qualifier in Groningen, which is the starting point of the next chapter. Throughout the last few months of the year there was much speculation that the event would not take place, which might have been because of genuine teething problems or disinformation by the chess media, but when it finally got under way it was clear that the PCA meant business.

Ironically, one year later the Greek government and FIDE had problems seeing eye-to-eye over the financing of the intended Thessaloniki Olympiad and the much-maligned PCA stepped-in to save the event. So in December 1994 the Moscow Olympiad came about (thank you Garry!) and the political playing field has again had its goal posts realigned. But now I'm jumping ahead; for the purposes of our story we start with the PCA Qualifier over Christmas in Groningen.

2 The PCA Cycle

The PCA had come into being as a result of wrangling and power-struggling between some of the world's top names. If as 1994 approached it could get its own cycle into motion then the lay observer could then at least see something positive coming out of all the politics i.e. more top-quality chess.

Most of the leading grandmasters seemed to be willing to participate in both World Championship cycles; hysterical animosity between the two rival camps was not shared by players more naturally concerned by prize funds. The Intel Corporation had come up with over $200,000 for the Groningen 'Interzonal' plus the guarantee of megabucks for the seven qualifiers, so it was no surprise that three-quarters of the world's fifty-odd 2600 players were there.

Groningen in December 1993 was to be the first tournament run by the Professional Chess Association but it bore great similarity to FIDE's Biel Interzonal run a few months earlier. The main difference is that the FIDE cycle has an additional earlier stage; the regional Zonal tournaments which allow lesser mortals the chance to qualify.

PCA qualifier, Groningen

The qualifiers:
1	M.Adams	2630	ENG	7½/11
2	V.Anand	2725	IND	7½
3	G.Kamsky	2645	USA	7
4	V.Kramnik	2710	RUS	7
5	S.Tiviakov	2635	RUS	7
6	B.Gulko	2635	USA	7
7	O.Romanishin	2615	UKR	7

Those in the world's top ten that didn't make it:
8	A.Shirov	2685	LAT	6½
23	E.Bareev	2660	RUS	5½

45 Kir.Georgiev 2660 BUL 4½

The seven qualifiers were joined by Nigel Short for the next stage. The Trump Tower, New York in June was the venue for the PCA Candidates matches, quarter-finals.

PCA Candidates quarter-finals, New York (matchplay)

G.Kamsky	1 1 = = = 1	V.Kramnik	4½-1½
V.Anand	= 1 1 = = = 1	O.Romanishin	5-2
N.Short	= 0 1 = = = = =	B.Gulko	4 - 4
Play-off (30 mins each)			
N.Short	= = 1 =	B.Gulko	2½-1½
M.Adams	1 1 0 0 = 1 0 =	S.Tiviakov	4 - 4
Play-off (30 mins each)			
M.Adams	= = = = = 1	S.Tiviakov	3½-2½

(n.b. throughout the book the reporting of match results has been presented in standard form. Thus in Kamsky-Kramnik, Kamsky won the first two games, then there were three draws and Kamsky won the last game, etc.)

The United States was a home draw for two players: Kamsky, who won the first two games, both of which were rather wild encounters, and thereby essentially finished-off Kramnik; and Gulko, who took an early lead against Short, only to be caught and then lose in the lottery of the play-offs.

England's two participants showed their prowess at half-hour chess. Many would feel that half-an-hour for all one's moves is an inappropriate way to decide such important matches but it's certainly exciting for the public.

Anand's one-sided match was the only predictable result. He plays astonishingly quickly and even won one game (on time!) after using only 24 minutes of his allotted two hours.

So no players from the former Soviet Union (Kamsky was born in Tatarstan in Russia but defected some years ago and is now considered American) survived to the semi-finals. This fact alone virtually guaranteed Western media interest and another high profile final when Kasparov meets the winner of the series in 1995 for the PCA title.

When the pairings were made Kramnik had been widely tipped to beat Kamsky and along with Anand was strongly favourite to get a chance at Kasparov. His demise at the hands of Kamsky became less of a surprise with the benefit of hindsight; the American proving himself to be exceptionally good at matchplay and the only survivor in both cycles as the year came to a close.

The Candidates semi-finals of September in Linares saw the following matches

PCA Candidates semi-final, Linares (matchplay)

| G.Kamsky | 1 1 1 0 1 1 = | N.Short | 5½-1½ |
| V.Anand | 1 1 1 = 1 = = | M.Adams | 5½-1½ |

English hopes of a Short-Adams final were rudely dashed as both players were completely overwhelmed, making the latter stages of the semi-finals almost irrelevant.

Nigel Short's form in 1994 has been well below his best, perhaps he needs to set new goals as financial insecurity and his career peak are probably both behind him. He has to rediscover his enthusiasm for the game if he is to maintain his top ten ranking.

Michael Adams also never came into his match and didn't seem to really have any confidence in his defence to 1 e4 (he tried four openings in four games). Both he and Kramnik will go further next time given more thorough preparation in their approach.

So will it be Kamsky or Anand? In their recent match in the FIDE cycle (see Chapter 3) Kamsky sensationally came back from a two-point deficit to turn the tables. Will 'Vishy' (Anand) be that much tougher next time?

Game One
Michael Adams-Sergei Tiviakov
2nd match game
PCA Candidates quarter-finals, New York 1994

Michael Adams originally comes from Truro in Cornwall, England. In his early years he certainly got to know the British Rail network, covering the length and breadth of the country in his hunger for the game. Once he became established on the international scene, a base in London, with easy access to Heathrow Airport, became imperative, and he now lives a stone-throw away from his good friend and second, Grandmaster Julian Hodgson. This liaison has helped both players to advance; and the following game is an example of their meticulous research.

Having won the first game, his first ever victory over Tiviakov, Michael Adams must have approached this game with some confidence.

1	e4	c5
2	♘f3	d6
3	♗b5+	♘c6

I believe that 3...♗d7 is a sounder choice.

| 4 | 0-0 | ♗g4 |

The Russian has had some success with this line but he must already have suspected that his opponent had something new prepared.

5 h3!

Although 5 c3, after 5...♕b6, is similar to the game, the inclusion of first 5 h3 ♗h5 and only then 6 c3 turns out to be very important, as we shall see. After 5 c3 ♕b6 one of Tiviakov's previous games continued as follows: 6 ♗a4 ♘f6 7 d4 0-0-0 8 ♗xc6 ♕xc6 9 d5 ♕a6 10 ♖e1 e6 11 ♘a3 ♘d7 12 ♗f4 ♗e7 13 h3 ♗h5 14 c4 g5 15 ♗h2 g4 and Black had good play; Ulibin-Tiviakov, Oakham 1992.

| 5 | ... | ♗h5 |

5...♗xf3 gives up the important bishop cheaply, e.g. 6 ♕xf3 e6 7 d3 ♘ge7 8 ♗g5 ♕d7 9 c3 a6 10 ♗a4 ♘g6 11♘d2 b5 12 ♗c2 ♗e7 13 ♗e3 0-0 14 ♕h5 d5 15 exd5 exd5 16 d4 and White has some advantage due to his light-square pressure; Larsen-

Bronstein, Moscow 1962.

6 c3

The alternative 6 c4!? was tried by another of Tiviakov's opponents, but after 6...♘f6 7 g4!? ♗g6 8 e5 dxe5 9 ♘xe5 ♖c8 10 ♘c3 e6 11 ♕a4 ♕c7 12 ♖e1 ♗d6 Black had good counterplay against White's loose kingside; Oll-Tiviakov, St Petersburg 1993.

| 6 | ... | ♕b6 |

Adams and Hodgson (his second) had anticipated this variation in their pre-match preparation. The rest of the game should be a good lesson for those who always play the same way and leave themselves open to prepared improvements.

7	♘a3	a6
8	♗a4	♕c7
9	d4	b5

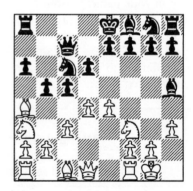

White can now retreat to b3 but, with the pin on the a4-e8 diagonal then broken, the pressure would be off.

10 ♘xb5!

An enterprising piece offer which, of course, would have

failed without the preparatory 5 h3 ♗h5; pushing the bishop back and therefore denying Black recourse to a defence based on ...♗d7.

| 10 | ... | axb5 |
| 11 | ♗xb5 | 0-0-0 |

White threatened 12 d5 so Black is forced to castle into open space.

12   b4!

A powerful novelty, worked out by Julian Hodgson, which essentially wins the game.

Less convincing is 12 ♕a4 when 12...♘b8 13 dxc5 ♗xf3 14 gxf3 dxc5 15 ♗f4 e5 (15...♕xf4 16 ♗a6+ looks immediately drawn as Black can hardly escape the threat of perpetual check) 16 ♖fd1 is rather unclear; Iskov-Larsen, Copenhagen 1979.

| 12 | ... | ♗xf3 |
| 13 | gxf3 | |

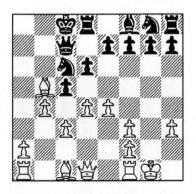

White has sacrificed a piece for two pawns. Black's kingside remains undeveloped and White threatens to open further lines against Black's king. Few players would relish the task of defending the black position.

| 13 | ... | ♘b8 |
| 14 | ♕a4 | |

After 14 bxc5 dxc5 15 ♕a4 e6 White opens up the queenside for the attack but also allows Black to more space for his defence. Instead, Adams is happy to allow the centre to become blocked as his opponent then suffers from being severely cramped.

| 14 | ... | c4 |
| 15 | d5! | |

Further restricting his opponent.

15	...	♘f6
16	♗e3	♘fd7
17	♗c6	e6
18	b5!	

White is less concerned with grabbing the c-pawn than carrying out the threat of playing 19 b6.

| 18 | ... | exd5 |
| 19 | exd5 | ♘b6 |

After 19...♗e7 White wins after 20 b6! ♘xb6 21 ♗xb6 ♕xb6 22 ♖ab1 ♕c7 23 ♕a8 as there is no defence to the threat of 24 ♖b7 (23...♖d7 is met by 24 ♗xd7+ ♔xd7 25 ♖b7).

20   ♕b4

White must avoid 20 ♕a5? in view of 20...♘xd5! etc.

20	...	♗e7
21	a4	♗f6
22	a5	

Black is totally swamped.

22	...	♘xc6
23	bxc6	♘xd5
24	♕b5	♖de8

25   ♗b6   1-0

After 25...♕e7 26 ♕a6+ (26 ♕xd5 also wins) 26...♔b8 27 ♖ab1 leads to mate. I suspect that

White's new move (12 b4) already gave him a winning position.

Game Two
Vladimir Kramnik-Gata Kamsky
2nd match game
PCA Candidates quarter-finals, New York 1994

Gata Kamsky's father, Rustam, was a boxer in his youth. His rather abrasive approach towards Gata's opponents is more typical of the fight game than the chess world, but despite widespread unpopularity Rustam has made his son into a tough chess battler, who is at home in many different openings and types of positions.

In this game the world's top two under-20's fight it out with the American Gata Kamsky successfully refuting Kramnik's aggression and taking a practically decisive two-nil lead.

1   ♘f3   ♘f6
2   c4

Kramnik's move-order leads to an English Opening, while avoiding those variations following 1 c4 e5.

2   ...   e6
3   ♘c3   ♗b4
4   g3   0-0
5   ♗g2   c5
6   0-0   ♘c6
7   d4

The opening can also arise via the Nimzo-Indian Defence, e.g. 1 d4 ♘f6 2 c4 e6 3 ♘c3 ♗b4 4 g3

c5 5 ♘f3 0-0 6 ♗g2 ♘c6 7 0-0.

7   ...   cxd4!?

Kamsky introduces a double-edged plan involving a timely ...♗xc3, crippling the white queenside pawns at the risk of problems on the dark squares. A solid alternative is 7...d6 maintaining the tension.

8   ♘xd4   ♕e7
9   ♘c2

If White doesn't wish to allow ...♗xc3 his last chance is to play 9 ♘a4(!?).

9   ...   ♗xc3
10   bxc3   ♖d8
11   ♗a3   d6

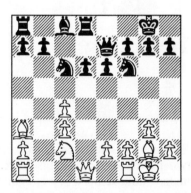

This particular position has

been seen before but is fairly un-usual. In this variation, White has two powerful bishops but the doubled c-pawns give Black a target for counterplay.

12 &b1

A natural developing move which had been previously sug-gested by Tukmakov, who con-tinues his analysis thus: 12...e5 13 ♘e3 ♗e6 'unclear'.

He also considers 12 ♘d4 and after 12...♘e5 13 ♕b3 ♘fd7 14 ♕b4 ♘c5 15 ♘b3 a5 16 ♘xa5 ♗d7 he again stops with the ubiquitous unclear assessment. Is White tangled-up (17 ♘xb7 ♖a4) or simply picking off pawns? The variation is rich in possibilities but probably White's best try is 12 ♕d2! when the continuation 12...♕c7 13 ♖fd1 d5 14 ♘e3 dxc4 15 ♗d6 ♕b6 16 ♖ab1 ♕a6 17 ♕b2 keeps Black rather pas-sive, as in Ribli-Ernst, Subotica Interzonal 1987, which was definitely better for White after the further 17...♘d5!? 18 ♘xd5 exd5 19 ♗c7 ♖e8 20 ♖xd5 ♗g4 21 ♕xb7.

12 ... ♕c7!

Getting off the a3-f8 diagonal and preparing for play on the c-file.

13 ♘d4 ♘xd4
14 cxd4!?

This pawn sacrifice is enter-prising but risky and was no doubt partially provoked by his loss in the previous game and the desire to immediately strike back. Kramnik was probably not im-pressed by the alternative 14 ♕xd4 as 14...e5 15 ♕d3 ♗e6 16 ♖xb7 ♕xc4 looks comfortable for Black. There the bishops compensate for the pawn weak-nesses and the chances would be more or less equal.

14 ... ♕xc4
15 ♕d2 ♕a6!

Covering the sensitive b7 and d6 squares with gain of tempo.

16 ♖b3 ♖b8

Black is now ready for 17...♗d7 followed by 18...♗c6.

17 e4?!

This natural move is uncon-vincing as the game continuation suggests. Interesting is 17 g4! intending to switch the rook on b3 over to the kingside. After 17...♗d7 (17...♘xg4? fails to 18 ♕g5 ♘f6 19 ♖g3 winning im-mediately) 18 g5, or 18 ♖h3 first, White has sufficient activity to compensate his pawn deficit.

17 ... ♗d7
18 ♖e1

White now only has vague threats for the sacrificed pawn but he must act quickly before the American is fully deployed.

18 ... ♗a4
19 ♖f3 ♖bc8

The intention is clear; to play ...♖c2 when possible.

20 ♗f1 ♗b5
21 ♗h3 ♕a4

Again preparing the invasion of c2.

22 d5

Defending against the imme-diate invasion by 22 ♖c3 is possible, but this abandons hope of mounting an attack on the king-side, and further, 22...♖xc3 23 ♕xc3 c4 24 ♕a5 b6 25 ♕xa7 ♕xd4 26 ♕c7 ♖a8 leaves White with absolutely no compensation for his efforts.

22	...	♖c2
23	♕e3	

23 ♕g5 is clearly unsatisfactory: 23...h6 24 ♕h4 ♖e2 25 ♖xe2 (25 ♖b1 ♖xe4 wins) 25...♕d1+ and Black wins.

23	...	exd5

Good enough is 23...e5?! as White's attack would probably fail, but 24 ♖xf6 gxf6 25 ♕h6 ♖e2 26 ♖c1! (rather than 26 ♗f5? ♖xe1+ 27 ♔g2 ♗f1+ 28 ♔f3 ♕d1+) could still cause a few awkward moments.

24	e5	

Desperate but dangerous. Now, after 24...dxe5 25 ♗e7 Black would suffer from the opening up of his king. However, Gata Kamsky was now able to coolly calculate a long forced win despite the tension of time trouble.

24	...	d4
25	♕g5 (D)	

Now comes a real blow.

25	...	♖e2!

White is forced to sacrifice as 26 ♖c1 ♖xe5 is hopeless.

26	exf6	♖xe1+
27	♗f1	♖xf1+
28	♔g2	♖g1+!
29	♔h3	

Of course 29 ♔xg1 ♕d1+ 30 ♔g2 ♕f1 is mate.

29	...	♗d7+

Being a rook up is fine but Black must still parry the mate!

30	♔h4	g6
31	♕h6	d3+
32	♖f4	♕xf4+!

The point of Black's play; he gives his queen but now it is White's king in the mating net.

33	♕xf4	

After 33 gxf4 Black wins by 33...♖g4+ 34 ♔h3 ♖g5+ 35 ♔h4 ♖h5+ etc.

33	...	♖h1
34	g4	h6!

Gaining time to surround the White monarch as 35 ♕xh6 is met by 35...♖xh2+.

35	♔h3	g5
36	♕d4	d2!
37	♕xd2	♖g1
38	f3	♗b5
	0-1	

White must give his queen to stop 39...♗f1 mating. An exciting game which virtually finished off Kramnik's chances of reaching the semi-finals.

Game Three
Viswanathan Anand-Michael Adams
1st match game
PCA Candidates semi-finals, Linares 1994

'Vishy' Anand, a Hindu and vegetarian, is a master tactician and the quickest thinker and player amongst the world elite. A popular and friendly person, he may lack the mean streak and killer-instinct necessary, it seems, to become world champion.

Very often the first game of a match between two equally-strong opponents can set the tone of the whole contest.

1   e4   ♘f6

A surprise, but this experiment wasn't repeated in later games.

2   e5   ♘d5
3   d4   d6
4   ♘f3   dxe5

The so-called Larsen variation is less popular than either 4...g6 and 4...♗g4. Black provokes the knight forward in order to seek its later exchange.

5   ♘xe5   g6

5...♘d7?! can be met by the aggressive 6 ♘xf7 ♔xf7 7 ♕h5+ ♔e6 8 c4.

6   g3!?

This solid move was mentioned by Hort in 1980 but has been largely ignored since. Anand uses the idea to channel the game away from likely pre-match preparation.

6   ...   ♗g7
7   ♗g2   0-0

8   0-0   c6
9   ♖e1   ♗f5
10   c3   ♘d7

By delaying this move until now, Black avoids anything unpleasant in the opening. Anand has cautiously avoided any outright attempt at refutation and settled for a nagging edge: pressure on the semi-open e-file and better central pawn deployment.

11   ♘f3!

Exchanges would ease Black's defence.

11   ...   ♖e8
12   ♘bd2

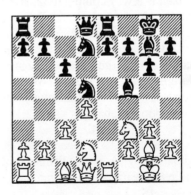

12   ...   ♘7f6?!

Black would like to break out with ....e7-e5, and if he can get away with it then it should be played. Can 12...e5!? be playable? White should try 13 ♘c4 (dull is 13 dxe5 ♘xe5 14 ♘xe5

♖xe5 15 ♖xe5 ♗xe5 16 ♘c4 ♗g7 with a level position) 13...♗g4 (after 13...exd4 14 ♖xe8+ ♕xe8 15 ♘d6 ♕e6 16 ♘xf5 ♕xf5 17 ♘xd4 the bishop pair guarantees a continuing edge for White) 14 ♘d6?! (14 dxe5! is best when the continuation 14...♘xe5 15 ♘cxe5 ♗xe5 16 ♕b3 probably forces 16...♗xf3 conceding the bishop pair) 14...♖e6 15 ♘xb7 ♕b6 16 ♕b3 with interesting complications favouring Black, e.g. 16...♗xf3 17 ♗xf3 exd4 18 ♖xe6 fxe6 19 cxd4 ♗xd4 20 ♕xb6 axb6 21 ♘d6 ♔f8 and despite the bishop pair White is tied up. So 12...e5 is playable but White can still claim a pull (with 14 dxe5). After the text move White puts a stop to Black's natural pawn-break and Black is always on the defensive.

13 ♘c4 ♕c7
14 ♘ce5 ♘g4?!

Adams again seeks the exchange of the strong central knight but overlooks White's next. 14...♘d7 was a better way of seeking exchanges.

15 ♘h4!

This must have been underestimated by Adams; White now gains a clearly superior game.

15 ... ♘xe5
16 ♘xf5 gxf5
17 dxe5 e6

Snatching a pawn by 17...♗xe5? actually loses one after 18 ♗xd5 cxd5 19 ♕xd5 ♗g7 20 ♕xf5 when White has a clear pawn more. Otherwise

17...♖ad8 18 ♕e2 e6 changes very little; White has his bishops and Black's kingside is compromised.

18 ♕e2 ♘e7

Michael decides on a slightly passive regrouping strategy rather than risk 18...b5 which would maintain the d5 outpost at the risk of further weaknesses.

19 f4 ♘d5

This seems like a waste of time. He should have preferred 19...♖ad8 20 ♗e3 ♖d7.

20 c4

With the bishop pair against him and space becoming a problem Michael has obviously lost the opening stage. This depressing scenario may have put him off the Alekhine (for the time being!) despite the improvement at move twelve.

20 ... ♘e7
21 ♗e3 ♖ad8
22 b4

After 22 ♗c5 then 22...♘c8 avoids an immediate invasion and, as in the game, Black will delay or omit ...b7-b6 which weakens the a8-h1 diagonal.

22 ... ♖d7
23 ♕f2 ♘c8
24 a4

The general expansion of the queen's wing is well supported by the bishop pair. A refinement is the exchange of one pair of rooks by 24 ♖ad1 or 24 ♖ed1 before the general queenside advance is implemented. This preempts any counterplay that

Black's doubled rooks on the d-file might generate.

| 24 | ... | ♖ed8 |
| 25 | a5 | |

White is finally threatening 26 ♗xa7 which up to now could earlier have been met by ...b7-b6.

| 25 | ... | f6! |

Striking back at the centre is Black's best hope. Now that he is better organized he can afford to weaken the e6-point to liberate his bishop.

26	exf6	♗xf6
27	♖ab1	♗c3
28	♖f1	♖d3
29	♔h1	

Necessary in view of the threat 29...♖xe3 30 ♕xe3 ♗d4.

| 29 | ... | ♗d4 |
| 30 | ♗xd4 | |

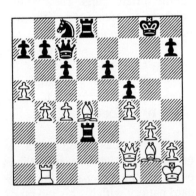

Black has been able to cause some general mischief, temporarily distracting his opponent from active operations. Now he must decide how to recapture.

| 30 | ... | ♖3xd4? |

A poor move allowing White to cut the communication between the black rooks.

Evidently 30...♖8xd4 was a better try meeting 31 ♕e2 by 31...♕d7 (intending 32...♖xc4 or 32...♘d6 followed by a later ...♘e4) although with 32 c5! and ♕e5 to follow White keeps the better prospects.

| 31 | ♖fe1! | |

The immediate 31 ♗d5 is less clear after 31...cxd5 32 ♕xd4 dxc4 with some play for the exchange.

| 31 | ... | ♕f7 |

31...♖xc4 permits 32 ♕e2 ♘d6 33 ♕xe6+ ♔g7 34 ♕e5+ ♔g6 35 ♖bd1 when White has a powerful attack.

| 32 | ♗d5! | ♕g7 |

32...♖4xd5 33 cxd5 exd5 was objectively better but 34 ♖e5 ♘d6 35 ♖be1 ♘e4 36 ♕xa7 ♕h5 37 ♔g2 is also hopeless.

| 33 | ♖e5 | |

33 ♗xe6+ was simple and good, but the text is stronger.

33	...	♖4xd5
34	cxd5	cxd5
35	g4!	

Moving in for the kill. Black loses his queen if he captures the g-pawn.

35	...	♘e7
36	♖xe6	fxg4
37	♕h4	♖d7
38	♖be1	♔f8
39	f5	1-0

The loss of the first game was the beginning of a one-sided match as the Indian grandmaster convincingly outperformed the Englishman.

Game Four
Gata Kamsky-Nigel Short
5th match game
PCA Candidates semi-finals, Linares 1994

For family reasons Nigel Short has recently moved from London to Greece. Perhaps the controversy associated with his involvement as a founder-member of the PCA has affected him more than he anticipated. Several previously close colleagues condemned his actions, and this may have affected his form. Certainly the magic of his matchplay in 1992-93 has not been so evident in the past twelve months.

Having dominated the first three games, Kamsky's progress to the Candidates final had been temporarily halted by a loss in the fourth game. If Short was to have a chance he could not afford to lose another game.

1	d4	♘f6
2	c4	e6
3	♘c3	

Kamsky has a very wide repertoire and is willing to play just about anything. Short, on the other hand, used to stick to only a few variations. However, in recent matches, to broaden his once rather limited range of openings, he has tried several defences to the queen's pawn. Nowadays, in the computer-age, the top echelon must adapt to rapid changes in opening theory to stay ahead of their contemporaries.

| 3 | ... | ♗b4 |

The Nimzo-Indian has always been in his repertoire despite flirtations with the Dutch, Queen's Gambit Accepted and Orthodox Queen's Gambit.

4	e3	c5
5	♗d3	♘c6
6	♘ge2	

The Hübner variation (6 ♘f3 ♗xc3+ 7 bxc3 d6 with ...e6-e5 to follow) has proven to be very sound, Black gives up the bishop but stations his central pawns on dark squares. Indeed, the closed centre often suits the 'knight pair', so in recent years the text move has been preferred.

6	...	cxd4
7	exd4	d5
8	cxd5	♘xd5
9	0-0	♗d6
10	♘e4	♗e7
11	a3	

All this has been seen at grandmaster level many times before. White prepares the standard battery with his bishop on c2 and queen on d3. Black can avoid immediate problems with ...g7-g6, but this inevitably loosens his control of some important dark squares.

11	...	0-0
12	♗c2	

Compared with many isolated

queen's pawn positions the knight on e2 is less active (than if it were on the typical f3 square) but White can still maintain some early pressure by avoiding exchanges.

12 ... 🗌e8

Black could have tried 12...e5!? immediately hitting back at the centre. Instead we have a typical isolated queen's pawn (IQP) game.

13 ♕d3 g6
14 ♗h6 b6
15 🗌ad1

Black would like to steady things down, exchange a few pieces and exploit the long-term weakness of the d4-isolani in the ending. White has to use his temporary activity to open up Black's king defences.

The alternative 15 🗌ac1 is less critical as this can lead to possible rook exchanges on the c-file, a course of action that would generally suit the second player. Semkov-Psakhis, Erevan 1988, then continued 15...♗b7 16 🗌fd1 🗌c8 17 ♕g3 ♘f6 18 ♘g5 ♕d6 and White's attack failed to breakthrough the black defensive set-up.

15 ... ♗b7
16 🗌fe1 🗌c8 (D)
17 ♗b3!

17 ♘2c3 ♘a5 18 ♕g3 ♘c4 19 ♗a4 ♗c6 20 ♗b3 was certainly very complex in the game Shirov-Psakhis, Klaipeda 1988. Black won this encounter and Kamsky must have prepared the text as a

refinement. See also the game Judit Polgar against Tiviakov (Chapter 7) for another example of this theme; the bishop redeploys now that ...g7-g6 has been provoked.

17 ... a6

After 17...♘a5, 18 ♗a2 keeps the black knight out of the important c4 square. The bishop has annoying pressure along the a2-g8 diagonal.

18 ♘2g3

Avoiding exchanges that may result from 18 ♘2c3 and heading towards the Englishman's monarch.

18 ... ♘b8?

It's true that the knight was rather in the way on c6 and redeploying the beast to d7 improves the scope of the queen's rook and bishop, but it's all too slow. Better is the prophylactic 18...♗h4 avoiding White's twentieth move and even allowing further support for his king by ...♘ce7 and ...♘f5.

19 ♕f3 🗌c7

Defending both b7 and (indirectly) f7, however in view of what now happens 19...♗h4 should still have been tried.

20　♘h5!　♘d7

20...gxh5? allows 21 ♕g3+ winning.

21　h4!

Intensifying the pressure. The pawn will later go onwards to h5, support a piece on g5 or play the role of a decoy.

21　...　♘7f6

21...♗xh4 has been given elsewhere as an improvement but in fact White wins by force: 22 ♘d6 ♖e7 23 g3 ♗f6 24 ♘xb7 ♖xb7 25 ♗xd5 exd5 26 ♘xf6+! (rather than 26 ♕xd5? with only an edge) 26...♘xf6 27 ♕xf6! ♖xe1+ 28 ♖xe1 ♕xf6 29 ♖e8 mate.

22　♘hxf6+　♘xf6
23　d5!

A decisive line-opening blow. There are now many options but no defence:

a) 23...exd5 24 ♘xf6+ ♗xf6 25 ♕xf6! and White mates in three;

b) 23...♘xd5 24 ♗xd5 ♗xd5 25 ♖xd5 exd5 (25...♕xd5 26 ♘f6+ etc.) 26 ♘f6+ ♗xf6 27

♖xe8+ ♕xe8 28 ♕xf6 ♖c1+ 29 ♔h2 ♕b8+ 30 g3 concludes neatly;

c) 23...e5 24 d6 ♗xe4 25 ♖xe4 ♗xd6 26 ♗g5 pins and wins.

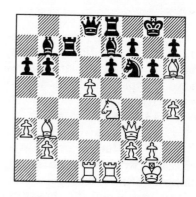

23　...　♘xe4
24　dxe6　f5

This is no defence but at least Short makes it past move 25!

25　♖xd8　♖xd8
26　♖d1　1-0

Enough is enough. Black only has a rook and minor piece for the queen and the enormous e6-pawn. White will transfer his queen to the a1-h8 diagonal with a quick mate. An excellent display in the handling of an IQP position by Kamsky.

3 The FIDE Cycle

Since the Second World War, FIDE, the international chess federation, has had total control over the World Championship. The events surrounding the formation of the PCA have, for the first time, seen competition in the form of an alternative cycle. The confused public has the right to ask the question: What are the differences?

A few players for personal reasons have preferred not to participate in one cycle or other (Salov, for instance, shunned the PCA Qualifier because he doesn't get on with Kasparov) but most top players see the PCA cycle as an opportunity for extra earnings and to double their chances! FIDE organize a first stage of world-wide Zonal tournaments which enables a few unlikely players to qualify for the Interzonal. The PCA do not and will eventually be accused of concerning itself only with the top echelon unless they intend to open it up.

In years gone by there used to be two or three closed Interzonal tournaments but in 1993 a lone Swiss system event in Biel determined the ten places in the 1993-95 FIDE World Championship. PCA's Groningen Qualifier was a very similar affair, as we saw in the last chapter.

The ten qualifiers plus Timman and Yusupov, as losing semi-finalists in the previous Candidates, received invitations for the first round of matches in Wijk aan Zee, January 1994. Note that Nigel Short was not invited nor was Garry Kasparov (hell hath no fury...) as they were deemed to have defaulted such privileges.

Karpov was to join in at the semi-final stage, a significant change, as earlier World Champions have only ever had to play one match (the final) to retain the title (as is still the case in the PCA event).

The PCA have announced a major coup in obtaining a sponsor for their cycle whereas FIDE have had a piecemeal approach for each stage with varying degrees of success.

The first round of the FIDE Candidates took place in Wijk aan Zee in the Netherlands in January:

FIDE Candidates first round, Wijk aan Zee (matchplay)

V.Anand	= 1 1 0 1 = =	A.Yusupov	4½-2½
B.Gelfand	= = = 1 0 1 = 1	M.Adams	5-3
G.Kamsky	1 0 1 1 = = =	P.van der Sterren	4½-2½
V.Kramnik	1 = = = 1 = =	L.Yudasin	4½-2½
V.Salov	1 = 1 1 = 1	A.Khalifman	5-1
J.Timman	= 1 0 = 1 = = =	J.Lautier	4½-3½

Several players managed to qualify for both the FIDE and the PCA Candidates matches. As an aside, I imagine that the most likely way of re-unifying the split in the chess establishment is if someone such as Anand or Kamsky were to battle his way through and overpower both Kasparov and Karpov! Already various challengers have complained about the tough task of winning four matches to become world champion, but to take both crowns the challenger will have to win seven!

There were only two matches that needed all eight games: Gelfand-Adams and Timman-Lautier. The young Cornish player was eliminated when Gelfand won the eighth and final game; Adams weakening his own queenside as he desperately sought a win with Black. Gelfand's extra experience in matchplay was probably the decisive factor in an otherwise even pairing.

Michael suffers from not really being a theoretical specialist. He gets round this by trying to 'pick and choose' his openings to avoid his opponent's preparation. His win in round five came from the c3 Sicilian (fairly unusual at 2600+ level) but his loss in round four resulted from a Queen's Gambit Accepted which transposed to a Petroff's Defence! Unfortunately it was Michael who seemed to be the more confused. Further, in round six 1 d4 d6 2 e4 ♘f6 3 f3 d5!? was an interesting idea but one with which he was unable to equalize.

Joel Lautier of France pushed Timman hard in perhaps the closest fought of the six matches. The Queen's Gambit Accepted featured in three games, the first was drawn, game three was won by Lautier but Timman won game five. Lautier adopted 1 d4 d5 2 c4 dxc4 3 e4 ♘c6!? on each occasion, a line frequently employed by his second, Matthew Sadler. The only other decisive result was in the second game where Timman, as Black, won a long struggle despite having had a very dubious position in the early middlegame. In the final game, Lautier needing a win to tie the score, adjourned with winning chances in a difficult ending. However, despite the extensive analytical efforts of

Matthew Sadler he didn't make the best of his chances and Timman gratefully held the draw. The other encounters went more or less as expected.

In the summer the FIDE cycle moved to Sanghi Nagar in India, where the locals had high hopes of their young star, Vishy Anand.

FIDE Candidates second round, Sanghi Nagar (matchplay)

B.Gelfand	= = 0 1= = = 1	V.Kramnik	4½-3½
V.Salov	0 = = 1 = = 1 =	J.Timman	4½-3½
G.Kamsky	= = 0 0 = 1 1 =	V.Anand	4-4
Play-off			
G.Kamsky	1 1	V.Anand	2-0

By a remarkable quirk of fate, all three second round matches all began in favour of the eventual loser. Kramnik took an early lead in his match against Gelfand but was pegged back to all-square in game four. As the tension mounted after three draws he was again criticized for the quality of his opening preparation, which cost him the eighth and final game as a result of a schoolboy blunder. Gelfand's nerve was again tested in this match but he remained solid and converted the final point to earn the right to play Karpov (who, as FIDE Champion, was exempt until the last four). Interestingly, in November in Cap D'Agde on the French Mediterranean, Gelfand defeated Karpov in the blitz play-off of a mini-match. Karpov was pressing but Gelfand took his chances to run out victor. I don't believe that Karpov will underestimate his opponent next time.

The Dutchman Timman has had a long and up and down career. By far the veteran of the six players in Sanghi Nagar, he has over the years produced more than his fair share of brilliant games and with his entertaining and provocative analyses he remains a good model player for the young enthusiast. However, his confident approach sometimes leads to over-optimism and he tends to be rather inconsistent, his name frequently appearing either at the very top or the very bottom of the tournament table. He is often drawn into playing fashionable variations in which he introduces his own brand of novelties and exciting chess. When on form this approach reaps dividends, but when below par... Always self-critical, Timman would be the first to admit that his best form has eluded him of late, and in particular in this match. In fact, Salov's early loss was due to the Russian overplaying his hand. After that Salov was almost always in control.

The Spanish-based Russian Valery Salov is an out-spoken critic of Garry Kasparov, the PCA and anyone who he judges to be in that camp. His White openings seem benign, but he scores very well with Black. In his youth Salov was something of a tactical theoretician, but nowadays, although still a young man, he has moved towards a slow manoeuvring style similar to that of the Swedish Grandmaster Ulf Andersson. It must be disconcerting for his opponents to see a youthful-looking Salov steering towards unspectacular endings and then outplaying them with the refined technique of a player many years older. In 1994 Salov made great strides, advancing to FIDE semi-finals and achieving an outstanding result at Tilburg. But, with his entrance into the political arena (with open letters to the powers-that-be with suggestions how to put the chess world's problems right) will he become distracted from his assault on the world title?

Anand seemed to be coasting to victory in his match with Kamsky, two up with three to play. However, Kamsky again showed his great fighting qualities to turn the Indian celebrations into mourning with an unlikely comeback. In the play-off a demoralized Anand was a shadow of his normal self and was dismissed easily. There is no doubt that Kamsky will be totally focused in his forthcoming match with Salov.

A number of the players in Sanghi Nagar were dissatisfied with the conditions arranged by the Indian authorities. With the semi-finals scheduled to take place at the same venue, the players' anxieties about health, food, climate, etc., could cause some problems for FIDE. In any case Indian support for the local hero Anand was the source of such great interest in the second round matches: with Anand eliminated, would there be the same enthusiasm?

Game Five
Leonid Yudasin-Vladimir Kramnik
1st match game
FIDE Candidates first round, Wijk aan Zee 1994

Both Yudasin and Kramnik were new to the Candidates stage of the World Championship. Kramnik settled first and won this, their opening encounter. Yudasin, now playing under the Israeli flag, did miss a win and the chance to equalize the match in the third game but otherwise Kramnik was in control. With White Kramnik made little headway but as Black in complex Sicilians (such as this one) his talent came to the fore.

1	e4	c5
2	♘f3	♘c6
3	d4	cxd4
4	♘xd4	♘f6
5	♘c3	e5

Kramnik employed this variation more frequently a few years ago when it was generally more popular. Although called by a variety of names modern practitioners call it the Sveshnikov after the Russian grandmaster who did so much to develop it.

6	♘db5	d6
7	♘d5	

The main line follows 7 ♗g5 a6 8 ♘a3 b5 9 ♘d5 when Black has active play but an inferior pawn structure. Black's early ...e7-e5 in the Sicilian gains time and challenges directly for the centre at the cost of potential problems on d5 and d6.

Yudasin's move saves a tempo but more importantly establishing a queenside majority. Black in compensation has an extra pawn on the other wing where his chances of counterplay lie.

7	...	♘xd5
8	exd5	♘e7

The other retreat 8...♘b8 is generally followed by 9 c4 ♗e7 10 ♗e2 a6 11 ♘c3 0-0 12 0-0 when Black will seek activity by ...f7-f5 and the redeployment of the knight to d7, where it will have influence over the important c5 and e5 squares. This was in fact the course of the seventh game of this match.

9	c3

Another try is to bolster the centre with 9 c4 but this weakens White's grip on d4 and the light-squared bishop has less scope. Still, 9...♘g6 10 ♕a4 ♗d7 11 ♕b4 ♕b8 12 ♗e3 is then the critical continuation where White has a queenside initiative.

9	...	♘f5

Overprotecting the d-pawn and preparing to develop the kingside.

10	a4	g6

This costs (yet another) tempo over the natural 10...♗e7 11 ♗d3 0-0 but in that case the continuation 12 0-0 ♘h4 (preparing ...f7-f5) 13 f4! may be slightly better for White, e.g. 13...f5 14 fxe5 dxe5 when 15 d6 disrupts the black camp, whereas 13...a6 14 ♘a3 f5 15 ♘c4 and 13...exf4 14 ♗xf4 both give White some central pressure.

11	♗e2

In the third game 11 ♗d3 ♗g7 12 0-0 0-0 13 ♕b3 ♖e8 14 ♖e1 b6 15 a5! gave Yudasin a strong queenside initiative. If White can obtain an advantage by force then 10...g6 may just be dubious and Kramnik was prudent to switch to 8...♘b8 in the seventh game.

11	...	♗g7
12	0-0	0-0
13	♕b3	

Aiming to pressurize d6. If Black reacts with 13...a6 then after 14 ♘a3 with ♘c4 to follow Black has a further weak point on b6.

13	...	♖e8
14	♕b4	e4

White was threatening to undermine the knight with 15 g4. Black could have played 14...h5 but the text is more dynamic.

15 ♗f4

A move such as 15 g4 would be viewed suspiciously by many grandmasters as White's kingside is seriously compromised. The cheeky 15...♗e5 16 gxf5 ♛h4 is refuted by 17 f4 when en passant allows 18 ♛xh4. Black could instead try 15...a6 16 gxf5 axb5 17 ♗xb5 ♛h4 with attacking chances and the threat of perpetual check or even 15...♞e7.

Risky would also be 15 a5 ♗e5 16 g3 h5 followed by 17...h4.

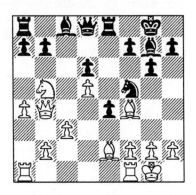

15 ... ♗e5

In this game Black exchanges both pairs of bishops in order to develop his attack. White's defensive pieces are eliminated one by one and his king is gradually exposed. This first exchange allows the rook to take up an attacking posture.

16 ♗xe5 ♖xe5
17 ♖ad1 ♞h4

Intending to threaten mate with 18...♛g5. Black could have first forced the white queen to commit herself by 17...a5 but whether this is desirable is a debatable point as Black may later regret not having the option of ...a7-a6.

18 ♔h1 ♛g5
19 ♖g1 ♗g4

Kramnik reduces further the white king's support.

20 ♗xg4 ♛xg4
21 ♖de1

After 21 ♛xd6 ♞f3! White has problems: 22 gxf3 ♛xf3+ 23 ♖g2 ♛xd1+ (hence the need to move this rook) or 22 ♖gf1 ♛f4 23 g3 ♖h5! 24 h4 ♛g4 with a quick mate in either case. The best try is 22 h3 but 22...♖h5 23 ♛g3 leaves White with insufficient compensation for the exchange.

21 ... ♛f4

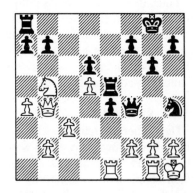

Inferior is 21...♞f3 22 gxf3 ♛xf3+ 23 ♖g2 ♖g5 as White can play 24 ♛xe4. Black can improve by first displacing the white queen and then forcing a draw: 21...a5 22 ♛xd6 ♞f3 23 gxf3

♛xf3+ 24 ♖g2 ♖g5 25 ♖g1 ♖xg2 26 ♖xg2 ♛f1+ with perpetual check. The text is an attempt to play for more.

Who is better? White can capture on d6 but can he then still defend his king? Is Black's attack worth a draw or even more?

22 ♛xd6?

An error but the position was very complicated:

a) 22 ♘d4 can be met by 22...♖h5 23 g3 ♘f3 24 ♘xf3 ♛xf3+ 25 ♖g2 e3! with an equal game; capturing on e3 is met by ...♛xd5 and 26 ♛xb7 is risky as 26...♖e8 27 fxe3 ♖xe3 28 ♛c8+ ♔g7 29 ♖g1 ♖e2 favours Black.

b) 22 ♘xd6 is best when the direct attack 22...♖h5 23 ♖xe4 ♘f3 fails to the clever resource 24 ♖e8+! ♖xe8 25 ♛xf4. Black does best to meet 22 ♘xd6 with 22...a5 when White has a difficult decision to make:

b1) 23 ♛xb7 ♖f8 (after 23...♖h5 White can defend with 24 ♛xf7+! obtaining four pawns for the piece after 24...♛xf7 25 ♘xf7 ♔xf7 26 ♖xe4) allows Black all the chances.

b2) After 23 ♛d4 White can survive to a nominally better ending after 23...♖h5 24 ♖xe4 ♛xd6 (24...♛xh2+ is attractive but unsound as 25 ♔xh2 ♘f5+ is met by 26 ♖h4 ♖xh4+ 27 ♛xh4 ♘xh4 28 ♘xb7 and White wins the ending) 25 ♖xh4 ♖xh4 26 ♛xh4 ♛xd5 27 b4 but after 27...♛b3! a draw is on the cards.

22 ... ♘f5!

Better than the typical draw with 22...♘f3 23 gxf3 ♛xf3+ 24 ♖g2 ♖g5, etc.

After 22...♘f5 White is lost. The best try is 23 ♛b4 but after 23...♛xf2 24 ♖xe4 ♖ae8 Black has a winning attack, e.g. 25 ♖f4 ♘g3+ 26 hxg3 ♛xg3 and there are too many threats.

23 ♛c7

Yudasin had obviously pinned his hopes on this pin. Now 23...♖ae8!? is interesting but Kramnik had prepared a spectacular *coup de grâce*.

23 ... e3!
24 ♖xe3 ♛xe3!!

Capturing the queen allows mate in two by 25 fxe3 ♘g3+ 26 hxg3 ♖h5 mate! A sensational combination, but Yudasin preferred to lose more prosaically.

25 ♘d6 ♖e7

The most efficient.

26 ♘xf5 gxf5
27 ♛d6

If 27 fxe3 then 27...♖xc7.

27	...	♛e5
28	♛b4	♖ae8
29	♛h4	f6
30	h3	♛xd5
	0-1	

Kasparov is on record as having stated that he believes that Kramnik will be his main challenger in the course of time. It's worth noting that this was his first game as a 'Candidate'. However, Kramnik surprisingly failed to make much impact in either cycle and his first game was to be his best.

Game Six
Paul van der Sterren-Gata Kamsky
5th match game
Candidates first round, Wijk aan Zee 1994

Kamsky must have felt very fortunate when the pairings for the first series of matches were made as Paul van der Sterren was generally considered by far the weakest qualifier. However, in the match itself van der Sterren, a renowned theoretician, consistently obtained excellent positions only to spoil his good work in time pressure. The final score may have been predictable but not the manner of it. In the following fighting game the Dutchman missed two wins.

1	d4	♘f6
2	c4	g6
3	♘c3	♗g7
4	e4	d6
5	f3	

The Sämisch variation of the King's Indian.

5	...	0-0
6	♗e3	e5
7	d5	c6
8	♗d3	

Sharper is 8...b5!? with an unbalanced game. In particular 9 cxb5 cxd5 10 exd5 ♘bd7 gives Black dynamic play for the gambit pawn.

8	...	cxd5
9	cxd5	♘h5

White has a space advantage but Black can obtain play with the typical King's Indian counter ...f7-f5.

10	♘ge2	f5
11	exf5	gxf5
12	0-0	

The Sämisch is often associated with queenside castling and attacks on opposite wings. In the present game van der Sterren prefers a more cautious approach, tucking his king away on h1 before commencing active operations.

12	...	a6

A useful move in such positions (preparing ...b7-b5 or simply stopping White using the b5 square). The main alternative 12...♘d7 13 ♖c1 ♘c5 looks slightly better for White after 14 ♗c4! (threatening 15 b4 and 15 ♗xc5 dxc5 16 d6+); Timman-Kasparov, Paris (25-minute game) 1991.

13	♔h1	♔h8

In Brunner-Gallagher, Bern 1993, (a game in which White needed to win for a GM norm) the natural 13...♘d7 was met by 14 ♗xf5!? (compared to our game White is missing ♖c1 and Black ♔h8) when 14...♖xf5 15 g4 ♖f7 16 gxh5 ♕h4 17 ♘g3 ♘f6 18 ♘ce4 ♘xe4 19 ♘xe4 ♗h3 20 ♖f2 ♕xh5 21 ♘xd6 ♖f6 22 ♘e4 ♖g6 23 ♕e2 ♖d8 24 ♖d1 ♔h8 gave Black good compensation for the pawn.

14	Rc1	Nd7
15	Bxf5!	

Van der Sterren introduces a 'novelty' although the idea is known; Timman-Thipsay, Thessaloniki Olympiad 1984 continued 15 Qd2 b5 16 Bxf5 Rxf5 17 g4 and White had the advantage. After the text White has a more active position than in the Brunner-Gallagher game above, essentially having the extra move Rc1.

15	...	Rxf5
16	g4	Rf8
17	gxh5	Qh4
18	Ne4	Nf6

This is more active than 18...Qxh5 as White can then snatch the pawn on d6: 19 Nxd6 Rxf3? (19...Nf6 is objectively better but Black is a pawn down for no compensation) 20 Ng3 Rxf1+ 21 Qxf1 and White wins a piece.

19	Nxd6	

The critical choice. Instead of this White could try 19 N2g3, a solid alternative.

19	...	Bh3
20	Rg1	Rad8

A complicated struggle that is worth comparison with the Brunner-Gallagher encounter above. White's chances are better here because of the rook on the c-file and indeed it seems that he has a clear advantage. From this observation it becomes clear that 13...Kh8 was inferior and the immediate 13...Nd7 should be preferred.

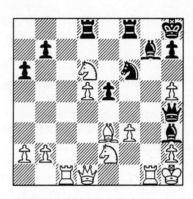

21	Rc7	

Also promising is 21 Rc4 as both 21...e4? 22 Nxe4 Rxd5? 23 Nxf6! and 21...Qxh5 22 Ng3 Qg6 23 Ngf5 win material. In the latter case Black can put up a serious defence with 23...Bxf5 24 Rxg6 Bxg6.

21	...	Bg4

After 21...Nxh5 White has 22 Nf7+, while the natural 21...Rxd6 is met by 22 Rgxg7 Bd7 (23...Rxd5 fails to 24 Qxd5!) 23 h6 Rxd5 24 Qg1 when White threatens mate in two starting with 25 Rxh7+ and finishing with 26 Qg7.

The wild 21...Ng4 (blocking the g-file) is refuted by 22 fxg4 Bxg4 23 Nf7+ Kg8 24 Nh6+ Bxh6 25 Nc3 with a deadly pin on the g-file (25...Rf1 26 Qxf1 Bxe3 27 Qf7+ and mate next move).

The text is a desperate attempt to find salvation through complications.

22	Nc3	

After 22 fxg4 ♘xg4 23 ♖xg4 ♕xg4 24 ♘f7+ ♖xf7 25 ♖xf7 Black has 25...♕e4+ winning back the piece with a good game.

22 ... ♗xh5

Now White meets 22...♖xd6 with 23 fxg4 maintaining a two pawn advantage.

23 ♖gxg7?

Up to this point the Dutchman had performed admirably but now 23 ♖cxg7! was required: 23...♖xd6 24 ♗c5 e4 is then met by the beautiful 25 ♗xd6! ♗xf3+ 26 ♕xf3 exf3 27 ♗xf8 h5 (27...f2 allows 28 ♖g8+ ♘xg8 29 ♗g7 mate!) 28 ♖g6 f2 29 ♗g7+ ♔h7 30 ♖h6+ ♔g8 31 ♖h8+ ♔f7 32 ♖f8+ ♔e7 33 ♗xf6+ winning. Very missable in time pressure!

23 ... ♖xd6
24 ♗c5

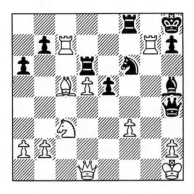

24 ... e4?

Kamsky had a fascinating possibility in this position; 24...♘d7! when best play could be 25 ♖cxd7 ♖h6 26 ♕d2 ♖ff6! 27 ♖g5 ♖hg6 28 ♖d8+ ♔g7 29 ♖d7+ taking a perpetual. Of course this line only scratches the surface of a very sharp position but Black's attack has to be taken seriously and White can't seem to profit from his extra material.

25 ♖g3 ♕f4
26 ♗xd6?

A natural move but one that overlooks Black's resource. By playing 26 ♖xb7 first, White comes out two pawns ahead after 26...♗xf3+ 27 ♖xf3 exf3 28 ♗xd6 ♕xd6 29 ♕xf3.

26 ... ♕xd6
27 ♖xb7 ♕xg3!

Van der Sterren was probably expecting 27...♗xf3+ 28 ♖xf3 etc., when the two pawns and significant simplification should guarantee victory. The text must have been a terrible blow.

28 hxg3 ♗xf3+
29 ♔g1 ♗xd1
30 ♘xd1 ♘xd5
31 ♖b3!

A necessary move as 31 ♖d7? would lose to 31...e3!

31 ... ♖c8
32 ♘c3 ♘xc3
33 ♖xc3 ♖d8
34 ♖e3 ♖d2
35 ♖xe4 ♖xb2
36 ♖a4 ♖b6
37 ♔g2 ½-½

A fascinating battle. Had van der Sterren managed to convert this game he would have clawed back to one down and might have put Kamsky under real pressure. As it was, the American teenager managed to halve out to win the match.

Game Seven
Vishwanathan Anand-Artur Yusupov
5th match game
FIDE Candidates first round, Wijk aan Zee 1994

The Russian-born Artur Yusupov has been one of the most consistent players over the past ten years, during which he has regularly appeared in the final stages of the world championship. A few years ago Yusupov moved to Germany and he even represented his adopted country in the Moscow Olympiad. In fact, the Tatar Yusupov must have unpleasant memories on the Russian capital as when he lived there he was shot and seriously wounded after disturbing burglars one evening, an incident which may have prompted his move to the comparative safety of the West.

This game took place in the critical stage of the match in which Anand's two-point lead had just been halved. A further defeat for Anand at this stage would have well and truly handed the initiative to his highly experienced opponent.

1	e4	e5
2	♘f3	♘c6
3	♗b5	a6
4	♗a4	d6

Yusupov has frequently used the 'Open' variation (4...♘f6 5 0-0 ♘xe4) in his matches in recent years and his adoption of 4...d6 during this match was quite a surprise.

5	c3	f5

This so-called 'Siesta' variation is named after a Budapest sanatorium, which was in fact the venue of a 1928 tournament, where Capablanca used the idea. In fact Marshall had introduced the variation against the Cuban 19 years earlier but he already had a certain variation of the Spanish named after him! (see the next game).

6	exf5	♗xf5
7	0-0	♗d3
8	♖e1	

The complications following 8 ♕b3 b5 9 ♕d5 ♘d4! should only be entered into after some thorough homework.

8	...	♗e7
9	♗c2!	

The main problem with this tactical line for Black is that White simply exchanges off the bishops, avoiding complications, and obtains the better prospects due to Black's weaknesses on the light squares.

9	...	♗xc2
10	♕xc2	♘f6
11	d4	0-0

After 11...exd4 12 cxd4 0-0 13 ♘c3 ♔h8 White can create some interesting complications: 14 ♘g5 ♘xd4 15 ♕d3 h6 (15...c5

fails to 16 ♘d5) 16 ♕xd4 hxg5 17 ♗xg5 ♕d7 18 ♘d5 ♘xd5 19 ♗xe7 ♖f5 (19...♘xe7 is worse due to 20 ♕h4+ ♔g8 21 ♖xe7) 20 ♗h4 with some advantage due largely to his superior minor piece; Glek-Vorotnikov, USSR 1986.

12   d5!?

Anand introduces a favourable tactical sequence which no one seems to have played before. This may be simply because the straightforward 12 dxe5 guarantees an edge after 12...♘xe5 13 ♘xe5 dxe5 14 ♘d2 ♗c5 15 ♘b3 ♗b6 16 ♗e3 when White has a comfortable game and the better structure. Not everyone would wish to defend such a position, but players such as Hübner and Yusupov have great faith in their defensive abilities, and a draw is a draw even if you've had to suffer a little!

Tactical players might wish to investigate 15...♘g4 (instead of the passive 15...♗b6) but the game Bannik-Estrin, USSR Spartakiad 1963, destroyed this move's credibility: 16 ♘xc5 ♕h4 17 h3 ♖xf2 18 ♖e2 ♖af8 19 ♗f4! ♖2xf4 (19...♖8xf4 fails to another fork 20 ♘d3) 20 ♘e6 ♘e3 21 ♖xe3 ♖f2 22 ♖e2 ♖xe2 23 ♕xe2 1-0.

12   ...   e4

Other moves are clearly inferior for Black: 12...♘xd5? 13 ♕b3, 12...♘b8 13 ♘g5 ♕d7 14 c4 and 12...♘a5 13 ♘g5 ♕d7 14 ♘a3.

13   ♘g5   ♘e5

13...♘xd5 is met not by 14 ♕b3 because of 14...♖f5, but rather 14 ♕xe4 which wins after 14...♘f6 15 ♕e6+ ♔h8 16 ♘f7+.

14   ♘e6   ♕d7

As is typical in this line the light squares in general and e6 in particular are a problem for the second player. However, Black can still generate some useful kingside counterplay after the text. Less good is 14...♕e8 15 ♘xf8 ♗xf8 16 ♘d2 ♕g6 17 ♖e3 ♘eg4 18 ♘xe4! (giving the exchange back for a clear extra pawn) 18...♘xe3 19 ♘xf6+ ♕xf6 20 ♗xe3.

15   ♘d2

It is dangerous to take immediately on f8: 15 ♘xf8 ♕g4 16 ♔h1 ♖xf8 and 16 ♖e3 ♖xf8 17 ♖g3 ♕h5 both give Black good practical compensation.

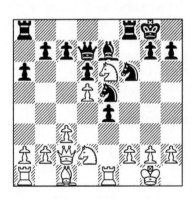

Black has several ways of trying to avoid drifting into a bad game.

15   ...   e3!

Yusupov picks the best. Others

all have their downside:

a) 15...♘d3 16 ♖xe4! and after simplification White ends up with an extra pawn, i.e. 16...♘xe4 17 ♘xe4 ♘xc1 18 ♘xf8 ♖xf8 19 ♖xc1.

b) 15...♖fc8, aims to meet 16 c4 with 16...c6, so White should content himself with a small edge after 16 ♘xe4 ♘xd5 17 ♘4g5 ♗xg5 18 ♘xg5.

c) The other significant rook move 15...♖f7 can be met by 16 c4. If Black then seeks complications by 16...♘d3 17 ♖e2 ♘xf2 18 ♖xf2 e3 then 19 ♖xf6! e2 20 ♖xf7! e1♕+ 21 ♖f1 ♕e3+ 22 ♔h1 must favour White with two pieces and a rook for the second queen.

d) Unsatisfactory is 15...♘xd5 16 ♘xf8 ♖xf8 17 ♕xe4 c6 18 ♘f1 when Black has insufficient compensation.

16   ♖xe3

Anand could have contemplated 16 fxe3!?, when he retains an extra pawn but yields the initiative to Black, e.g. 16...♖f7 17 e4 ♘fg4 18 ♘f1 (not 18 ♖f1? as 18...♘e3 would be embarrassing) 18...♗h4 19 ♖e2. It is of course academic to discuss whether there is enough play or not as most players would prefer to keep the initiative in such a sharp position.

16   ...   ♘xd5
17   ♘xf8!?

Safer is the attempt to play positionally: 17 ♖xe5 dxe5 18 ♘xf8 ♖xf8 19 ♘e4 but Anand

(the world's strongest vegetarian) was looking for blood!

17   ...   ♘xe3
18   ♕xh7+   ♔xf8
19   fxe3

There was a draw on offer (19 ♕h8+ ♔f7 20 ♕xa8 ♘xg2 21 ♔xg2 ♕g4+ with perpetual check) so the Indian probably felt that he was better at this point.

19   ...   ♖e8

19...♕g4 must have been sorely tempting but after 20 ♕h8+ ♔f7 21 ♕xa8 ♕e2 22 ♕xb7 Black has remarkably no way of punishing White's materialism. After the further 22...♕xe3+ 23 ♔f1 ♘d3 (23...♗h4 is coolly met by 24 g3) 24 ♕f3+ White exchanges queens to victory.

20   e4

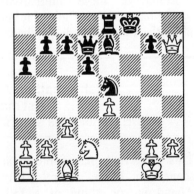

White has an extra pawn but his queenside needs some untangling.

20   ...   d5?!

20...♗f6 has been universally recommended as giving Black enough compensation but I still prefer White after 21 ♕h8+ ♔e7 22 ♕h5.

21 ♘b3 dxe4?!

Tricky was 21...♕g4. After 22 ♗e3 ♘f3+ 23 ♔h1 ♘h4 24 ♖f1+ ♗f6 25 g3! (rather than 25 ♖xf6+ ♔e7! when White loses control of events) 25...♘f3 26 h3!! (easy to miss!) 26...♕xg3 27 ♗c5+ ♔f7 28 ♕h5+ g6 29 ♕xf3 and White mops up.

Another try was 21...♘g4 when White should avoid 22 ♕h8+ ♔f7 23 ♕h5+ ♔g8 24 ♕xd5+?? ♕xd5 25 exd5 ♗c5+ when he must ditch a piece by 26 ♗e3 in order to avoid mate. Better is 22 e5! ♘xe5 23 ♗e3! (23 ♕h8+ ♔f7 24 ♕h5+ ♔g8 25 ♕xe5 fails to 25...♗h4) with real practical problems for Black now that White is fully organized.

Either of these alternatives would have made a fight of it but now Black is swiftly despatched.

22 ♗e3 ♗f6
23 ♖f1 ♘g4
24 ♗d4

White exchanges into a winning ending after 24 h3 ♘xe3 25 ♖xf6+ ♔e7 26 ♕xg7+ ♔d8 27 ♕xd7+ ♔xd7 28 ♘c5+ ♔c8 29 ♖f4 but the game continuation is even stronger.

24 ... ♕c6

For the record it should be mentioned that 24...♕e6 survives longer but 25 ♘c5 ♕f7 (25...♕c6 26 ♗xf6 ♘xf6 27 ♖xf6+! wins the black queen) 26 ♘xe4 is hopeless.

25 ♗c5+ 1-0

After 25...♔f7 White picks up the knight with 26 ♕h5+.

Anand is at home in complications as he sees variations faster than probably anyone else in the world and he is invariably able to get his opponents into time trouble!

Game Eight
Vishwanathan Anand-Gata Kamsky
1st match game
FIDE Candidates second round, Sanghi Nagar 1994

This game took place amid great scenes in India, where Vishy Anand is something of a folk hero. The potential for chess in the next century is enormous if the game reallly takes off in the most populated countries, China and India. The development of chess in these countries would appear to be in good hands with women's world champion Xie Jun and Anand acting as ambassadors.

This encounter could easily be judged game of the year. Hold on to your hats!

1	e4	e5
2	♘f3	♘c6
3	♗b5	a6
4	♗a4	♘f6

5	0-0	&e7
6	&e1	b5
7	&b3	0-0
8	c3	

Allowing a dangerous gambit known as the Marshall Attack. Anand has never been afraid of taking on this line, which was introduced by the innovative Frank Marshall in a game against Capablanca (New York 1922). Kamsky is also not one to back down from a challenge.

| 8 | ... | d5 |

Those seeking a quieter game play 8...d6 here.

9	exd5	&xd5
10	&xe5	&xe5
11	&xe5	c6
12	d4	&d6
13	&e1	&h4
14	g3	&h3
15	&e3	&g4
16	&d3	&ae8
17	&d2	&e6
18	a4	&h5
19	axb5	axb5

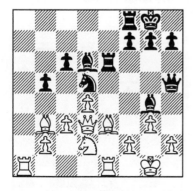

These moves have all been played before. Standard opening theory doesn't always take us this deep into the game!

White has an extra pawn but Black has active pieces ranged at the white monarch, the overall consensus suggests that Black has more or less enough play for his material deficit.

| 20 | &e4!? | |

The first surprise, generally 20 &f1 or 20 &f1 have been played. The text had been played only once before in a game of note; Anand-Kamsky, Monaco (quickplay) 1994, a game in which Kamsky soon seized the advantage. Naturally, Anand has an improvement prepared and Kamsky must have been bracing himself to face his opponent's home preparation over the board.

| 20 | ... | &c7 |

The plan to pin with 20...&f5 is ineffective after 21 &d2 &fe8 22 f3 &g6 23 &c2 threatening 24 &f6+.

| 21 | &d2 | &fe8 |
| 22 | &d1! | |

So here it is; Anand's new move. Some may ask, why do top players involve themselves in long variations such as in this game? Is modern chess only a game of memory and home preparation? Well, to answer the first question, I would say that main lines and long variations are frequently repeated because experience tells us that these are the best and most reliable moves, and to answer the second, I would say far from it, and then invite the sceptic to play through this game!

The previous encounter between these two players, with a rapidplay time-limit, continued as follows: 22 ♘c5? ♖xe1+ 23 ♖xe1 ♖xe1+ 24 ♗xe1 ♘f4! 25 gxf4 ♗xf4 26 h4 ♗f3? (with a slower time limit Kamsky would no doubt have found the forced win following 26...♕xh4 27 ♕e4 ♕h2+ 28 ♔f1 ♕h3+ 29 ♕g2 ♗e2+ 30 ♔g1 ♗h2+ 31 ♔h1 ♗f3 32 ♕xf3 ♕xf3+ 33 ♔xh2 ♕e2) 27 ♗xf7+! ♔xf7 28 ♘e4 ♕g4+ 29 ♘g3 g6 30 b3 ♗d5 31 c4 bxc4 32 bxc4 ♕f3 and Black's bishops gave him enough play for a draw in the ending.

| 22 | ... | ♗xd1 |
| 23 | ♖exd1 | |

The right rook! 23 ♖axd1? loses to 23...♖xe4 24 ♖xe4 ♕xd1+.

| 23 | ... | f5 |

Anand had naturally foreseen 23...♖xe4? 24 ♕xe4 (so that if 24...♖xe4 White mates with 25 ♖a8+) 24...♕xd1+ 25 ♔g2! (winning, whereas 25 ♖xd1 ♖xe4 26 ♖e1 only gives an endgame advantage) 25...♔f8 26 ♕xe8+! ♔xe8 27 ♖xd1 and Black can of course resign.

Kamsky finds the best chance to generate some play.

| 24 | ♘g5 | ♖e2 |
| 25 | ♘f3? | |

Anand was probably very pleased with his opening (he may even still have been following his home preparation!), but here he becomes complacent and overlooks his opponent's resource.

Safer than the text was 25 ♕f3 ♕g6 26 ♘h3 but most ambitious, and probably best, was 25 ♕xf5! introducing very favourable complications. After 25...♖f8 26 ♕h3 ♕g6 White has 27 ♕g4! ♖fe8 (27...♖fxf2 fails to 28 ♖a8+ ♖f8 29 ♖xf8+ ♔xf8 30 ♕xe2 and 27...♖exf2 to 28 ♕e6+ ♔h8 29 ♕xg6 hxg6 30 ♘e6 ♖8f5 31 ♖a8+ ♔h7 32 ♘g5+) 28 ♖a8! (better than 28 f3 as Black has good drawing chances in variations such as 28...h6 29 ♘h3 ♕xg4 30 fxg4 ♘e3 31 ♗xe3 ♖8xe3 32 ♖a7 ♗xg3! 33 hxg3 ♖xg3+ 34 ♔f1 ♖xb2 35 ♘g1 ♖gg2) 28...♖xd2? (28...♖xa8 is objectively better but still not really satisfactory after 29 ♕xe2 ♖e8 30 ♕f3) 29 ♖xe8+ ♕xe8 30 ♖xd2 ♕e1+ 31 ♔g2 ♘e3+ 32 fxe3 ♕xd2+ 33 ♔h3 and White is winning.

This doesn't cover all possibilities, but instead of being on the road to victory the Asian No.1 found himself facing a difficult defence after...

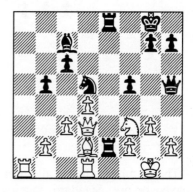

25 ... ♖8e3!
26 ♖a8+

Capturing on e3 fails (26 ♗xe3 ♕xf3 27 ♗g5 ♖e1+ and 26 fxe3 ♕xf3) and 26 ♘e5 ♗xe5 27 ♗xe3 gives Black excellent winning chances after 27...♗xg3! 28 hxg3 ♘xe3 29 ♕xe2 ♕xe2 30 fxe3 ♕xe3+.

26 ... ♔f7
27 ♘g5+ ♔g6

Kamsky is forced to further expose his king as 27...♕xg5 is refuted by 28 ♕xe2! etc.

28 ♗xe3 ♘xe3

White's chances looks grim: 29 h4 ♗xg3 30 fxg3 ♕g4, 29 ♖a6 ♔xg5 30 h4+ ♔h6 31 ♖xc6+ g6 32 ♖xc7 ♕f3 and even 29 ♖e8 ♘g4! are all hopeless.

29 ♖f1!!

Now 29...♘xf1 30 ♔xf1 ♖xb2 31 h4 h6 32 ♘e6 probably favours White but...

29 ... ♔xg5

looks difficult to cope with. How can White defend?

30 ♖e8!!

Defending and now causing some difficult problems in the American's camp.

30 ... f4

Now Kamsky had to avoid capitulation after 30...♕xe8 31 ♕xe2, 30...♕f3 31 ♖xe3 or 30...♘xf1 31 h4+.

31 ♕e4 fxg3!

Avoiding 31...♘xf1 32 h4+ ♔h6 33 ♕xe2 when White wins material, and 31...♕xh2+ 32 ♔xh2 ♘xf1+ 33 ♔g2 ♖xe4 34 ♖xe4 ♘d2 35 ♖e7 when White has a strong initiative in the ending.

32 h4+

Rather than 32 hxg3, which is met by 32...♗xg3.

32 ... ♕xh4

Necessary as 32...♔h6 is met simply by 33 fxe3.

33 ♕xh4+

Chasing the king by 33 ♕e7+ ♔h5 34 ♕f7+ ♔h6 35 ♖e6+ g6 36 ♕f8+ ♔h5 37 ♕f3+ ♘g4 would only help Black.

33 ... ♔xh4
34 ♖e4+

Better than 34 fxe3? ♔h3 and certainly better than 34 ♖xe3?? gxf2+. Now the ending starts to look drawish.

34 ... ♔h3
35 ♖xe3 ♖xb2
36 ♖e7 ♗f4

Also equal is 36...g2 37 ♖xc7 gxf1♕+ 38 ♔xf1 b4 39 cxb4 ♖xb4 40 ♖xg7.

37 fxg3

There are still opportunities to go wrong: 37 ♖xg7? gxf2+ 38 ♔h1 (38 ♖xf2 allows a quick

mate after 38...♖b1+ 39 ♖f1
♗e3+ etc.) 38...h5 and White is
already probably lost.

37	...	♖g2+
38	♔h1	♖h2+
39	♔g1	♖g2+
40	♔h1	♖h2+
41	♔g1	♗g5

An unusual move that is less
testing than the obvious
41...♗xg3! 42 ♖xg7 h5 43 ♖g6!
(but not 43 ♖f6? ♖c2 44 ♖xg3+
♔xg3 45 ♖g6+ ♔h3 46 ♖xc6 b4

47 ♖c5 b3 48 ♖xh5+ ♔g4 49
♖b5 b2 winning for Black)
43...h4 44 ♖xc6 ♖g2+ 45 ♔h1
♗f2 46 ♖xf2 ♖xf2 47 ♔g1 ♖c2
48 ♖c5, although White draws all
the same.

| 42 | ♖e5 | ♖g2+ |
| 43 | ♔h1 | ½-½ |

Only a draw, but any other result would have been unjust. A
game involving difficult complications, tricks and resources of
the highest calibre.

Game Nine
Boris Gelfand-Vladimir Kramnik
4th match game
FIDE Candidates second round, Sanghi Nagar 1994

In common with Alexei Shirov
and Vassily Ivanchuk, Boris Gelfand has the disconcerting habit
of looking away from the board,
staring into space as if dreaming.
Apparently this helps them focus
their thoughts, and actually
looking at the chessboard might
distract them from something
important. However, this is not
necessarily recommended for
ordinary mortals!

Kramnik had just gone ahead
after winning the third game.
Naturally Gelfand was determined to come bouncing back
with a win. Was it time to test his
opponent's main openings or to
set new problems elsewhere?

1	c4	c5
2	♘f3	♘c6
3	♘c3	♘f6

4   e3   e6
It seems as if Gelfand chose
the second option. The opening
starts quietly.

5   d4   d5
6   a3
In symmetrical positions such
as this one, Black always faces
the tricky task of choosing the
moment to deviate from simply
copying the first player. Although
there seems no immediate danger, achieving full equality can be
a difficult task.

6   ...   a6
Playable is 6...cxd4 7 exd4
♗e7 but White keeps some initiative with 8 c5 ♘e4 9 ♗b5.

7   b3
More forcing is 7 dxc5 ♗xc5 8
b4 but Gelfand waits for his opponent to break the tension.

7   ...   cxd4

If Gelfand's novelty on move nine proves to be strong then Black should delay this capture with 7...♗e7 8 ♗b2 0-0 9 ♗d3 cxd4 10 exd4 and now 10...dxc4 or 10...b6 as recommended by *ECO*.

8   exd4   ♗e7
9   c5!?

Gelfand varies from standard theory with this move, although the idea is fairly well known without ...a7-a6 from Black and b2-b3 from White. In fact this ploy works; Kramnik fails to find a convincing route to equality.

9   ...   b6
10   cxb6

After 10 b4 bxc5 11 bxc5 Black can try to exploit White's loss of tempo (7 b3 and 10 b4) by playing actively with 11...♘e4. After the text White has more pawn islands (in particular, b3 and d4 may become weak) but Gelfand is relying on good piece play to retain the initiative.

10   ...   ♘d7!?

Presumably 10...♕xb6 11 ♘a4 ♕a7 12 b4 intending ♘a4-c5 was not to Kramnik's taste.

11   ♗d3   a5
12   ♘b5!?

After 12 0-0 Black eases the pressure with 12...♗a6 and the plausible 12 ♘a4 ♘xb6 13 ♗b5 ♗d7 14 ♘c5 is attractively refuted by 14...♘xd4! when Black gets away with an extra pawn.

12   ...   ♕xb6
13   ♗f4   0-0

14   0-0

Murky complications follow both 14 ♗c7 ♕b7 15 ♕c2 ♘f6 16 ♘e5 ♘xe5 17 dxe5 ♘e8 18 ♗xh7+ ♔h8 and 14 ♖c1 ♗a6 15 ♘c7 ♗xa3. So Gelfand naturally castles intending to meet 14...♗a6 with 15 ♘c7 ♗xd3 16 ♘xa8 winning material. Black should probably settle for 14...♘f6 15 ♖c1 ♗d7 when he's not doing too badly

14   ...   ♘a7?!

By trying to punish White's ambitious play Kramnik gets rather tangled up.

15   ♘c7   ♖b8
16   b4   ♗b7

Capturing on b4 twice with 16...axb4 17 axb4 ♗xb4? allows 18 ♘a6! and 16...♖b7 fails to the eccentric 17 ♘a8 ♕d8 18 ♕c2 ♘f6 19 ♗c7 ♕e8 when White simply takes the a-pawn. The white queen's knight is a real thorn in Black's side.

17   bxa5   ♕xa5
18   ♕e2

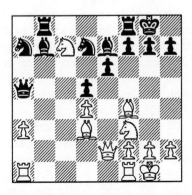

Kramnik has serious problems

as White threatens havoc in the black camp with ♘xe6, e.g. 18...♖bc8 19 ♘xe6! fxe6 20 ♕xe6+ or 18...♔h8 19 ♘xe6 fxe6 20 ♗xb8 ♘xb8 21 ♕xe6 ♘ac6 22 ♘e5. To avoid such unappetizing lines Kramnik tries to confuse the issue.

18	...	e5!?
19	♗xe5	

Interesting is 19 ♘xe5 when Black can try to defend with 19...♕xc7 20 ♖ac1 ♕d6 21 ♘g6 hxg6 22 ♗xd6 ♗xd6.

19	...	♘xe5
20	♕xe5	♘c6
21	♕f4	♖bc8

Black has shed a pawn but has liberated his position. He's worse but can make a fight of it.

22	♘b5	♗a6
23	a4	♘b4
24	♗f5	

Gelfand opts to keep active whereas 24 ♕d2 would try to consolidate his pawn at the risk of going on the defensive.

24	...	♖cd8
25	♖fe1	

25 ♘e5! is the most dangerous for Black as 25...♗xb5 26 axb5 ♕xb5 27 ♖a7 is more than troublesome and the better 25...h6 26 ♗b1 ♗c8 27 ♖a3 ♗f6 28 ♖g3 ♔h8 is defensible but unpleasant.

25	...	♗f6
26	♘e5	♗xe5

Taking off a possible attacking piece but at the cost of parting with the king's main defender. After 26...♗xb5 White can keep it simple with 27 axb5 ♕xb5 28

♖ab1, but this may not be enough and 28 ♖a3 as in the game would be more to the point. The dangerous try 27 ♘g4!? (instead of recapturing on b5) is safely diffused by 27...♕b6 28 axb5 ♕xd4 29 ♘xf6+ ♕xf6 30 ♗xh7+ ♔xh7 31 ♕xb4.

27	dxe5	♗xb5
28	axb5	♕xb5
29	♖a3!?	

29 ♖ab1 looks insufficient for an advantage after 29...♖b8 30 ♖b3 ♕c4.

29	...	♕c4

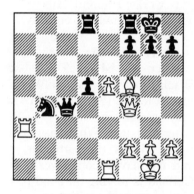

White now has to sacrifice if he is still serious about winning.

30	♗xh7+	♔xh7
31	♕f5+	♔g8

After 31...g6 White wins by 32 ♖h3+ ♔g8 33 ♕f6 with mate to follow.

32	♖h3	♖fe8

The text is the best try as after 32...♕c2? 33 ♕h5 f6 with 34 e6 White threatens mate on h8.

33	♕h7+?	

This should even lose whereas 33 ♕h5! keeps the advantage

with every prospect of victory:
33...♔f8 34 ♕g5 ♔g8 35 ♖g3 g6
36 ♖h3 ♕c6 37 ♕h4 ♔f8 when
White wins back the piece with
38 ♕xb4+ to emerge a pawn up.

33 ... ♔f8
34 ♕h8+ ♔e7
35 ♕xg7 d4?

Both 35...♖g8 (because of 36
♕f6+ ♔e8 37 e6) and 35...♔d7
(after 36 e6+ ♔c8 37 ♖c3) lose
immediately.

However, best is 35...♕f4! as
White fails to break through: 36
♖f3? allows 36...♕xf3 37 gxf3
♖g8 and 36 e6 is defused after
36...♔d6 37 ♖f3 ♕d2 38 ♕e5+
♔c6 39 ♖c3+ ♔b5 40 ♖ec1 ♖xe6
41 ♖c5+ ♔a6 or even 41...♔a4
42 ♕a1+ ♕a2 43 ♕d4 ♖de8. If
this is the case, Kramnik could
well have won this game having
earlier been a pawn down for
nothing. A good example for us
all in that we should 'never give
up hope' and play accordingly.

36 e6 ♔d6
37 e7

In a complex position Kramnik
must find the right square for his
rook.

37 ... ♖d7?

Evidently 37...♖xe7?? loses a
rook after 38 ♕f6+.

After 37...♖c8! White can take
a perpetual check but has no
more. If 38 ♖h4 then 38...♘c6
and Black can wriggle out of the
checks so 38 ♕e5+ ♔d7 39 ♕f5+
♔c7 40 ♕a5+ ♔d7 (40...♔b7?
goes down to 41 ♖h5!) 41 ♕f5+
would be best play for both sides.

Another try 38 ♖h6+ only risks
losing after 39...♔d7! 39 ♕g4+
♔c7.

38 ♕e5+ ♔c6
39 ♖h6+ ♔b7
40 ♕a5!

Suddenly there is no defence:
40...♖exe7 41 ♕b6+ ♔c8 42
♖h8+, 40...♘c6 41 ♖b1+ ♔c8 42
♕a8+ ♔c7 43 ♖b7+ and 40...♖c7
41 ♖b6+ ♔c8 42 ♖xb4 are all
hopeless.

40 ... ♖dxe7
41 ♖xe7+ ♖xe7
42 ♕b6+ 1-0

Black resigned as 42...♔c8 43
♖h8+ ♔d7 44 ♖d8 is mate.

An exciting scrap but hardly a
smooth victory. If Kramnik had
taken his chance at move 35 then
he may have gone two up, but as
it was, Gelfand equalized and
later won the match after cashing
in on an opening blunder in the
eighth game.

4 Quickplay and Novelty Tournaments

In most walks of life the media has had a significant impact. Naturally, chess has not been immune from these developments as organizers and sponsors look for different ways to encourage more interest, and, ideally, television coverage. In the past the imagination of the public has been captured by title matches between the top Western player and the top Russian (Fischer-Spassky and Short-Kasparov) but barring that television companies have rarely become involved. One form of chess that has been seen increasingly on television in recent years is quickplay or rapidplay chess (usually with 25 or 30 minutes for each player for all their moves).

In fact, quickplay events are becoming more popular at all levels; they are exciting for players and spectators alike. Over the past ten years there have been any number of blitz and rapid chess tournaments, some of which have attracted the top players. Even World Blitz (five minutes each) titles have been banded about.

The most significant (and spectator-friendly) quickplay tournament over the past few years has been Immopar, run every November in Paris as a sixteen player knock-out event. The top players in the world competing in the sumptuous surroundings of the Champs-Elysées theatre with no expense spared on visual aids and high-tech paraphernalia.

Intel, the PCA sponsors, have modelled their new speed chess Grand Prix on the successful Immopar formula. Four events, in Moscow, New York, London and Paris, with big prizes, and bonuses for the most consistent performers. The possibility of battling with the big guns (and earning the minimum first-round losers purse of $5000) by succeeding in the qualifying tournament encourages interest for the 'average' grandmaster, an encouraging development when 75 GMs turn up as they did in Moscow!

The Grand Prix rules included a rather controversial tie-breaking system, which had already been tried out at Immopar. If, after the two 25-minute rapidplay games, the scores are level, then one game of blitz is played to decide the bout. White has six minutes to Black's five but must win, Black being declared the winner in the case of a draw on the chessboard. This was used throughout the Grand Prix, but unfortunately White very rarely seems to win in practice (something like 20% of White players were successful) and many players are unhappy about this rule. The 'powers that be' naturally require a quick decision (for reasons of scheduling, media coverage, crowd interest, etc.) but there must be room for a rethink on this one. There has been talk of giving White seven minutes, but as yet nothing has been decided.

Intel Grand Prix first leg, Moscow

The choice of Moscow as the first venue of the Intel Grand Prix cycle was remarkable in itself, but even more remarkable was the fact that the tournament would be played within the Kremlin itself. For a few days in April the antics of the chessboard took over one of the twentieth centuries centres of world statesmanship.

The Grand Prix itself was preceded by a powerful qualifying tournament in which dozens of grandmasters competed.

Qualifiers
8/11   Z.Azmaiparashvili, L.Yudasin, I.Smirin, J.Ehlvest,
             A.Vyzmanavin, V.Malaniuk

A Georgian, two Israelis, an Estonian, a Russian and a Ukrainian made it to the Grand Prix proper, all of whom are products of the Soviet school of chess. Another Russian, Bareev, surprisingly failed to qualify as a result of his last round loss to Vyzmanavin.

The quarter-finals saw the total domination of youth over experience. Rapid chess is more a game of instinct and quick reactions than one of erudition and carefully weighted judgements, and these qualities are more suited to the Anand's of this world than the Korchnoi's.

The most remarkable incident of the whole event (and perhaps of the Grand Prix series as a whole) occurred at the end of the semi-final match between Vyzmanavin and Kramnik. After two draws all was to be decided in the six minutes vs five minutes play-off. Kramnik, as Black, had slipped into a lost ending with both players having very little time remaining on the clock, and must have been very surprised when his opponent offered him a draw. Of course Kramnik gratefully accepted the gift, automatically eliminating his opponent from the competition. In the heat of the battle, the relatively unknown Russian had had a momentary brain-storm, believing that a draw was sufficient for he himself to progress to the final. Students of the Russian language could have extended their vocabulary if they had been there when Vyzmanavin realised what a blunder his draw offer had been.

V.Anand 1 0 =
I.Smirin   **V.Anand** 1 1
                            V.Malaniuk

V.Malaniuk 1 =
G.Kamsky   **V.Anand** 1 =
                                            V.Ivanchuk
J.Ehlvest
N.Short = 1
                            N.Short
Z.Azmaiparashvili   **V.Ivanchuk** 1 1
V.Ivanchuk = = =
                                                        V.Anand = = = 1
                                                        V.Kramnik
A.Vyzmanavin 0 1 1
A.Shirov   **A.Vyzmanavin** 1 =
                            V.Korchnoi
V.Korchnoi = = =
M.Adams   A.Vyzmanavin = = =
                                            V.Kramnik
J.Timman
G.Kasparov = 1
                            G.Kasparov
L.Yudasin   **V.Kramnik** = 1
V.Kramnik 1 =

Intel Grand Prix second leg, New York

A total of 69 grandmasters participated in the New York qualification tournament in June, which was won outright by the Russian Sergei Tiviakov (bouncing back from his defeat by Michael Adams in the Candidates earlier in the week) with nine others finishing equal second. A play-off was required to determine the other five qualification places.

Qualification tournament
8/11   S.Tiviakov

7½   G. Kamsky, P.Nikolic, M.Adams, J.Ehlvest, L.Oll,
           J.Speelman, A.Khalifman, I.Smirin, A.Vaiser.

Play-off (5 mins)

5½/9	I.Smirin, A.Vaiser
5	P.Nikolic
4½	M.Adams, G.Kamsky
4	L.Oll
3½	A.Khalifman
2	J.Speelman
1½	J.Ehlvest

In the heat of the Manhattan summer, Kamsky faced Kasparov in front of his own public with a new tactic - a shaven head. Unfortunately this *bold* decision was accompanied by a disappointing chess effort on his part and he was eliminated.

Having qualified for the Grand Prix in the five-minute play-off, Predrag Nikolic certainly confirmed that he is one of the world's leading blitz players by overcoming both Vyzmanvin and Adams in the tie-break. Unfortunately for the Bosnian, he didn't get as far as a tie-break in his semi-final with Kasparov, going down 2-0.

Nowadays Judit Polgar is a popular invitee at some of the world's top events, and she was given a 'wild-card' to compete in New York. No longer the 'circus-act' of a few years ago, she is rightly regarded as a dangerous opponent. After her performance here Nigel Short can vouch for her ability to generate attacking chances out of practically nothing.

In the top half of the draw Vladimir Kramnik demolished Joel Benjamin and Judit Polgar, and then held his nerve well in a dramatic blitz finish against the wild man of the Ukraine, Vassily Ivanchuk. The stage was set for a dramatic finale between Kasparov and his heir apparent Kramnik.

In fact the final more than lived up to everyone's expectations. In the first game a magnificent array of multi-sacrifices by Kasparov was negated by counter-sacrifices and accurate defence from his resourceful opponent with a drawn outcome, but in the second Kramnik outplayed his mentor so totally that spectators were astonished by the ability of the young gentle giant.

V.Kramnik 1 1
J.Benjamin
    V.Kramnik 1 1
    J.Polgar
J.Polgar 1 1
N.Short
        V.Kramnik = = 1
        V.Ivanchuk
A.Vaiser
V.Korchnoi = 1
    V.Korchnoi
S.Tiviakov
V.Ivanchuk = 1
    V.Ivanchuk 1 =

           V.Kramnik 1 =
           G.Kasparov
P.Nikolic = = 1
A.Vyzmanavin
    P.Nikolic 1 0 =
    M.Adams
M.Adams 1 1
V.Malaniuk
        P.Nikolic
        G.Kasparov 1 1
I.Smirin
V.Anand = = 1
    V.Anand
G.Kamsky
G.Kasparov 1 1
    G.Kasparov 1 =

Intel Grand Prix third leg, London

There were to be five qualifiers for the third leg, held in August/September. The London Lloyds Bank open played at normal speed was deemed to be also the qualification event. A.Morozevich 9½/10 and R.Mainka, clear second on 8 points, obtained two of the coveted places. Those players finishing equal third participated in a round robin blitz play-off:

6/8 U.Adianto, 5½ V.Tkachiev, 4½ R.Akesson, A.Miles, 4 T.Markowski, J.Nunn, 3 D.Norwood, 2½ A.Yermolinsky, 2 P.Wells.

A further play-off was required to split Akesson and Miles, and Tony Miles became another victim of the notorious PCA tie-splitting rule; A.Miles = R.Akesson.

The history of chess took a surprising twist in the London leg of the PCA cycle with the loss of the world No.1 Garry Kasparov to a computer, followed by the defeat of positional master Predrag Nikolic to the same inhuman, unfeeling Pentum Genius. The other games between mortals paled into insignificance as the public came to terms with such drama until eventually Vishy Anand gained revenge for mankind in the semi-final by showing that despite the Pentium Genius's ability to calculate extremely accurately, it lacked endgame judgement and the ability to plan ahead - one has just to get the right sort of position against it.

The final between Anand and Ivanchuk, who had reached that stage after a blitz play-off with Kramnik, the New York champion, was a real ding-dong battle. After two draws the players embarked on two fiercely contested five-minute games. After winning the first of these Ivanchuk only needed a draw to win the tournament, but became embroiled in a wild melee in which both players kings were under attack. After getting on top Ivanchuk incredibly missed a trivial 'mate in one' that had been spotted by every spectator in the hall, eventually losing on time to put the match into a final six minutes vs five 'White must win' play-off. Fortunately for Ivanchuk, he comfortably clinched the title in the tie-break, otherwise he would still be kicking himself now.

V.Ivanchuk = 1
R.Akesson   **V.Ivanchuk** = 1
            V.Tkachiev

V.Tkachiev 1 1
V.Malaniuk   **V.Ivanchuk** = = =
                         V.Kramnik

R.Mainka
A.Vyzmanavin 1 0 =
          A.Vyzmanavin
U.Adianto   **V.Kramnik** = 1
V.Kramnik = = 1
                         V.Ivanchuk = = 1 0 =
                         V.Anand

Pentium Genius 1 =
G.Kasparov   **Pentium Genius** 1 1
            P.Nikolic

P.Nikolic 1 0 =
N.Short   Pentium Genius
                    V.Anand 1 1

A.Morozevich
V.Korchnoi 1 1
          V.Korchnoi
M.Adams   **V.Anand** 1 =
V.Anand 1 0 1

Intel Grand Prix fourth leg, Paris

The fourth and final Grand Prix held in November had many similarities to the Immopar formula which had been so successful in previous years. Many of the staff worked in both and comparisons were inevitable. The atmosphere was heightened by a series of nail-biting play-offs (e.g. Vaiser won on time against Milov with only one second remaining on his own clock) and the calculations for the overall title.

The four main contenders were soon only two, as Ivanchuk and Anand both lost rather tamely on the first day, and everything came down to the semi-final clash between Kramnik and Kasparov. Kramnik must have missed a win with the white pieces but after two draws we had the spectacle of his eighth sudden-death play-off. Kasparov, playing White and therefore obliged to win, seemed lethargic at first, but after winning a pawn had great chances in the ending. The tension in the hall reached fever-pitch as Kramnik was presented with an immediate draw which he amazingly failed to spot and Kasparov delivered mate with eleven seconds to spare. This missed opportunity cost the 19-year-old dear and he had to share the overall title with the PCA World Champion. After that, the final, in which Nikolic was comfortably despatched, was inevitably an anti-climax.

Qualifiers

Megeve, France (coinciding with the opening of 'The Kasparov University')

The six successful qualifiers from a field of 37 grandmasters were V.Arbakov, J.Hjartarson, V.Tkachiev, V.Milov, I.Smirin and M.Sadler (chosen rather controversially as the French qualifier although he is resident in England and plays under the English flag).

G.Kasparov 1 1
V.Arbakov   **G.Kasparov** 1 1
                           J.Hjartarson
J.Hjartarson 1 1
M.Adams   **G.Kasparov** = = 1
                                              V.Kramnik
J.Polgar
V.Kramnik = = 1
                           V.Kramnik = = 1
M.Sadler   A.Vyzmanavin
A.Vyzmanavin = 1
                                              G.Kasparov 1 1
                                              P.Nikolic
A.Vaiser 1 1
V.Anand   **A.Vaiser** 1 0 1
                           V.Milov
V.Milov 1 1
V.Korchnoi   A.Vaiser
                                              P.Nikolic 1 =
V.Ivanchuk
I.Smirin = = 1
                           I.Smirin
V.Tkachiev   **P. Nikolic** = = 1
P.Nikolic = 1

In May Intel also introduced the World Chess Express Challenge in Munich, a blitz style tournament, again run with a preliminary qualification stage, with some of the world's leading players and a powerful computer. Kasparov finished equal first with *Fritz3* (run on an Intel, Pentium processor) and lost his individual encounter with the machine. Kasparov won the play-off comfortably but a day later, by losing a skittles game against the machine on German television, the PCA World Champion still had a bruised ego.

A number of the top players are not keen on playing against machines, Ivanchuk for instance, whose infamous 'no computers please' remark at the closing ceremony in London in front of the Intel sponsors certainly caused a stir. Computers are now becoming more than a nuisance(!) and will soon be too strong for humans in quickplay but sponsors of the powerful computers are obviously pleased to take the big scalps. However, I can see them being withdrawn from the actual tournaments and sidelined to exhibition matches, under pressure from the leading players, but there again, money talks.

Intel World Chess Express Challenge, Munich

Qualifiers from group A
15/18	O.Cvitan
12	J.Hjartarson, A.Wojtkiewicz, P.Nikolic

Qualifiers from group B
14/18	A.Chernin, M.Petursson, A.Dreev, Kir.Georgiev

Final
12½	G.Kasparov, Fritz 3/Pentium
12	V.Anand
11	N.Short, B.Gelfand, A.Dreev
10½	Kir.Georgiev
10	V.Kramnik
8½	O.Cvitan
8	P.Nikolic, G.Hertneck
7	R.Hübner
6	A.Chernin, A.Wojtkiewicz
5	E.Lobron, J.Hjartarson
4½	M.Petursson, P.Leko

G.Kasparov won the 'best of six' game play-off 4-1.

During 1994 there were also several other strong rapidplay tournaments:

Munich, Germany, January
8½/9	A.Raetsky

Aubervilliers, France, January
11/12	O.Korneev, R.Vasquez, A.Vaiser, O.Renet, Kr.Georgiev, A.Haik

The Parisian suburb of Aubervilliers was host to the year's largest two-day tournament with over 900 participants.

Eupen, Belgium, March
6½/7	A.Khalifman, V.Jansa

Garmisch-Partenkirchen, Germany, October

11½/16	M.Adams
10½	I.Sokolov
9	N.Short, M.Stangl
8½	G.Hertneck
8	W.Hug, C.Landenbergue
7½	K.Bischoff, R.Hübner, S.Kindermann
7	C.Lutz
6½	V.Korchnoi
6	L.Brunner
5½	A.Yusupov, L.van Wely
2½	E.Lobron

There was no quickplay in Oviedo this year as the normal dates would clash with the Olympiad. This Spanish extravaganza had certainly been the most important open quickplay event in 1993 but in the age of the Intel Grand Prix the organizers may have to think of new ideas for the next one, presumably to be held in December 1995.

Melody Amber, Monaco, March/April

The strongest novelty event of the year is Joop van Oosterom's annual 'Melody Amber' tournament in Monaco, held in March/April. The sponsor is a wealthy Dutch businessman who has named the tournament after his daughter. There is certainly a great deal of coverage of the event in the chess press, but van Oosterom's motivation as benefactor is essentially personal satisfaction with this and various other chess activities which he sponsors. The idea of getting several of the world's top players playing rapid blindfold chess with the 'Fischer clock' is unique and quite feasible if you offer lucrative enough conditions!

The 1994 tournament consisted of two round-robins (quickplay and blindfold) with a combined total at the end.

Quickplay

9/11	V.Anand, V.Kramnik
7	V.Ivanchuk, J.Polgar
6½	G.Kamsky
5	L.Ljubojevic
4½	J.Nunn, J.Piket

4	A.Karpov, V.Korchnoi
3	Zsu.Polgar
2½	Y.Seirawan

Blindfold

8/11	V.Anand
7½	V.Ivanchuk, G.Kamsky
7	V.Kramnik, Y.Seirawan
6½	A.Karpov
5	L.Ljubojevic, J.Nunn
4½	Zsu.Polgar
4	J.Polgar
2	V.Korchnoi, J.Piket

Combined

17/22	V.Anand
16	V.Kramnik
14½	V.Ivanchuk

Karpov only finished sixth overall. In fact, despite Karpov and Kasparov's domination of 'normal-speed' chess, the World Champions have struggled at the quicker time limits. The younger players, in general, and the three that headed the overall Melody Amber standings, in particular, have really emerged this year as major contenders in top rapidplay competitions.

No games in this section, there were so many good games played with the traditional time-limit that I have preferred to concentrate on those.

5 Important Round Robins

Nowadays, there are so many events worldwide that I have decided to give only the results of category XII or stronger (average strength at least 2526) tournaments, the stronger of which are given in greater detail. This book is about grandmaster chess and 2526 represents 'average grandmaster strength'. Coverage may not be complete; the reporting of some tournaments, particularly from Eastern Europe, can sometimes be patchy.

Anatoly Karpov achieved one of the great results of his superb tournament career at Linares but in a particularly active year he failed to win any other strong events, e.g. Dos Hermanas, Las Palmas and Dortmund.

On the other hand Garry Kasparov consistently finished first where games were played with the slower-time limit, except of course for Linares where he still obtained his expected score. Overall results suggest that Kasparov is still the world's No.1.

The other most notable round-robin achievement was by Judit Polgar, who won her strongest-ever event to register a best-ever female all-play-all performance; two games from the Madrid event can be found in Chapter 7.

As for the chasing group of younger players Kamsky has probably done enough to be considered the world No.3 at the time of writing.

Hastings (England), December/January, cat XII
7/9   J.Nunn
The traditional New Year event was much weaker this time due to financial constraints.

Bonn, Godesberger (Germany), January, cat XII
6½/9   O.Romanishin

Wijk aan Zee (A) (Netherlands), January, cat XIV
7/9   P.Nikolic
Once one of the main closed tournaments, Wijk aan Zee is now

definitely overshadowed by the sheer numbers of category XVI events around.

Linares (Spain), February/March, cat XVIII

11/13	A.Karpov
8½	G.Kasparov, A.Shirov
7½	E.Bareev
7	J.Lautier, V.Kramnik
6½	V.Topalov, G.Kamsky, V.Anand
6	V.Ivanchuk
5½	B.Gelfand
4½	M.Illescas
4	J.Polgar
2	A.Beliavsky

Although Novosibirsk was to have a higher category, the 14-player Linares event is really the round-robin that most caught the public's imagination in 1994. Arguments about such-and-such being the world's strongest ever tournament are very subjective, and comparing generations rarely proves very much, but without doubt, FIDE World champion Anatoly Karpov achieved one of the best results of all time in this tournament.

Alusta (Russia), February, cat XII

6/9	V.Malaniuk, A.Onischuk

Ter Apel, Kloster (Netherlands), March, cat XV

3/5	R.Dautov

Dos Hermanas, Seville (Spain), April/May, cat XVI

6½/9	B.Gelfand
6	A.Karpov
5½	V.Epishin
4½	V.Topalov
4	M.Illescas, J.Lautier, B.Gulko, J.Polgar
3½	I.Morovic
3	M.Rivas

Leon (Spain), May, cat XII

7/9	A.Beliavsky

Madrid (Spain), May, cat XVI

7/9	J.Polgar
5½	I.Sokolov
5	G.Kamsky, M.Illescas, A.Shirov
4½	S.Tiviakov, V.Salov
3½	J.Magem
2½	P.San Segundo, E.Bareev

This was the world's best-ever result by a female player. Of course Judit is still young and she's not finished yet!

Alusta (Russia), May, cat XIV

5½/9	A.Morozevich

The strongest of several closed tournaments organized in Alusta in 1994.

VSB Amsterdam (Netherlands), May, cat XVIII

4/6	G.Kasparov
3½	V.Ivanchuk
2½	J.Timman
2	N.Short

Lark, Las Palmas (Spain), May, cat XVII

6½/9	G.Kamsky
6	A.Karpov
5½	V.Topalov, J.Lautier
4½	J.Polgar
4	M.Adams, M.Illescas, I.Morovic
3½	A.Shirov
1½	V.Epishin

The fifth category XII or more on Spanish soil this year.

Credit Suisse, Munich (Germany), May/June, cat XVI

7½/11	V.Ivanchuk
7	A.Beliavsky, R.Hübner
6	E.Bareev
5½	B.Gelfand, E.Lobron, P.Nikolic
5	A.Yusupov, C.Lutz, G.Hertneck
3½	P.van der Sterren, J.Benjamin

Malmo (Sweden), June, cat XII
7/9   F.Hellers, C.Hansen

Jagodina (Yugoslavia), cat XII
6/9   V.Spasov

Dortmund (Germany), July, cat XVI
6½/9   J.Piket
5½   M.Adams
5   V.Epishin
4½   A.Yusupov, A.Dreev, V.Korchnoi, A.Karpov
4   J.Timman
3   C.Lutz, P.Leko

Pardubice (Czech Republic), July, cat XV
6/9   E.Bareev

Altensteig (Germany), July, cat XII
7/11   V.Zviaginsev, J.Speelman
The fourth German event to feature here.

PCA, Novgorod (Russia), August, cat XIX
7/10   G.Kasparov, V.Ivanchuk
5   V.Kramnik
4   N.Short, A.Shirov
3   E.Bareev
One of the strongest tournaments of all time (but only six players)!

Donner Memorial, Amsterdam (Netherlands), August, cat XV
5½/9   M.Adams, J.Piket, A.Yusupov

Barbarela Cup, Brno (Czech Republic), August/Sept, cat XIII
6/9   V.Epishin and A.Dreev

Credit Suisse, Horgen (Switzerland), September, cat XVI
8½/11   G.Kasparov
7   A.Yusupov, A.Shirov
6½   V.Korchnoi, J.Lautier
5½   B.Gelfand
5   P.Leko

4½ J.Benjamin, P.Nikolic
4   A.Miles, C.Lutz
3   V.Gavrikov

Jelenite (Bulgaria), September/October, cat XV
5½/9 I.Smirin, A.Khalifman, V.Epishin, V.Topalov
The strongest tournament ever held in Bulgaria and another success for the local star Topalov.

Linares (Mexico), October/November, cat XII
9/13 M.Illescas
The strongest closed tournament in the Americas this year.

Kasparov is the only player to come first or equal first three times in the tournaments featured above.

Those players finishing twice at the top include Epishin, Ivanchuk and Piket but not Karpov.

Game Ten
Anatoly Karpov-Judit Polgar
Linares 1994

Judit Polgar had an excellent year in 1994 and has now shown herself to be capable of inflicting serious damage to the egos of most of the world's best. Against the 'big two' she has yet to impose with the classical time limit, but nearly everyone else has proved vulnerable. Perhaps the 'two K's' try just that little bit harder against the young Hungarian in order not to be the first World Champion to fall victim to a woman!

Karpov has certainly sharpened his style in recent years, but this games collection would be incomplete without one game in which he wins *à la Karpov*.

1 e4   c5
2 c3

Later in the year Karpov used the same line to defeat Judit in another Spanish tournament, Dos Hermanas. In fact she became so tired of losing against 2 c3 that she even included it in her repertoire as White (see Chapter 7, game 29)!

2 ...   e6
3 d4   d5
4 exd5 exd5
5 ♘f3 ♘c6
6 ♗b5 c4

The conventional move is 6...♗d6 when the position is

analogous to a type of French Defence, Tarrasch variation. This quiet line suits Karpov who purposely avoids the type of game that would suit Judit's tactical imagination.

6...c4 is Judit's attempt to vary from such typical French-style positions but it proves to be probably too slow, although it requires a Karpov to show us why!

7 ♘e5 ♛b6

7...♗d7 is the most accurate way to develop: 8 ♗xc6 bxc6 (on 8...♗xc6 the pawn structure doesn't lend itself to pawn breaks and after 9 0-0 ♗d6 10 ♛g4 White has the more active pieces and a pleasant initiative) 9 0-0 ♗d6 10 ♖e1 ♘e7 is natural when White has the slightly better pawn structure and a timely b2-b3 will give him an edge, as in the game.

8 ♗xc6+

Simplest. Naturally 8 ♛a4 comes into consideration but then 8...♗d7 9 ♘xd7 ♔xd7 10 0-0 a6 11♗xc6+ ♛xc6 12 ♛d1 ♘f6 is probably not too bad for the second player; White has some difficulty in mounting an attack.

8 ... bxc6
9 0-0 ♗d6
10 b3!

After the inevitable exchange on b3 Black's weaknesses on the queenside become exposed. Opposite-coloured bishops do not represent much of a drawish factor here as White can pressurize

his opponent on the dark squares.

10 ... cxb3
11 axb3 ♘e7
12 ♗a3 ♗xe5?!

A better try was 12...♗xa3 although, with no counterplay and sensitive pawns, Black will have some difficulties in the middlegame. After 13 ♖xa3 0-0 14 ♘d2 for instance, Black doesn't equalize after 14...c5!? because of 15 dxc5 ♛xc5 16 b4 or 15 ♘df3.

13 dxe5 ♗e6

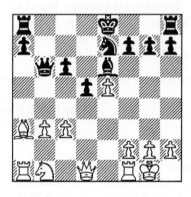

Critical is 13...c5 when in order to keep Black's king in the centre White has to try 14 b4 c4 15 b5!? with great play but no obvious breakthrough: 15...♛xb5 16 ♗xe7 (16 ♛h5 is also dangerous but perhaps not fatal for Black after 16...♗e6 17 ♘d2 ♛d7!) 16...♔xe7 17 ♛d4 ♗f5 18 ♖xa7+ (or 18 ♛h4+ ♔e6) 18...♖xa7 19 ♛xa7+ ♛d7 20 ♛c5+ ♔e6.

14 ♛d4! ♘f5

Now 14...♛xb3? is too risky after either 15 ♘d2 or the more forcing 15 ♗xe7 ♔xe7 16 ♖xa7+ ♖xa7 17 ♛xa7+ ♗d7 18 ♛c5+

♔e8 19 ♘d2 ♕b5 20 ♕d6 and wins.

15 ♕c5 h5

Black lacks central control, so here she at least tries to stabilize the knight on f5.

16 ♘d2 f6

This gives access to the f7 square and a little breathing space in the black camp.

17 exf6 gxf6

18 ♗b4

Karpov could in fact win a pawn here with 18 ♕xb6 axb6 19 ♗c5! as 19...♖b8 fails to 20 ♗xb6 ♖xb6 21 ♖a8+ and 19...♖xa1 20 ♖xa1 ♔f7 21 ♗xb6 ♖b8 22 ♗c5 ♖b5 leaves Black with no compensation, but of course the ending would still have to be won. One of the most difficult dichotomies in chess is the decision whether to keep the bind or win material but in the process reduce the pressure.

18 ... ♔f7

19 ♖a4

Preparing to double or even switch along the fourth rank if need be. Black has to find a way to avoid losing the a-pawn as there is a threat of 20 ♖fa1 followed by 21 ♖xa7.

19 ... ♕xc5

20 ♗xc5 a6

20...a5 simply loses the a-pawn after 21 ♖fa1.

21 f3

Karpov first improves the position of his king before making further headway on the queenside.

21 ... h4

Judit could again ditch the a-pawn by 21...♖ae8 22 ♖xa6 ♗c8 but it all looks to no avail after 23 ♖a7+! (possible but more double-edged is 23 ♖xc6 ♖e2 24 ♖f2 ♖e1+ 25 ♘f1) 23...♔g6 24 ♔f2 stopping any penetration by the rook.

22 ♖fa1 ♗c8

23 ♔f2 ♖b8

24 b4 ♖e8

25 ♘b3 ♗b7

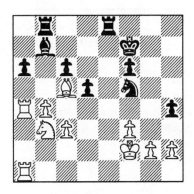

26 ♘a5

Karpov keeps his bind. Again he can win a pawn but this would enable Black to liberate herself after 26 ♗a7?! ♖a8 27 ♗b6 ♘d6! (heading for c4) 28 ♘c5 ♗c8! (28...♘c4? fails to 29 ♘xb7 ♘xb6 30 ♖xa6) when 29 ♘xa6? loses to 29...♘c4 30 ♗d4 ♘b2 31 ♖4a2 ♖xa6! 32 ♖xa6 ♗xa6 33 ♖xa6 ♘d3+ 34 ♔f1 ♖e1 mate!

26 ... ♗a8

27 ♖4a2 ♖e6

28 ♗a7!

Now this idea works. Karpov first putting his rook on a2 to

avoid any tactical surprises.

28　...　♖b5?!

Bad, but the pressure was difficult to live with. Resistance can be extended with 28...♖be8 29 ♘b3 ♖6e7 (after 29...♗b7? 30 ♘c5 ♖6e7 31 ♘xb7 ♖xb7 32 ♗c5! White picks up the a-pawn but keeps total control) but 30 ♗c5 (rather than 30 ♖xa6?! ♖e2+ 31 ♔f1 ♖b2 and Black is out of the box) 30...♖e6 31 g4 hxg3+ 32 hxg3 ♗b7 33 g4 turns the screw a little tighter.

29　♘b3　♗b7
30　g4!

Switching flanks in order to finally push back the knight. The threat of the knight coming to d4 is decisive.

30　...　hxg3+
31　hxg3　♖e8
32　g4　♘d6
33　♘d4　1-0

The rook is mated!

Game Eleven
Anatoly Karpov-Vaselin Topalov
Linares 1994

Karpov is a real master of the type of patient game, in which he probes away at his opponent's sensitive points until they give way, that we saw above. This has led many ordinary chess enthusiasts to classify Karpov as a technical or even boring player, but he is also more than capable of playing in combinative style (as the next game illustrates). In fact, the world No.2 is just as ready as anyone else to sacrifice material and play for the attack given the right circumstances.

Topalov has established himself in a short period of time as a world top-twenty player. Three to four years ago he played extensively in opens and smaller closed tournaments, primarily in Spain. His apprenticeship complete, he obtained the magic 2600-rating two years ago and started getting invites to the top events. This year he achieved a creditable 50% in his first Linares and led an inspired Bulgarian team that finished 5th in the Moscow Olympiad. The twenty-year-old topped off a good year with an individual victory over Kasparov that can be found in Chapter 9.

1　d4

Karpov is equally happy playing this move as he is in indulging in king's pawn openings (see game 10). This is true of most of the world's top players, Nigel Short being a notable exception in that he exclusively plays 1 e4.

1　...　♘f6
2　c4　c5

A move that Karpov cannot have expected as the young Bulgarian is not known as a Benoni player. Critical is now 3 d5, but both 3...b5 (Benko Gambit) and 3...e6 (Modern Benoni) are complex openings requiring good preparation. Therefore Karpov side-steps any special preparation with his next, more cautious, developing move.

| 3 | ♘f3 | cxd4 |
| 4 | ♘xd4 | e6 |

Club and weekend tournament players often like to indulge in the speculative 4...e5 5 ♘b5 d5!? 6 cxd5 ♗c5, but this is rarely seen at top level.

| 5 | g3 | ♘c6 |
| 6 | ♗g2 | ♗c5 |

An alternative way of striking at the white knight is 6...♕b6!? when 7 ♘b5 (or 7 ♘b3 ♘e5 8 ♕c2 ♕b4+ 9 ♘1d2 d5!) 7...d5! 8 ♗e3 ♕a5+ gives Black active play. I believe that Black does best to try and 'mix-it' early on with these more combative lines, otherwise he usually ends up with a rather passive position, as we see in the game.

7	♘b3	♗e7
8	♘c3	0-0
9	0-0	d6

Black would like to liberate his position by ...d7-d5, but this is impossible in the short term as White's whole development has been geared to keeping Black restrained.

| 10 | ♗f4 | ♘h5 |
| 11 | e3!? | |

Natural is 11 ♗e3 ♗d7 12 ♖c1 when White maintains an edge

after 12...♕b8 13 ♕c2 ♘f6 14 ♖fd1 ♖d8 15 ♘e4 ♕c7 16 ♗f4, though Black has a solid enough position; Pekarek - Schulz, Berlin 1988.

The text is certainly a surprising new idea: Karpov envisages pressure on the d- and e-files with his rooks. In this way Topalov's bishop pair is reduced to a purely defensive role.

| 11 | ... | ♘xf4 |

11...♘f6 is inconsistent and loses time after 12 e4.

| 12 | exf4 | ♗d7 |
| 13 | ♕d2 | ♕b8 |

Slightly awkward looking but 13...a6 14 ♖fd1 ♕c7 15 ♘e4 hits d6 very quickly.

| 14 | ♖fe1 | |

The bishop on e7 is exposed to an early f5 by White, hence Black's next.

| 14 | ... | g6 |
| 15 | h4! | |

Now that ...g7-g6 has been played Karpov decides to soften up the black kingside.

| 15 | ... | a6 |

15...h5 would be far too weakening.

| 16 | h5 | b5? |

Naturally seeking counterplay and trying to distract his opponent from any kingside ambitions. However, better was the patient 16...♖d8 aiming to defend by 17 hxg6 hxg6 18 ♖ad1 ♗e8 as now ...b7-b5 will be appropriate. The text allows Karpov to switch to combinative mode!

| 17 | hxg6 | hxg6 |

18   ♘c5!   dxc5

After 18...♗e8 White has 19 ♘xa6! ♖xa6 20 cxb5 ♖b6 21 bxc6 ♖xb2 22 ♖ab1! and Black has no compensation for the pawn.

19   ♕xd7   ♖c8

20   ♖xe6!

A shock! Black's pieces can more or less cope with the threats on the queenside but are not well placed to rescue the king. The Bulgarian had probably anticipated 20 ♗xc6 ♖a7 (evidently 20...♖c7? 21 ♕xc7 ♕xc7 22 ♗xa8 leaves White with far too much for the queen) 21 ♕d3 ♖xc6 22 cxb5 axb5 23 ♘xb5 ♖a4! (inferior are 23...♖b7 allowing White to consolidate the extra pawn with 24 a4 and 23...c4 leading to a dubious ending after 24 ♘xa7! cxd3 25 ♘xc6 ♕d6 26 ♘xe7+ ♕xe7 27 ♖ad1 where White would have excellent winning chances) with active play for the pawn.

20   ...   ♖a7

20...fxe6 loses a tempo over

the game continuation: 21 ♕xe6+ ♔g7 22 ♗xc6 ♖a7 23 cxb5 and White has three pawns plus an attack for the exchange.

21   ♖xg6+! fxg6

Other moves lose swiftly: 21...♔f8 can be met by 22 ♕h3! when 22...fxg6 23 ♕h8+ ♔f7 24 ♗d5 is already mate and after 21...♔h7 22 ♕h3+! ♔xg6 23 ♗e4+ Black can avoid immediate mate only by 23...f5 when 24 ♕xf5+ ♔g7 25 ♕g6+ ♔f8 26 ♗d5 ♗d6 27 ♖e1 is crushing.

22   ♕e6+   ♔g7
23   ♗xc6   ♖d8

Hopeless is 23...bxc4 in view of 24 ♗e4! ♗f6 25 ♕g4 and in this variation 24...♕d6 fails to 25 ♕xc8.

24   cxb5   ♗f6

Desperately trying to hide the denuded king away from the attacking pieces. Black loses material after both 24...♕d6 25 ♕xd6 ♗xd6 26 b6 and 24...axb5 25 ♘xb5.

25   ♘e4   ♗d4

Topalov could hardly have taken on b2 as after 25...♗xb2 26 ♖b1 ♗d4 27 b6 ♖f7 28 ♘g5 the black defences are again breached.

26   bxa6

If we summarize the tally, White temporarily has four(!) pawns for the exchange. Topalov will surely pick some of them off but in the meantime Karpov can move in for the kill.

26   ...   ♕b6

The Bulgarian No.1 must have

spent some time considering 26...♕xb2. After 27 ♖d1 ♖f8 the cheeky 28 ♗e8 looks strong at first sight because 28...♗f6 is inadequate, e.g. 29 ♘xf6 ♕xf6 30 ♖d7+ ♖xd7 31 ♕xd7+ ♔h8 32 a7 ♕a1+ 33 ♔g2 ♕xa2 34 ♕e7 ♕d5+ 35 f3 and the a-pawn wins the game for White.

A better try is 28...♖xe8! 29 ♕xe8 ♕xa2 30 ♔g2 ♕g8! with some hope of a successful defence.

So the real reason for his rejection of 26...♕xb2 (after 27 ♖d1 ♖f8) was probably 28 ♗b7! keeping Black tied down as 28...♖xb7 29 axb7 ♕xb7 fails to 30 ♘xc5(!).

27   ♖d1   ♕xa6

27...♗xf2+?? would be a blunder as 28 ♘xf2 defends the white rook.

28   ♖xd4!

Black's best piece is eliminated and his king is open to the winds.

28   ...   ♖xd4
29   ♕f6+   ♔g8

Even worse are 29...♔h6 (because of 30 f5 ♖d1+ 31 ♔h2 ♖g7 32 ♕h4 mate) and 29...♔h7 (30 ♘g5+ etc.).

30   ♕xg6+   ♔f8

30...♖g7 allows mate in three by 31 ♕e8+ ♔h7 32 ♘f6+ ♔h6 33 ♕h5.

31   ♕e8+   ♔g7
32   ♕e5+

32 ♘xc5 is suggested by Karpov as an easier win. It's true that 32...♖d1+ 33 ♔h2 ♕f1 34 ♕e5+ ♔h6 35 ♕g5+ ♔h7 36 ♗e4+ ♔h8 37 ♕h5+ ♔g8 38 ♕e8+ ♔g7 39 ♘e6+ ♔f6 40 ♕g6+ ♔e7 41 ♕g7+ ♔xe6 42 ♕xa7 is winning but the text is in fact simplest.

32   ...   ♔g8
33   ♘f6+   ♔f7

34   ♗e8+?

It is here that Karpov complicated his task as 34 ♗d5+ wins easily: 34...♔f8? (34...♖xd5 is the only move to delay the inevitable but 35 ♘xd5 wins slowly but surely) 35 ♕e8+ ♔g7 36 ♕g8+ ♔xf6 37 ♕g5 is mate.

| 34 | ... | ♔f8 |

34...♔g7 35 ♘d7+ ♔g8 36 ♕g5+ leads to a forced win after 36...♔h8 37 ♕h5+ ♔g7 38 ♕f7+ ♔h6 39 ♕f8+ ♔h7 40 ♘f6+ ♕xf6 41 ♕xf6.

| 35 | ♕xc5+ | ♕d6 |
| 36 | ♕xa7 | ♕xf6 |

Black should have played for an unlikely draw with 36...♖d1+

37 ♔g2 ♖g1+ 38 ♔h3! (38 ♔xg1 ♕d1+ 39 ♔g2 ♕h1+ 40 ♔xh1 stalemate!) 38...♕e6+, however 39 ♘g4 is ugly but effective; White has knight and five pawns for a rook.

37	♗h5	♖d2
38	b3	♖b2
39	♔g2	1-0

Game Twelve
Vladimir Kramnik-Garry Kasparov
Linares 1994

This game was a prelude to a rather mediocre (by his very high standards) year for Kasparov. He later suffered unexpected losses to Lautier (also at Linares, see game 14), Shneider (in November) and Topalov (at the Moscow Olympiad in December, see game 34) and had rather mixed results in the Intel Grand Prix.

Kramnik is another of the 'computer generation' who has arrived on the scene in double-quick time. Kramnik-Kasparov encounters invariably produce thrilling chess, no doubt with added spice from the fact that Kramnik was a student of the world champion, who has tipped Kramnik as his eventual successor.

1	♘f3	♘f6
2	c4	g6
3	♘c3	♗g7
4	e4	

White's move-order is directed at avoiding the Grünfeld Defence, but Kasparov is happy to play his favourite King's Indian.

4	...	d6
5	d4	0-0
6	♗e2	e5
7	d5	♘bd7!?

This, the old-fashioned line, may now see a revival as a result of Kasparov's interest.

Most grandmasters prefer 7...a5 when 8 ♗g5 h6 9 ♗h4 ♘a6 10 0-0 ♕e8 (unpinning without weakening the pawn structure) 11 ♘d2 ♘h7 12 a3 ♗d7 13 ♔h1 h5 14 f3 ♗h6 represents typical play. This was how the game Illescas-Gelfand proceeded one round later (another recent example is the game Shirov-J.Polgar from Chapter 7).

| 8 | ♗g5 | h6 |
| 9 | ♗h4 | g5 |

It's natural to chase the bishop but the downside is that if, and when, Black plays ...f7-f5 he can no longer recapture on f5 with a pawn after White's likely exf5. White can in this case lay claim to the important e4 square. Kasparov aims to remain active so that any light square problems won't become a major factor.

10	♗g3	♘h5
11	h4	g4
12	♘h2	

More natural would seem to be 12 ♘d2 as, in the game continuation, the knight on h2 is rather out of play. However, with less pressure on g4 Black can then consider 12...f5!? 13 exf5 ♘df6 or even 12...♘df6 13 ♘f1 ♘f4 14 ♘e3 h5 to seek counterplay.

12	...	♘xg3
13	fxg3	h5
14	0-0	f5!

Kasparov typically chooses the most aggressive course of action. After 14...♘f6 15 ♕d2 ♘e8 16 ♗d3 Black has a passive game and it is unlikely that he will ever have another chance to play the ...f7-f5 break (here 16...f5? just loses a pawn).

Another idea is 14...♗h6!? repositioning the bishop on a more active diagonal but after 15 ♗d3 it may again be difficult to organize the right conditions to play ...f7-f5.

15	exf5	♘c5
16	b4!?	

The most critical. Black has a good game after the slower 16 ♖f2 ♗xf5 17 ♘f1 ♗g6 18 ♖xf8+ ♕xf8 19 b4 e4.

| 16 | ... | e4 |

17	♖c1	♘d3

Kasparov is not one to retreat! The alternative 17...♘a6 18 ♘xe4 ♗xf5 19 ♘g5 ♘xb4 at first sight looks playable but after 20 ♕d2 a5 21 a3 ♘a6 22 ♗d3! (rather than 22 ♕xa5? ♘c5 23 ♕b4 ♖a4 which favours Black) White exposes the light squares around the black king, e.g. 22...♕d7 23 ♕c2, etc.

18	♗xd3	exd3
19	f6!	

Easy to miss. The inferior 19 ♕xd3 ♕f6 allows Black to solve all his problems and the bishops will start to dominate after ...♗xf5, etc.

19	...	♖xf6
20	♕xd3	

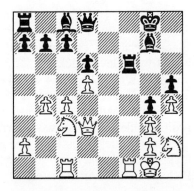

Kramnik is facing the bishop pair with two knights in an open position. Furthermore, his knight on h2 is out of play for the present, but he does have a strong threat of ♘c3-e4-g5 and the safer king.

20	...	♕f8

Kasparov is intending to meet

21 ♘e4 by 21...♖xf1+ 22 ♖xf1 (instead 22 ♘xf1 allows Black good counterplay with 22...♗f5 23 ♘e3 ♗g6!? 24 ♖f1 ♕e7 25 ♘f5 ♗xf5 26 ♖xf5 ♖e8) 22...♗f5 when 23 ♘f6+ ♕xf6 24 ♖xf5 hoping to win the h-pawn is too slow: 24...♕d4+ 25 ♕xd4 ♗xd4+ 26 ♔f1 (or 26 ♔h1 ♖e8) 26...♖f8 27 ♖xf8+ ♔xf8 and White's extra pawn is useless.

| 21 | ♘b5 | ♗f5 |
| 22 | ♖xf5! | |

Too tempting to resist! Kramnik sacrifices the exchange for some good outposts for his cavalry.

22	...	♖xf5
23	♘xc7	♖c8
24	♘e6	♕f6
25	♘f1	

The obvious 25 ♖f1 aiming to exchange pieces and reduce Black's chances of counterplay, is met by a clever trick: 25...♖f8! 26 ♘xf8 ♕d4+ 27 ♕xd4 ♗xd4+ 28 ♔h1 ♖xf1+ 29 ♘xf1 ♔xf8 and White cannot improve his position, despite his two pawn advantage, due to his king being locked permanently out of play. Perhaps Black is even better!

| 25 | ... | ♖e5 |

Not intending the counter-sacrifice by ...♖xe6, as Black remains a pawn down and would still have the more exposed king, but rather the exchange of queens by ...♕f5 as the rooks then become more powerful.

| 26 | ♖d1 | |

Unfortunately for Kramnik, 26 ♘d2 ♕f5 27 ♕xf5 ♖xf5 28 ♘e4 fails to 28...♖xd5 exploiting the pin on the c-file hence the need to reposition the rook. After 26 ♘e3? White loses material to 26...♗h6.

| 26 | ... | ♕f5 |

Now after 26...♗h6 White expands in the centre with 27 c5 dxc5 28 bxc5.

| 27 | ♕xf5 | ♖xf5 |
| 28 | c5 | ♗f8! |

The bishop defends well on the a3-f8 diagonal.

| 29 | ♘e3 | ♖f6 |
| 30 | ♘c4! | |

Sacrificing a pawn to keep the initiative. Things are hotting up!

| 30 | ... | dxc5 |
| 31 | b5 | ♗h6? |

An unfortunate move for Kasparov when there was a good alternative available. After 31...♖e8! if Black is allowed to capture twice on e6 then he would have no problems. So logical would then be 32 ♖e1 ♖f5 33 ♖d1 ♖f6 with a repetition. Was the world No.1 looking for more?

White can in turn try and win with 32 ♘f4 when 32...♗d6 33 ♘xh5 ♖h6 34 ♘xd6 ♖xd6 35 ♘f4 ♖e3!? (35...♖e5 is simplest as 36 ♔f2 ♔f7 37 ♖e1? ♖xe1 38 ♔xe1 ♔f6 39 ♔d2 a6! even favours Black.) 36 ♔f2 ♖a3 gives Black adequate counterplay. So 31...♖e8 equalizes.

| 32 | ♖e1 | |

Preparing 33 d6.

| 32 | ... | ♖e8 |

33 ♖e5

The d-pawn is stymied (33 d6?? ♖fxe6 34 ♖xe6 ♖xe6 35 d7 ♖e1+ 36 ♔f2 ♖d1 wins for Black) but the black h-pawn now catches Kramnik's attention!

33 ... ♖e7
34 ♖xh5 ♖ef7
35 ♔h2 ♗c1
36 ♖e5

36 ♘e5?! is met by 36...♖f5! when the knights and passed pawns are no match for Black's rook and bishop: 37 ♖xf5 ♖xf5 38 ♘xg4 (insufficient is 38 d6? as following 38...♖xe5 39 d7 ♖d5 40 d8♕+ ♖xd8 41 ♘xd8 c4 42 ♘e6 ♗e3 it is Black who queens) 38...♔f7 Black picks up the d-pawn and the open position suits him well, and after the further 39 ♘xc5 ♖xd5 40 ♘xb7 ♗a3 41 ♘a5 ♖xb5 42 ♘c6 a6 Black has the dangerous plan of picking up the white a-pawn.

36 ... ♖f1
37 ♖e4

The g-pawn falls. Kasparov's attempt to activate at all costs was evidently too optimistic.

37 ... ♖d1
38 ♖xg4+ *(D)*
38 ... ♔h7?

The alternative 38...♔h8 would give the PCA World Champion a fighting chance! For instance, 39 ♘e5? only draws after 39...♖ff1 40 ♘g6+ ♔h7 41 ♘gf8+ ♔h8. Better is 39 ♖e4! (in order to meet 39...♖ff1 with 40 ♔h3 and White avoids mate). After 39...♖xd5 40 ♘e5! (40 g4? im-

mediately is less good as 40...♖e7 41 ♘xc5 ♖xe4 42 ♘xe4 ♖d4 43 ♘cd6 ♗f4+ or 41 g5 ♖d4! even win for Black) 40...♖f6 41 ♘f3 with g3-g4-g5 to follow. White's pieces are beautifully placed to support his pawns. The consensus of opinion after the game was that Black should still lose and a deeper investigation seems to support this: 41...♗b2 (41...c4 is inadequate due to 42 ♖xc4!) 42 g4 c4 43 g5 c3 (43...♖g6? 44 ♘f4 wins) 44 gxf6 c2 45 f7 ♖f5 46 ♖f4! ♖xf4 (also losing are 46...c1♕ 47 ♖xf5 and 46...♖xf7 47 ♖xf7 c1♕ 48 ♘fg5 and after chasing the white king up the board Black will be mated) 47 ♘xf4 ♔g7 48 ♘d3 ♔xf7 49 g4 c1♕ 50 ♘xc1 ♗xc1 51 ♔g3 and White wins the ending.

So with best play Kasparov was still in trouble.

39 ♘e5 ♖e7

Equally hopeless is 39...♖ff1 40 ♖g7+ ♔h6 41 ♘f7+ (simplest) 41...♖xf7 (41...♔h5 42 g4+ ♔xh4 43 g3 mate) 42 ♖xf7

♖xd5 43 g4 and White wins routinely.

40　♘f8+　　1-0

40...♔h8 loses a rook after 41 ♘fg6+ and 40...♔h6 permits mate in three by 41 ♖g6+ ♔h8 42 g4+ ♔xh4 43 g3.

Game Thirteen
Garry Kasparov-Vishwanathan Anand
Linares 1994

Meetings between the strongest-ever Asian player and the leading player in the world often generate sharp complications. This game was certainly no exception.

1　e4　　c5
2　♘c3　d6
3　♘ge2

Not the prelude to a closed game, just jockeying for position.

3　...　♘c6
4　d4

That's better!

4　...　cxd4
5　♘xd4　♘f6
6　♗c4

In an analogous position Nigel Short frequently tried this move against Kasparov in their 1993 match.

6　...　♕b6

An early ...♕b6 has the advantage of forcing the knight to retreat but if Black intends to play the thematic ...b7-b5 he has to again move his queen, losing back any temporary gain of time.

7　♘b3　e6
8　♗f4!?

An unexpected move. One would anticipate 8 ♗e3 with f2-f4 to follow but this in fact occurs after further transpositional play.

8　...　♘e5

Naturally 8...♕c7 9 ♘b5 would not do, and 8...e5 would be ugly after 9 ♗g5 when White will play for control of d5.

9　♗e2　♗e7
10　♗e3　♕c7
11　f4

If we count the superfluous moves, both sides have expended the same three tempi: for White one with each bishop and one with the knight. Black's three came about as the knight loses two and the queen one.

Many opening books concentrate on the theory once the standard positions are reached but ignore the importance of move-orders and transpositional possibilities that are common in grandmaster play. Trying to channel the game away from your opponent's pet-lines and into your own preparation is typical of top-class praxis.

11　...　♘c6

After 11...♘c4?! White has 12 ♘b5 when after 12...♕c6 13 ♗xc4 ♕xc4 the simple 14 ♕d3 gives Black an unpleasant choice between consolidating the white centre with 14...♕xd3 15 cxd3 (when White threatens both the a-pawn and 16 ♘c7+) or 14...♕c6 and after 15 ♘3d4 retreating with the ugly 15...♕d7 (when White has the more harmonious position after 16 0-0).

12 ♗f3 a6
13 0-0 0-0

Leaving the king in the centre and starting queenside play with 13...b5!? is interesting but not recommended in beginner's books. Kasparov indicates that this is not advised but White must open lines immediately with 14 e5 dxe5 15 fxe5 ♘d7 16 ♗xc6 ♕xc6 17 ♘d4 when he has a strong initiative: 17...♕c7 (17...♕b7 is worse as 18 ♕g4 g6 19 ♖xf7! yields a fantastic attack) 18 ♖xf7 ♔xf7 19 ♕f3+ ♔g8 20 ♘d5! when Black can only hope for a rotten ending a pawn down after 20...♘xe5 (20...exd5? loses to 21 ♕xd5+ ♔f8 22 ♘e6+ and White takes the queen with check) 21 ♘xe7+ ♕xe7 22 ♕xa8 ♕b7 23 ♕xb7 ♗xb7 24 ♘xe6.

14 a4

A standard move to restrain ...b5-b4.

14 ... b6
15 g4!

Despite his own king becoming exposed by this push Kasparov goes for an immediate attack.

15 ... ♖b8

The 'magician from Madras' gets himself organized but gives the 'butcher from Baku' time for the attack to really get underway. Instead he could have tried 15...d5 based on the principle that 'an attack on the flank should be met with a counter in the centre' but its specific variations that count. Here 16 exd5 ♖d8 17 dxc6! ♖xd1 18 ♖axd1 gives White full material compensation for the queen and a positional advantage in view of the strength of the c6 pawn.

16 g5 ♘d7
17 ♗g2

Moving out of the way of the heavy pieces.

17 ... ♖e8
18 ♖f3 ♘c5!?

Desperately trying to get active as 18...b5 19 axb5 axb5 fails to the unlikely 20 ♗f1 b4 21 ♘b5 winning the d6 pawn. The problem with 18...g6 19 ♖h3 ♗f8 20 ♕g4 ♗g7 is that its rather passive and as such White is set few problems.

19 ♖h3 g6
20 ♕g4

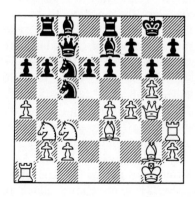

20 ... ♘b4?

The problem for Anand is to defend his kingside while creating some play for himself. The text tries to keep Kasparov occupied elsewhere but the knights are straying away from the defence of his king. With the benefit of hindsight it seems that Black should try and club together his defences on the kingside first, before chasing confusion on the other wing. There are two methods:

a) he can instead seek to defend patiently by 20...♗f8 21 ♖f1 h5 22 gxh6 ♔h7 where the knight on c6 is ready to come to e5 in the case of f5 by White. This may be rather passive but there is no immediate breakthrough for White.

Or he can try and provoke his opponent into a risky sacrifice with

b) 20...h5 when Kasparov would have been sorely tempted by 21 ♖xh5 gxh5 22 ♕xh5 ♗f8 23 f5 and after the best defence 23...♗b7 24 ♖f1 f6 Kasparov considers the position to be unclear. Its hard to disagree with him at the best of times but here variations like 25 gxf6 (25 ♕g6+ ♕g7 26 gxf6 ♘e5) 25...♕h7 26 ♕g6+ ♔h8 27 ♘xc5 bxc5 28 f7 ♖e7 are given by him to justify his claim. The rook sacrifice is fascinating but impossible to fully calculate, so would Kasparov have played it? The alternative 21 gxh6 allows Black to hide behind the pawn with

21...♔h7.

| 21 | ♕h4 | h5 |
| 22 | ♗f3 | ♗f8 |

22...♔g7, hoping for 23 ♗xh5? ♖h8, is refuted by first playing 23 f5! exf5 24 ♗d4+ and only after 24...♔g8 then 25 ♗xh5.

23 ♗xh5!

Kasparov immediately goes for gold. Lesser players would have first defended c2 and thereby allowed their opponent a crucial extra tempo for the defence.

23 ... gxh5

The main alternative 23...♗g7 could be met by 24 ♗d1 holding onto an extra pawn but giving up on the attack. Then 24...♗b7 would give Black play by hitting at White's other soft target, the e4 square. However, 24 ♗d4! is more in Kasparov's style when 24...gxh5 proves to be inadequate as 25 ♕xh5 ♗xd4+ 26 ♘xd4 ♔f8 27 ♕h8+ ♔e7 28 ♕f6+ ♔d7 29 ♖h7 is too strong. After 24...e5 White crashes through after 25 f5:

a) 25...gxh5 is again hopeless in view of 26 ♕xh5 ♔f8 27 ♕h7 ♔e7 28 ♗xc5 bxc5 29 ♕xg7 and White is even ahead on material;

b) 25...exd4 26 ♗xg6 fxg6 27 ♕h7+ ♔f8 28 ♖f1 gxf5 29 exf5 with f6 to follow and the attack is too strong;

c) 25...gxf5 is met by 26 ♗xc5 bxc5 27 g6! ♗e6 (on 27...f6 White can simply play 28 ♗e2 and not surprisingly Black has difficulty meeting all the threats, e.g. 28...♗e6 29 ♕h7+ ♔f8 30 exf5) 28 gxf7+ ♗xf7 29 exf5 and now my Fritz2 program prefers Black after 29...♘xc2 but in fact the attack is clearly too strong following either 30 f6 ♘xa1 31 ♘xa1 ♗xh5 32 ♖g3 or 31 ♖g3! ♗xh5 32 ♕xh5 ♘xb3 33 ♘d5 ♕d7 34 fxg7 ♕xg7 35 ♘f6+ ♔f8 36 ♖xg7 ♔xg7 37 ♘xe8+.

24	♕xh5	♗g7
25	♗d4	e5
26	f5	♘xe4

The only chance. Instead Black doesn't last long after capturing on d4, e.g. 26...exd4 27 ♕h7+ ♔f8 28 f6 ♘e6 29 ♕h8+(!).

27	♕h7+	♔f8
28	♘xe4	

Again immediately capturing on d4 is refuted by 29 f6 so Anand must first eliminate this most dangerous of pawns.

28	...	♗xf5
29	♕xf5	exd4
30	♘f6	

Still attacking, despite the simplification and open centre.

30	...	♕xc2
31	♘xd4!	

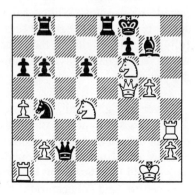

A good move, showing that White can continue his attack remorselessly even in a queenless middlegame. Now 31...♕xf5 sheds a piece after 32 ♘xf5 ♖ed8 33 ♘h7+! and 31...♕d2 loses the exchange after 32 ♘d7+ (32 ♖f1 sacrificing the knight for the attack is interesting but unnecessary) 32...♔e7 33 ♘b3 ♕c2 34 ♕xc2 ♘xc2 35 ♘xb8 as 35...♘xa1 is refuted by 36 ♖e3+ ♗e5 37 ♘c6+ ♔d7 38 ♘xe5+ ♖xe5 39 ♖xe5 ♘xb3 40 ♖f5 ♔e7 41 h4 with a winning ending. Instead 35...♖xb8 36 ♖c1 should win simply for White as 36...♖c8? loses to 37 ♘a1(!).

31	...	♕xb2
32	♖d1	

The simplest. White can now be sure of winning the exchange and of course the attack continues.

32	...	♖e5
33	♘d7+	♔e7
34	♘xe5	♗xe5
35	♕e4	1-0

This centralizing move prepares 36 ♘f3 and the activation of the rooks. Now on 35...♖g8 then 36 ♕b7+, or after 35...♘a2 then 36 ♘c6+. In fact Black can do nothing but wait for his demise hence Anand's immediate resignation.

One doesn't become World Champion by talent alone. Talent is wasted without a lot of hard work and this can be illustrated by the depth and incisiveness of

Kasparov's notes. He analyses in great detail and even his most fantastic of variations are very difficult to improve upon.

Game Fourteen
Garry Kasparov-Joel Lautier
Linares 1994

The multi-lingual Joel Lautier has the qualities of hard work and discipline, a good all-round education, with a touch of flair; the product of having a French father and a Japanese mother. Even when he was only fourteen I was astonished with his detailed knowledge of an opening variation that as far as I knew he didn't play! Polugayevsky, who is at present recovering from a serious operation, was his trainer in the crucial years when he graduated from being a promising junior into a potential world-beater.

Some of the year's best games are victories against one or other of the 'two K's'. To beat one of them you generally have to do something a little bit special. Here Lautier more than holds his own in wild complications, normally Kasparov's domain.

1	e4	e5
2	♘f3	♘c6
3	♗c4	

Kasparov would generally be expected to play 3 d4 or 3 ♗b5. With modern databases it's necessary for *la creme* to have a number of surprises in the locker, such as the introduction of this totally unlikely opening.

| 3 | ... | ♗c5 |
| 4 | c3 | |

Kasparov obviously hasn't yet found a way of reviving the dubious Evans' Gambit with 4 b4.

| 4 | ... | ♘f6 |
| 5 | d3 | d6 |

Interesting is 5...a6!? when White's queenside expansion with b2-b4 and a2-a4 can only be achieved with loss of time. But Kasparov has another scheme in mind.

| 6 | ♗b3 | |

A typical repositioning of the bishop to avoid its unfavourable exchange by ...a7-a6 and ...♘a5. With the game being of a fairly quiet nature (so far!) such a loss of time is forgivable.

6 b4 ♗b6 7 a4 a6 8 a5 is preferred by some; White gains space but if Black can successfully organize ...d6-d5 then the white pawn chain may come under pressure.

| 6 | ... | h6 |

Covering g5 and preparing ...♗e6. It's worth noting that both players refrain from early castling as there is a danger that the opponent would then leave the king in the centre and concentrate on kingside expansion.

7	h3	a6
8	♘bd2	♗e6
9	♗c2	

Kasparov is intent on keeping the tension as 9 ♗xe6 fxe6 10 ♕b3 ♕c8 leads nowhere for White, who has no way to exploit the doubled pawns. Lautier proposes instead 9 ♘c4 as after the text Black is ready to play the freeing ...d6-d5.

9	...	♗a7

The dubious 9...d5?! would allow a standard theme 10 ♘xe5! (as is known from many 1 e4 e5 openings) when both 10...♗xf2+ and 10...♘xe5 11 d4 ♗d6 12 dxe5 ♗xe5 13 ♘f3 give White the better of it.

10	♕e2	♕e7
11	b4	

Only now does Kasparov seek to expand on this wing as 11 ♘f1 d5 12 ♘g3 offers no advantage.

11	...	d5
12	a4	

Lautier is now faced with the awkward threat of 13 b5, hitting the knight and undermining the e5 square, hence his next move.

12	...	b5!
13	0-0	0-0

As the action has begun on the other side of the board both players hurry to castle as there is now little chance of anyone launching an immediate kingside attack.

14	axb5	axb5

Threatening 15...♗xf2+ which is best met by 15 ♗b2, simply completing development and de-

fending the weak c3 point, when after 15...♗b6 chances are about equal.

15	d4?	

Kasparov never lacks the courage to go in for the critical continuation, but here his opponent's pieces are more active and the young Frenchman is not to be ruffled by such brutal means. This blunder could have been brought on by frustration due to an opening that offered nothing at all for White.

15	...	exd4
16	e5	

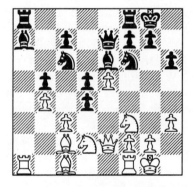

16	...	dxc3

A tempting piece sacrifice leading to fantastic complications.

Black had two worthwhile alternatives:

a) 16...♗d7! looks convincing for Black as 17 ♖e1 (17 cxd4 fails to impress as after 17...♗xd4 18 ♖xa8 ♖xa8 19 ♘xd4 ♘xd4 20 ♕d3 ♕xe5 Black should win) 17...dxc3 18 exf6 ♕xe2 19 ♖xe2 cxd2 20 ♗xd2

♗xf2+ wins;

b) 16...♘d7 looks playable. Kasparov would presumably have aimed for attacking chances with ♘b3 and ♕d3, etc., although I am sceptical that he has enough for the pawn even here. After 17 cxd4! ♘xb4 (not 17...♘xd4? as following 18 ♘xd4 ♗xd4 19 ♖xa8! ♖xa8 20 ♕d3 Black drops material) 18 ♗a3 c5 19 ♗xb4 (19 ♗b1?! cxd4 favours Black) 19...cxb4 20 ♕xb5 ♖fb8 21 ♕d3 ♘f8 Black is not worse.

Including the text, Black has three favourable continuations so it's evident that for once Kasparov's instinct led him down with the howler 15 d4(?).

17　　exf6　　♕xf6
18　　♘b3　　♘xb4

With four pawns and good pieces Lautier has more than enough for the sacrificed knight.

19　　♗b1

The continuation 19 ♗e3 ♗xe3 20 fxe3 ♘xc2 21 ♕xc2 b4 would simplify the position but not the difficulties for White.

19　　...　　d4

Activating the light-squared bishop and embarrassing the knight on b3. White has chances with a timely ♕e4 but these are insufficient against precise play.

20　　♖xa7

After 20 ♘bxd4 ♗xd4 21 ♕e4 (after 21 ♖xa8 ♖xa8 22 ♕e4 Black has 22...♖d8 diffusing any white hopes) 21...♗f5!, when both 22 ♕xa8 c2 23 ♗xc2 ♗xa1 and 22 ♕xf5 c2 23 ♕xf6 ♗xf6

lose immediately.

Critical is 20 ♗a3, when after 21...d3 21 ♗xd3 ♘xd3 22 ♗xf8 (22 ♕xd3 fails, according to Lautier, to the strong kingside attack generated after 22...♖fd8 23 ♕c2 ♗f5 24 ♕c1 ♗xh3! 25 ♗b4 ♗xg2 26 ♔xg2 ♖d3) 22...♘f4 23 ♕xb5 Black keeps a clear advantage with 23...♘xh3+! 24 ♔h1 (24 gxh3 is worse as 24...♕xf3 25 ♖xa7 ♗xh3 26 ♕b7 ♕g4+ 27 ♔h2 ♖xa7 wins easily for Black) 24...♘xf2+ 25 ♖xf2 ♖b8, as White has two defensive tries but neither equalize: 26 ♕f1 ♗xf2 27 ♕xf2 (on 27 ♗c5!? Black still maintains four pawns for the piece) 27...♔xf8! 28 ♘c1 ♔g8! keeping a clear edge or 26 ♕xb8 ♗xb8 27 ♖a8 ♕d8 and White's position is just too loose.

20　　...　　c2?!

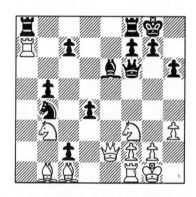

It's worth remembering that it is very easy for the annotator, in the quiet of his study, to criticize other players when armed with the benefit of hindsight. Over the board, if given only a few minutes to think, many of this game's best moves would be almost impossible to accurately calculate.

Using the advantage of limitless time we can conclude that 20...♖xa7! is more accurate. After 21 ♘bxd4 ♖a1! 22 ♕e4 ♕g6! 23 ♕xg6 fxg6 24 ♗xg6 (24 ♘xe6 ♖xf3 25 ♗b2 also fails to hold after 25...cxb2 26 gxf3 ♘d5 27 ♗xg6 ♘c3! 28 ♔g2 b4 and Black wins by queening both b-pawns) 24...♗c4 25 ♖e1 c5 and the passed pawns plus rook should beat the minor pieces.

Here Kasparov seizes his best chance to create confusion with unusual complications.

21   ♖xa8!

Astonishingly allowing his opponent to capture and queen at the same time! However, this was the only hope in view of 21 ♗xc2 ♖xa7 22 ♘bxd4 ♗c4 23 ♕e4 and now 23...♘xc2 (one of the points of the intermediate 20...c2, the bishop can be captured) 24 ♘xc2 ♗xf1 25 ♔xf1 and Black's two rooks plus passed pawns will overcome the ineffective minor pieces.

21	...	cxb1♕
22	♖xf8+	♔xf8
23	♕xb5??	

Kasparov cracks! For the second time in one game he blunders, this time as a result of time pressure.

23 ♗g5! is the move that immediately comes to mind when 23...♕xf1+ 24 ♕xf1 hxg5 25 ♕xb5 ♘d5 26 ♘bxd4 would

leave Black a pawn up but with few prospects of retaining either the pawn or an advantage.

23 ♘c5 was suggested by Kasparov as an improvement that would give Black serious practical difficulties. This seems to be the case, but with accurate play the pair of queens(!) should enable Black to retain the better chances, but not by 23...d3 as 24 ♕e4 ♕fa1 25 ♖e1! ♕xc1 26 ♕xb4 d2 27 ♘xe6+ ♔g8 28 ♕xd2 (note that g7 is defended so 28 ♕f8+ leads nowhere) 28...♕xd2 29 ♖xa1 ♕d5 30 ♘xc7 ♕c6 31 ♘xb5 ♕xb5 32 ♖e1 should permit White to hold. Best is 23...♕bg6! 24 ♘e5 ♕gf5 25 f4 ♕d8! as suggested by Lautier. Black has the advantage of queen and three pawns for rook and knight, starts to untangle himself and retains some winning chances after the further 26 ♗a3 ♗c4 27 ♕f2 ♗xf1 28 ♗xb4 ♕d5 29 ♕xf1 ♕c2.

| 23 | ... | ♕xb3 |

Did Kasparov simply forget about this move, defending the knight?

24	♕b8+	♔e7
25	♕xc7+	♔e8
26	♗d2	

On 26 ♕b8+ checks will soon run out after 26...♕d8.

26	...	♕d8
27	♕e5	♔f8!

A practical move although a correspondence player (not under the stress of limited time and not facing the physical presence of a dangerous opponent!) would have had time to calculate 27...♘c6!? 28 ♕xg7 ♗xh3 29 ♖e1+ ♗e6 30 ♗xh6 ♕b4 31 ♖c1 ♗c4. There is always the danger in such a line that you may overlook something, so I prefer the text move.

28 ♘xd4?

The final error. More robust was 28 ♕c5+ ♔g8! (28...♕e7? throws away the advantage as after 29 ♕xe7+ ♔xe7 30 ♘xd4

♕b2 31 ♗xb4+ Black dare not capture on b4) 29 ♗xb4 ♕c4 but Black exchanges queens and retains the d-pawn with an eventual win.

28	...	♘d3!
29	♕e3	♕c4

The complications have fizzled out and queen for rook is a decisive advantage.

0-1

Game Fifteen
Boris Gelfand-Vladimir Epishin
Dos Hermanas 1994

Boris Gelfand, who is now firmly established in the world's top ten, had his best tournament result of the year in this year's Dos Hermanas (the sisters) tournament in Spain. The Belarussian, having battled through to the FIDE Candidates semi-final will meet Karpov in his biggest test yet.

Karpov lost to the American Gulko in this event and didn't quite have enough time in nine rounds to catch an in-form Gelfand. This was the start of a run of less impressive results for Karpov whose excellent form of the previous year or so had seemingly come to a close.

1	d4	♘f6
2	c4	e6
3	♘c3	♗b4
4	e3	

Fifteen years ago, when I was building a 1 d4 repertoire, this

was the most important variation against the most fashionable Nimzo-Indian, but nowadays the King's Indian and Semi-Slav have overtaken the 'Nimzo' in popularity and the 'Classical' 4 ♕c2 is by far the most critical anti-Nimzo line. Today 4 e3 is no longer 'standard' but more of a surprise sideline. How things have changed!

4	...	0-0
5	♗d3	d5
6	♘f3	c5
7	0-0	

Black now has many options depending on how he releases the tension in the centre and develops his queen's knight, but the main line is probably 7...♘c6 8 a3 ♗xc3 9 bxc3 dxc4 10 ♗xc4 ♕c7 when White tries to activate his bishops but Black has good counterplay with the plan of an early ...e6-e5.

7	...	dxc4
8	♗xc4	♘bd7
9	♕e2	a6

Karpov used to play 9...cxd4 10 exd4 b6, Epishin is in fact one of his seconds and this could well be a line they have investigated together but Karpov decided not to use.

10	♗d3	b5
11	a3	♗a5
12	b4!	

The most testing move as slow development allows ...♗b7, etc., with no particular problems.

12	...	cxb4

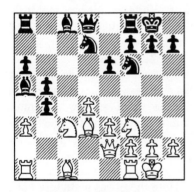

13 ♘xb5!?

Theory up to now has continued 13 axb4 ♗xb4 14 ♘xb5 when White has the slightly superior pawn structure but it's hard to prove a concrete edge in practice, e.g. 14...♗b7 15 ♖b1 (or 15 ♗a3 ♗xa3 16 ♘xa3 ♘d5 17 ♕d2 ♘5b6 18 e4 a5 19 ♖fc1 ♘f6 20 ♕f4 a4 with counterplay; Danner-Kochiev, Reggio Emilia 1979) 15...♗e7 16 ♘c3 ♗xf3 17

♕xf3 e5 18 ♘e4 exd4 19 exd4 a5, as in Scheeren-Korchnoi, Wijk aan Zee 1983. These 'ancient' references clearly show that this line hasn't recieved much attention in recent years.

13 ... ♗b7

After 13...axb5 14 axb4 the pin on the a-file enables White to win back the piece with interest.

Some commentators have suggested 13...b3!? 14 ♘d6 ♘d5 as a better method of defence intending to meet 15 ♗b2?! with 15...♘7b6, when Black is already threatening 16...♘a4. Interesting is instead 15 e4! keeping some chances of an advantage, e.g. 15...♘c3 (not 15...♘5b6? due to 16 ♖b1) 16 ♕b2! (16 ♕e3 ♖b8 17 ♘c4 with a complex game is less clear) 16...♖b8 17 a4 intending to undermine the advanced black forces.

After the text the knight is really en prise.

14	♘d6	♗xf3
15	♕xf3	♗c7

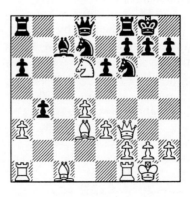

It is now too late for 15...b3 as

16 ♖b1 ♖b8 17 ♕d1 will lead to the loss of the b-pawn.

Now most of us would concentrate our thoughts on either 16 ♘c4 or 16 ♘e4 but Gelfand has an original idea in mind.

16   ♘b7!

The win of a tempo enables White to capture on b4.

16   ...   ♕e7

Gelfand had of course foreseen 16...♗xh2+? (a 'Greek gift' that is gratefully accepted) 17 ♔xh2! (thank you!) 17...♕c7+ 18 ♔g1 ♕c3 19 ♕e2! ♕xa1 20 ♗b2 ♕a2 21 ♗c4 b3 22 ♖a1 (very much indeed!) and with queen and minor piece for two rooks White would be winning.

The alternative 16...♕b8 17 axb4 ♗xh2+ 18 ♔h1 ♗c7 19 ♗xa6 would still leave Black a pawn light.

17   axb4   e5

Naturally the b-pawn is off-limits for the black queen, so Epishin starts central operations quickly before White is fully organized.

18   ♗xa6

Avoiding the fork by a possible ...e5-e4 and grabbing a further pawn.

18   ...   exd4

19   exd4   ♕xb4

What is the difference, why can Black now take the pawn, surely he loses the exchange? As so often in chess the answer is 'yes, but...'

20   ♗e3?!

Gelfand prefers instead to retain the material advantage of an extra central pawn. Evidently 20 ♗a3 ♕xd4 21 ♗xf8 ♖xf8 leaves White a clear exchange ahead, but with all the pawns on one wing there would be technical problems in converting the advantage.

Both continuations keep good winning chances but 20 ♗a3 has the advantage of avoiding unnecessary complications. It's true that White's minor pieces are offside but this should only be a temporary problem.

20   ...   ♖fb8

21   ♖ab1   ♕e7

After 21...♕a3 22 ♗b5 ♖a7 23 ♗c6 White avoids any major difficulties with the wayward knight.

22   ♗b5

Gelfand would like to safety his pieces and gradually exchange them off for a winning ending, a pawn to the good. However, things are rarely that simple in chess!

22   ...   ♖a3

Here there was a slightly better option in 22...♘b6, and not just because it sets the trap 23 ♗g5?? ♖xb7! and Black wins material. After the more prudent 23 ♗c6 ♘c4 24 ♗g5 ♖a3 25 ♕f5 White remains in control, but only just! He is still a long way from converting his extra pawn, although 25...♘d6 now only aids White's task as 26 ♘xd6 ♕xd6 27 ♖xb8+ ♗xb8 28 ♕c8+ introduces welcome simplification.

23 &c6 ♘b6
24 ♖fc1

Now Gelfand is able to avoid the irritating ...♘c4, the main reason why 22...♘b6 should have been preferred.

24 ... h5

Creating 'luft' (breathing-space) for the king, with ideas of using the g4 square for aggressive purposes.

25 h3 ♕e6!?

A tricky move.

26 ♖b5?!

This move imperceptibly weakens White's own back rank. 26 ♘c5! instead would have speeded-up the process of reorganization as Black's best move is probably to go back to e7. Gelfand probably didn't want to indulge in any risky complications but 26...♕e7 (with a clear head we can see that 26...♕d6 can be dealt with by 27 &f4! ♕xf4 28 ♕xa3 ♕h2+ 29 ♔f1 and White has no concrete problems, but in time trouble...) 27 ♘e4 and White has successfully redeployed his worst placed piece.

26 ... ♕a2

Keeping out of harm's way, or so it seems, but straying from the kingside.

The courageous 26...♘c4! is surprisingly difficult to refute. At first sight 27 ♘c5 ♕e7! 28 ♖xc4?? looks good but 28...♖a1+ leads to mate after 29 ♖c1 ♖xc1+ 30 &xc1 ♕e1 so if White cannot capture the knight on c4 then he will be embarrassed on e3. His best continuation could be 28 ♖xb8+ &xb8 29 ♘e4 ♘xe3 30 fxe3 ♘xe4 31 &xe4 &c7 32 &d5 which still gives good winning chances despite the presence of opposite-coloured bishops.

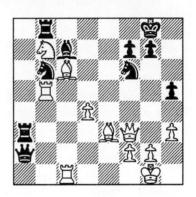

27 ♕d1?!

Now Epishin finds a way to significantly complicate White's task, so Gelfand should have preferred 27 &e4! when Black is struggling: 27...♘xe4 (27...♘a8 is far too passive and gets punished by 28 ♘d6! ♖f8 29 ♘f5 with a strong attack for White) 28 ♖xc7 (28 ♕xe4 also looks good) 28...♘d2 (not 28...♘a8? as 29 ♘c5 yields a decisive attack, e.g. 29...♖e8 30 ♖e7! or 29...♖f8 30 ♘xe4 ♘xc7 31 ♘f6+!) 29 ♕d1 ♘bc4! (29...♘dc4 30 ♕xh5 ♘xe3 31 fxe3 and Black has no compensation for his two-pawn deficit) would then be the best chance for Black but 30 ♘c5 (30 &xd2 is less good as 30...♕xd2 31 ♖b1 ♕xd1+ 32 ♖xd1 ♖a7 33 ♖xc4 would be difficult to win) 30...♖e8 31 ♖e7 and White will consolidate.

Gelfand instead recommends 27 ♖f5 preparing a dangerous exchange sacrifice on f6.

27 ... ♘bd5!

A clever resource, his queen may be trapped but the game is far from over.

28 ♖c2

After 28 ♗d2 then 28...♖d3 is unpleasant.

28 ... ♘c3!

Exploiting White's sensitive back rank to obtain two rooks for the queen.

29 ♖xa2 ♖xa2
30 ♕f1 ♘xb5
31 g4 ♘d6?

Epishin, despite time trouble, has staged a remarkable comeback, but with limited time it is particularly difficult to cope with a rapidly changing situation on the board and here he makes a crucial imprecision. 31...♘a7! was better when 32 ♗f3 hxg4 33 hxg4 ♘xg4! (rather than 33...♖b2?! 34 g5 ♘d7 35 ♕a6 - 35 ♕h3? fails to 35...♖8xb7!- 35...♘b5 36 g6 and White keeps the initiative) 34 ♗xg4 ♖xb7 35 ♗f3 White's advantage would be difficult to convert.

32 ♘xd6 ♗xd6
33 g5

Material is balanced but White's pieces are poised to attack and his king always has a safe haven on g2, so he retains the advantage.

33 ... ♘e8
34 g6

A good move but 34 ♗d5 ♖a7 35 g6 was even stronger.

34 ... ♘f6
35 gxf7+ ♔f8
36 ♕c4

Now it is clear why 35...♔xf7 was avoided.

36 ... ♖a7
37 ♕e6 ♖d8
38 ♗b5

Not 38 ♗h6? because of 38...♖xf7, but now if Black captures on f7 the combined attack of White's three pieces will be too strong, e.g. 38...♖xf7 39 ♗c4 ♖e7 40 ♕f5 ♖c7 41 ♗e6 ♔e7 42 ♗g5 ♗b4 43 ♗b3 ♖f8 44 ♕e6+ ♔d8 45 ♗f4 and Black is in total disarray and must lose material.

38 ... ♖e7
39 ♕f5 1-0

Black now lost on time but he really had no real option but to transpose into the previous note with few chances of holding the game. A real fight; Epishin made Gelfand's task very difficult indeed.

Game Sixteen
Garry Kasparov-Nigel Short
Amsterdam 1994

Now that they have met in a match for the (PCA) World

Championship title, all subsequent meetings between Kasparov and Short are viewed with great interest. This game has particular significance as many observers wanted to know why Short decided against employing the French Defence in the match (he preferred 1...e5 but without much success) and what had Kasparov prepared in this case. It was to be in Amsterdam six months after their London match that these questions could start to be addressed.

1	e4	e6
2	d4	d5
3	♘c3	♘f6

Perhaps the best move is 3...♝b4. However, Kasparov's most recent experiences in the Winawer are crushing wins over the normally solid Nikolic in Horgen (September) and Paris (November).

4	e5	♘fd7
5	f4	c5
6	♘f3	♘c6
7	♝e3	cxd4
8	♘xd4	♝c5
9	♕d2	0-0
10	0-0-0	a6
11	h4	

Pre-1990 books on the French don't deal with this continuation, which has now become the critical line.

White will press on the kingside by pushing his h-pawn quickly or using the rook on the third rank. Many lines of the French are characterized by

Black's poor light-squared bishop, so if Black seeks exchanges even endings tend to be in White's favour. Black does best to seek counterplay on the queenside.

11	...	♘xd4
12	♝xd4	b5
13	♖h3	

The immediate 13 h5 has also been tried.

13	...	b4

The obvious continuation, but 13...♝b7 has something to be said for it. After 14 h5 b4 White does best to retreat to e2, as following 15 ♘a4 ♝xd4 16 ♕xd4 ♕a5 17 b3 ♝c6 Black obtains excellent counter chances.

14	♘a4	

As in a number of similar positions White has the choice between e2 and a4 for this knight. On e2 this piece heads for d4 (central control) or g3 (kingside pretensions). Kasparov prefers to reduce Black's queenside options, hence the text.

14	...	♝xd4
15	♕xd4	f6

A new idea that unfortunately for the Englishman Kasparov had already foreseen in his preparation for their 1993 match! As the alternatives seem to favour White then this was certainly worth a try:

a) 15...a5 is met by the manoeuvre 16 ♝b5! (rather than 16 ♝d3 which allows the immediate exchange of bishops by 16...♝a6) 16...♖b8 17 ♝d3 which gave

White plenty of time to get his kingside moving before Black could create any threats of his own; Fogarasi-Luther, Hungary 1993;

b) 15...♕a5 is also unsatisfactory, as in a game from 1992 where Ketevan Arakhamia had White against Mihail Gurevich, i.e. 16 b3 ♗b7 17 ♖g3 ♖fc8 18 ♖d2 ♗c6 19 f5! and White's attack proved to be the more significant.

16   ♕xb4   fxe5

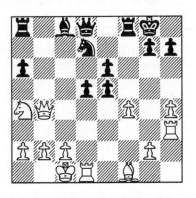

Is White's centre in the process of disappearing? Perhaps we should first look at Black's relatively undeveloped position and ask is it possible for White to punish him? Who is better?

Do not despair! Kasparov has all the answers!

17   ♕d6!   ♕f6

If Black's e-pawn falls then so does his d-pawn, hence the text. Now Kasparov unleashes his prepared tactical thrust.

18   f5!   ♕h6+

The immediate captures on f5

don't hold-up to scrutiny; 18...exf5 19 ♕xd5+ wins a rook and 18...♕xf5 19 ♖f3 ♕g4 20 ♖xf8+ ♘xf8 21 ♘b6 and White wins material.

19   ♔b1   ♖xf5?!

Short grabs the pawn but is then never able to complete his development. The aggressive 19...♘f6!, playing for complications, may be the key to solving Black's problems: 20 fxe6 ♘e4 21 ♕xd5 ♘d2+! 22 ♖xd2! ♖xf1+ (22...♕xd2 is inadequate as 23 ♕xd2 ♖xf1+ 24 ♕c1 ♖xc1+ 25 ♔xc1 ♗xe6 just leaves Black a pawn down) 23 ♖d1 ♗b7! (23...♖xd1+? 24 ♕xd1 ♗xe6 25 ♘c5! ♗xh3 26 ♕d5+ and 23...♕xe6?? 24 ♕xe6+ ♗xe6 25 ♖xf1 ♗xh3 26 gxh3 win for White) 24 ♕d3 ♖xd1+ 25 ♕xd1 ♗xg2 (25...♕xe6 allows 26 ♘c5 and White exchanges off into a comfortably won ending) 26 ♖g3 ♗c6 27 ♘c5 (27 e7 ♖e8 covers everything nicely) 27...♕xh4 with unclear play. If this improvement is indeed playable then Short's novelty 15...f6 may be good after all, despite Kasparov giving it a "?".

20   ♖f3

Kasparov had apparently prepared this line some months before, intending to play 20 ♗e2 ♖f7 21 ♖b3!, threatening 22 ♕c6 and thus tying Black down to a passive defence after 21...♖f8 22 g4. A remarkable example of how deeply the top player goes into his lines looking for the truth. In fact, over the board he changed his mind (a player should not be a slave to his homework, but use it as a tool!) preferring the text, perhaps he saw 20 ♖f3 as even more convincing.

20 ... ♖xf3

20...♕f6 prevents the white bishop from coming to h3 but with Black's queenside pieces not going anywhere White can take his time: 21 ♖xf5 ♕xf5 22 ♗e2 (threatening 23 ♖f1) 22...♕f7 23 ♗g4 and after the black knight moves, 24 ♘b6 is decisive.

21 gxf3

White permits his pawns to be broken but he has the h3 square for his bishop.

21 ... ♕f6

There was no joy in 21...♕xh4 as 22 ♕xe6+ ♔f8 23 ♕xd5 ♖b8 24 ♗c4 would leave White in a winning position.

22 ♗h3 ♔f7

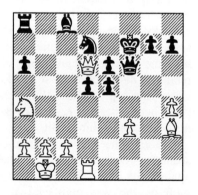

Ugly, but e6 must be defended and 22...♘f8? 23 ♘b6 ♕xf3 24 ♖f1 allows White to mate after

24...♕xh3 25 ♕xf8. Now with Black totally tied down it's time for strong-arm action and as usual Kasparov doesn't shirk from sacrificing pawns!

23 c4!

The more obvious breakthrough, 23 f4, trying to get directly at the black king, was also good. After 23...exf4 24 ♖e1 ♘f8 25 ♘b6 White wins material or 23...e4 24 f5! and the house of cards collapses. The most gritty defence is 23...♕e7 24 fxe5 ♕xd6 25 exd6 but Black has great difficulties despite the exchange of queens.

23 ... dxc4

After 23...d4 24 c5! ♕e7 25 ♕c7 the threat is 26 c6 and, after the knight moves, both the e5 and d4 pawns will fall.

24 ♘c3

For the record, Black has a two-pawn advantage. However, he has already been suffering from asphyxia for some time and with the last white piece joining the attack something vital has to give.

24 ... ♕e7
25 ♕c6 ♖b8
26 ♘e4

Threatening to come to both d6 and g5.

26 ... ♘b6

Hopeless is 26...♘f6 27 ♘d6+ ♔g6 28 ♖g1+ ♔h6 due to 29 ♕xc4!, threatening 30 ♕c1 mating and 30 ♘xc8 picking up a piece.

27 ♘g5+ ♔g8

28   ♕e4

Forking h7 and e5. White wins back the first pawn and keeps up the pressure.

28   ...   g6
29   ♕xe5   ♖b7
30   ♖d6!

This is stronger than the impatient 30 ♗xe6+ ♗xe6 31 ♕xe6+ ♕xe6 32 ♖d8+ ♔g7 33 ♘xe6+ ♔h6 which would just free the black position. After the text, the e6 pawn is attacked by all the white pieces.

30   ...   c3

The desperate 30...♘a4 31 ♗xe6+ ♗xe6 32 ♖xe6 ♖xb2+ loses to both the cheeky 33 ♔a1 and the prosaic 33 ♕xb2.

31   ♗xe6+

The other e-pawn falls and all routes are open to the black king.

31   ...   ♗xe6
32   ♖xe6   1-0

Black could have tried 32...♘c4 instead of resigning but Nigel obviously trusted his opponent to find 33 ♕xc3 (33 ♖xe7 ♖xb2+ 34 ♔c1 ♘xe5 35 ♖xe5 ♖xa2 should also win for White but is more complicated in view of the paucity of pawns) 33...♘a3+ 34 ♔c1 ♕d7 35 ♖c6 ♖b8 36 bxa3.

Kasparov has confirmed his domination over Short this year in registering other convincing wins over him in both Moscow and Novgorod.

Game Seventeen
Ivan Morovic-Gata Kamsky
Las Palmas 1994

The climate in the Canary Islands is pleasant all year round. This holds true not only for holiday-makers but also for chessplayers as there are many interesting tournaments in these parts. Most are held in Las Palmas, which has the ambience of a Latin American, rather than a Spanish, city which could be a good reason why the Chilean Ivan Morovic chooses to live there.

In 1993 Morovic surprised everyone by winning a category XVI in Las Palmas. This year he finished with a more predictable 4/9 including this loss with White to the top American player, Gata Kamsky. The most important success for Kamsky, this year, was the unique achievement of retaining his place in both World Championship cycles. His first place here (ahead of Karpov) was his best round-robin result.

Lautier started with four consecutive wins including one against the FIDE World Champion but he was outplayed and lost comfortably to Kamsky in round five. Both players have taken great strides forward in

1994 but, of the two, it is the American who is generally considered as a potential World Champion.

1	♘f3	♘f6
2	c4	g6
3	♘c3	♗g7
4	e4	

Morovic uses the 'Grünfeld-avoidance' move-order but Kamsky is adept at many openings and the double-edged King's Indian suits him well.

4	...	d6
5	d4	0-0
6	♗e2	e5
7	d5	a5

Currently fashionable now is 8 ♗g5 as discussed elsewhere in the book (see Shirov - J.Polgar, Chapter 7, game 28) but Morovic tries another idea.

8	♗e3	♘g4
9	♗g5	f6

It's never quite clear to me which player gains from this sequence. White loses some tempi with the bishop but in a few moves the knight on g4 will be obliged to recycle out of danger.

10	♗h4	h5

It was Kasparov who introduced the idea of playing ...h7-h5 before retreating the knight to h6.

11	♘d2	♘h6

After 11...♘a6 the English players Jonathan Speelman and Dharshan Kumaran have sometimes continued 12 a3 ♗d7 13 0-0 introducing a more cautious plan in which White makes his king safe before undertaking active operations. In this case 13...♕e8 would be normal rather than 13...♕e7 14 ♖b1 ♘c5 15 b4 axb4 16 axb4 ♘a4 17 ♘xa4 ♖xa4 18 h3 and White had some advantage in a recent game of Speelman's against Dutch No.1 Jeroen Piket.

12	h3

Black was threatening to win a piece with 12...g5 and 13...h4.

After 12 f3 best is 12...♕e8! intending a timely ...f7-f5 with typical King's Indian play rather than 12...g5?! 13 ♗f2 f5 14 exf5 when White has the e4 square for his knights.

12	...	♘a6
13	a3	♗d7
14	♖b1	♘c5

Kamsky is aware that White will play b2-b4 anyway and hurries to meet this move with 15...♘a4, in order not to have this piece locked out of play.

15	b4	axb4
16	axb4	♘a4
17	♘xa4	

In the original game from this variation Bareev (in Tilburg 1991) tried 17 ♕c2 ♘xc3 18 ♕xc3 g5 19 ♗g3 h4 20 ♗h2 f5 21 c5 g4 22 c6 against Kasparov, but Black's attack proved to be the stronger.

17	...	♗xa4
18	♕c1 *(D)*	
18	...	g5!

Played in Kasparov-style. Instead 18...♕e8 seems to allow White enough time to get fully organized: 19 f3 ♗d7 20 c5 f5 21

0-0 ♘f7 22 exf5 gxf5 23 f4! and White took the initiative and should have won in Kumaran-Shirov, Oakham 1992.

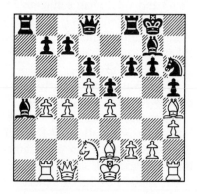

Kamsky has a reputation for trying out Kasparov's opening ideas, perhaps he is already putting extra effort into studying the PCA World Champion's games ready for their possible match!

19　♗g3　h4
20　♗h2　♗d7

The bishop has little future on the queenside.

21　f3

Black was already envisaging ...g5-g4 which White restrains with this move, whose principal purpose is to redeploy the bishop via g1.

21　...　f5

White could have considered castling (either here or the last move) but he instead continues with his plan.

22　♗g1　g4!
23　fxg4

23 ♗e3 is interesting (hoping to castle) but after 23...f4 24 ♗g1

g3 White's king's rook is imprisoned by his own bishop. It would be embarrassing to play such a position with White!

23　...　fxg4
24　♗e3

Nice bishop but what about the king!

24　...　♕f6
25　c5　♕g6

Eyeing g3 and g2.

26　♖g1　♘f7

After 26...♖ac8? White has 27 c6 bxc6 28 dxc6 ♗e6 29 ♗c4 and after the exchange of this bishop Black's attacking potential is significantly reduced.

27　cxd6　cxd6
28　♕c7

White's first aggressive stroke of the game, now Kamsky tests his opponent's willingness to take a draw.

28　...　♗c8
29　♕c3　♗d7
30　♕c7　♖fd8!

No thank you!

White has to be very careful about his king which will never be truly safe in any middlegame, whereas Black's only weakness is the rather irrelevant b-pawn.

31 ♕xb7

Probably an error as Black now has time to really get the attack rolling. However, the alternatives all seem insufficient due to the centrally placed king (if one mentally places the white king on h1 he would be okay).

31 g3 has been suggested (to rip open the kingside and give the black monarch something to think about) but after 31...gxh3 32 gxh4 ♕f6 White's king is the only one in danger.

31 ... ♗h6

Now the dark squares start to creak.

32 ♗xh6

On 32 ♕b6 Black wins with 32...♖db8.

32 ... ♕xh6

33 ♖f1 ♕e3

Amongst others, Black has the threat of 34...♖a2.

34 ♕c7

Hopeless are both 34 ♖b3 ♖a1 and 34 hxg4 ♖a7! (another of Black's threats!).

34 ... ♖ac8

35 ♕b7 ♖c2

36 ♖d1 ♘g5

The black pieces arrive from all parts of the board, honing in on the white king.

37 ♕a6 ♕g3+

0-1

White resigned as after 38 ♖f2 ♖f8 39 ♕b6 ♖xd2 40 ♖xd2 ♘xe4 Black has a decisive advantage.

Where did White go wrong?

Kasparov, in his notes to another game, hints that the whole line with the white king left in the centre favours Black (if this really is the case white players should consider Speelman's 13 0-0) and after playing through this efficient display by Kamsky one gets the feeling that he is right!

Game Eighteen
Christopher Lutz-Boris Gelfand
Munich 1994

In Germany this year there were two category XVI tournaments; Munich at the end of May and Dortmund in July. Next year Dortmund are setting their sights even higher, a category XVII.

Robert Hübner was for many years the top German but now he has competition; Yusupov has

taken out German citizenship and plays for the German team and the younger generation of Hertneck, Lobron and Lutz have gradually been catching him. Perhaps motivated by the desire to reaffirm his position Hübner, a renowned language expert, started in tremendous form in

Munich and looked as if he would give the sponsors a home-bred champion. However, by losing in the last round he allowed Ivanchuk to overhaul him, the Ukrainian putting together some useful tournament results in 1994 that helped compensate (financially and morally) his non-participation in the World Championship cycles.

The best game from the event was a hard-fought draw between Christopher Lutz and Boris Gelfand (who seems to be everywhere and is one of the most active of the top echelon). The youthful Lutz is only now becoming known outside German circles but is progressing rapidly.

1	d4	♘f6

Lutz is yet another player who opens with both 1 e4 and 1 d4, in modern chess to be successful you must be versatile.

2	c4	g6
3	♘c3	♗g7
4	e4	d6
5	♘f3	0-0
6	♗e2	e5
7	0-0	

The normal move, although this year the top players seem to have been mainly playing 7 d5 (of which there are several examples in this book).

7	...	♘c6
8	d5	♘e7
9	♘e1	

The main line. White's plan is generally to expand on, and then try to invade the queenside,

whereas Black aims for a kingside attack by pushing ...f7-f5 and often following up with ...f5-f4 and ...g6-g5 with his pieces supporting and urging the pawns on. The next few moves illustrate these plans well.

9	...	♘d7

Freeing the f-pawn and also restraining White's typical c4-c5 advance.

10	♗e3	

A provocative idea.

The main alternative method for White is 10 f3 f5 11 ♘d3 f4 12 ♗d2 ♘f6 13 c5 g5 14 ♖c1. This has some advantages over the game continuation; for instance, one tempo less is spent with the bishop and the f2 square is available for the knight, where it helps restrain Black's attack based on an early ...g5-g4.

10	...	f5
11	f3	f4
12	♗f2	g5
13	a4	

A typical space-gaining, but time-consuming idea, that came to the public's attention in the famous game Korchnoi-Kasparov from Amsterdam 1991. Since then this move has been played frequently at top level.

13	...	♘g6
14	a5	♖f7
15	c5!?	

Once White theoreticians started to feel that the more 'normal' continuation 15 b4 gave no advantage the positional gambit introduced by the text became the critical line. The final word has not been said on the older move but Black seems to be at least holding his own: 15 b4 ♘f6 16 c5 ♗f8! 17 cxd6 ♗xd6 18 ♘d3 ♖g7 19 ♘c5 ♘f8 20 ♘b5 g4 21 ♗h4 h5 and Black was okay although she went on to lose in Korchnoi-J.Polgar, Pamplona 1990. White's minor pieces seem well placed but Black has counterplay.

> **15** ... **♘xc5**
> **16** **♗xc5** **dxc5**
> **17** **a6?!**

Several games have followed 17 ♗c4 ♔h8 18 a6, when 18...bxa6 or 18...b6 have allowed White some initiative. However, after 18...♖f6! 19 axb7 ♗xb7 20 ♘d3 ♗f8 21 ♖a5 ♗c8 22 ♘xc5 c6 23 b4 ♖b8 24 ♕a4 g4 25 fxg4 f3 White has made progress on the queenside but Black has a dangerous counter-attack on the other wing; D.Gurevich-Sherzer, USA 1992.

The text is an attempt by Lutz to juggle with the move order to obtain a favourable position.

> **17** ... **b6**
> **18** **♗c4** **♗f8!**

Sacrificing the exchange brings any White initiative to an abrupt end. Instead 18...♔h8?! would fall-in with White's plans.

> **19** **g4!**

Shocked by the turn of events the German decides to seek solace in a positional blockade. The extra pawn on the queenside is not easy to use and if Black fails

to breakthrough against the white king he cannot hope for more than a draw.

The materialistic 19 d6 is inadequate after 19...c6! (covering the b5 and d5 squares) 20 ♗xf7+ ♔xf7. Black picks up the d-pawn, thereby obtaining two pawns for the exchange in the type of game where White's rooks have no play. Furthermore, he can manoeuvre his knight to d4 so, all-in-all, Black is better.

> **19** ... **♗d6**

Black prepares to open the h-file. The dark-squared bishop is hardly active on this square but it bolsters the centre in preparation for the flank attack.

Inferior is 19...fxg3 giving away his kingside space advantage and allowing White to free his game with 20 hxg3 followed by ♘e1-g2-e3.

> **20** **♕e2?!**

A rather routine and unnecessary developing move. White should already prepare the king flight without this waste of time. So 20 ♘g2 h5 21 h3 ♖h7 22 ♔f2 was more in tune with the position.

> **20** ... **h5**
> **21** **h3** **♖h7**
> **22** **♘g2** **♕f6**

Lutz was relieved that his opponent didn't find 22...♔g7! followed by 23...♘e7 with two ideas: ...♕h8 and ...c7-c6 intending ...♘xc6-d4 (if White captures) or ...b6-b5 (if he does not). The game suggests that kingside threats need to be combined with play elsewhere for Black to hope to breakdown the white defences.

23	♔f2	hxg4
24	hxg4	♖h2
25	♔e1!	

Worse is 25 ♖h1 ♕h8 26 ♖xh2 ♕xh2 27 ♖g1 ♘h4 28 ♔f1 as Black has the simple 28...♕h3 and the f3 pawn falls. So White has to try and live with the black rook on the seventh.

| 25 | ... | ♗xg4!? |

After 25...♘h4 26 ♖f2 ♘xg2+ necessary is the resource 27 ♔d2! (27 ♖xg2?? loses to 27...♖h1+) when White has little to fear after 27...♗xg4 28 ♖xg2! (but not 28 fxg4? as 28...♖h6! intending 29...♘h4 is very strong as if 29 ♖xg2 then 29...f3 wins due to the black queen being defended) 28...♖xg2 29 ♕xg2 ♗d7 30 ♖g1.

| 26 | fxg4 | ♘h4 |

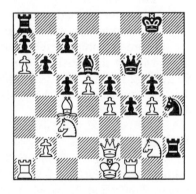

Gelfand has generated strong threats.

| 27 | ♘xf4! | |

The best way to defend is to give up the queen, but this is achieved under inferior circumstances after 27 ♖f2 when Black has two promising continuations:

a) 27...♖h1+ 28 ♖f1 f3 29 ♘xh4 (on 29 ♖xh1 Black wins by first playing 29...♘xg2+) 29...fxe2 30 ♖xh1 gxh4 31 ♗xe2 and the passed h-pawn should enable Black to win after 31...♕f4 32 ♔d1 ♗e7 as he has too many threats on the dark squares;

b) 27...♘xg2+ 28 ♖xg2 f3 29 ♖xh2 fxe2 30 ♗xe2 ♖f8 with good winning chances as Black can meet 31 ♘b5 with 31...c4(!).

| 27 | ... | ♖xe2+ |
| 28 | ♘fxe2 | |

Black has a queen but White's pieces defend all the important entry squares. The a6 pawn will now have an important role to play as Black cannot forever leave his rook on a8 to defend a7.

| 28 | ... | ♕h6? |

Losing all hope of an advantage and maybe even giving himself losing chances.

Necessary was 28...♘f3+! 29 ♔d1 ♕h6 with complex play. Then 30 ♖xf3? (30 ♔c2 has to be tried but now ...♘d4+ is unpleasant for White) 30...♕h1+ 31 ♘g1 ♕xg1+ 32 ♗f1 ♖f8! leads to the loss of White's g-pawn.

| 29 | ♔d2! | |

Given time, White can improve his position in a number of ways: king to the queenside, doubling rooks and ♘c3-b5. Therefore Gelfand decides that it is high time to force the pace.

29	...	♖f8
30	♘b5	♘f3+
31	♖xf3!	

The simplest. Instead the tempting 31 ♔c2 ♘d4+ 32 ♘exd4 exd4 33 ♘xa7 can be met by 33...d3+ preparing to introduce the long dormant bishop into the game with unclear complications.

31	...	♖xf3
32	♘xa7	♕h7
33	♘b5	

The natural move but the alternative 33 ♘c3! suggested by Lutz is a good winning try. After 33...♕h2+ 34 ♗e2 ♕f4+ 35 ♔c2 ♖f2 (after 35...♖xc3+?! Black is soon struggling; 36 bxc3 ♕xe4+ 37 ♗d3 ♕xd5 38 ♖a4!) 36 ♖e1! (excellent, instead neither 36 ♘c8 ♕xg4 37 a7 ♖xe2+ 38 ♘xe2 ♕xe2+ 39 ♔b1 ♕xe4+ 40 ♔a2 ♕xd5+, nor 36 ♔b3 c4+! 37 ♗xc4 ♕d2 38 ♖b1 ♕c2+ lead anywhere for White, indeed nor for that matter does 36 ♘ab5 in view of 36...♖xe2+) 36...♕xg4 37 ♘ab5 ♕c8 38 ♖a1! (38 a7? is premature; 38...♕a6) and with the black queen stuck on a8 White should win.

| 33 | ... | ♕xe4 |
| 34 | ♘xd6?! | |

A strange capture, exchanging the knight for such a poor bishop. 34 a7 seems to guarantee a draw 34...♕xc4!? (or 34...♕e3+ drawing as White can only escape the perpetual by losing his rook) 35 a8♕+ ♖f8 36 ♕c6 ♕b4+ 37 ♔c2 (37 ♔e3?! is a winning try

that looks too risky: 37...♕xg4 38 ♘xd6 cxd6 39 ♕xd6 ♖f3+ 40 ♔d2 ♕b4+ and only Black can win) 37...♕e4+ 38 ♔d2 ♕b4+ and the spoils are again shared.

| 34 | ... | cxd6 |
| 35 | a7 | ♖f8 |

Here Gelfand could have taken a draw with 35...♕e3+ but he was obviously still thinking of winning!

36	a8♕	♖xa8
37	♖xa8+	♔g7
38	b3	

Although many people tend to generally prefer the pieces, in my experience, an active queen plus pawns is adequate compensation for a rook and two minor pieces. For Gelfand to actually contemplate winning with the queen here is not just misplaced optimism but is based on exploiting the looseness of White's rook.

| 38 | ... | b5 |
| 39 | ♖a7+ | |

After 39 ♗xb5?? Black picks up the rook with 39...♕xd5+.

| 39 | ... | ♔f8?! |

After this move a draw would be the natural result. There did remain one last winning try: 39...♔f6! but Gelfand judged that by 40 ♗xb5 ♕b4+ 41 ♘c3 ♕d4+ 42 ♗d3 c4 43 ♘e4+ ♔g6 44 bxc4 ♕xa7 45 ♘xd6+ White has enough compensation for the queen. My guess is that most players would intuitively prefer Black.

| 40 | ♗xb5 | ♕xd5+ |
| 41 | ♔c2 | ♕e4+ |

42   ♔b2

Keeping out of harm's way.

42	...	♕xg4
43	♖a8+	♔e7
44	♖a7+	♔d8
45	♖a6	♔e7
46	♖a7+	♔f8
47	♖a8+	♔g7
48	♖a7+	♔g6?

Rather than allow a perpetual Gelfand loses his objectivity and overpresses. It has been said that the easiest way to win in chess is to be slightly worse(!); your opponent thinks only of winning and therefore takes excessive risks!

49   ♖a6

With the black king on the third rank White is able to organize his pieces and take the initiative.

49	...	♕e6
50	♘g3	♕d5

Following 50...e4, 51 ♔c2! threatens 52 ♘xe4 ♕xe4+ 53 ♗d3, after the further 51...e3 there follows 52 ♗d3+ and Black has no square, e.g. 52...♔f7 (or 52...♔g7 53 ♖xd6 winning) 53 ♗c4 and wins.

51	♔c2!	♕g2+
52	♘e2	g4

After 52...♕d5 White has 53 ♗c4 winning the d-pawn anyway.

53	♖xd6+	♔g5
54	♖d8	

With his rook checking from behind Black cannot find a shelter for his king.

54	...	♕e4+
55	♗d3	♕e3
56	♖g8+	♔h4

White now took a draw as he underestimated 57   ♘c3! (intending 58 ♘e4) and if then 57...♕f2+ the simple 58 ♗e2 leaves Black in trouble, e.g. 58...g3? 59 ♖h8+ ♔g5 60 ♘e4+.

57	♖h8+	♔g5
58	♖g8+	½-½

A missed opportunity for Lutz who put up one of the best defensive displays of the year. Curiously enough both his missed wins involved 'knight to the c3 square', at move 33 and at the end.

Game Nineteen
Anatoly Karpov-Victor Korchnoi
Dortmund 1994

The letter 'K' has great significance for chessplayers. Twenty years ago we had the Karpov-Korchnoi era, for the last ten years we have had a stream of Karpov-Kasparov matches and in a few years it could well be Kramnik and Kamsky who dominate.

Since the ever-enthusiastic Korchnoi is no longer in contention for World Championship honours, with his best form unfortunately behind him, Karpov has generated an enormous plus score against his old rival in tournament games. Recently, however, the veteran Korchnoi managed to outlast his younger opponent in an energy-sapping marathon of a game. The complications at the end are sensational!

1	d4	♘f6
2	c4	e6
3	♘f3	b6
4	a3	

White wants to play his knight to c3 without being pinned by ...♗b4.

4	...	♗b7
5	♘c3	d5
6	♗g5	♗e7
7	♕a4+	

A check aimed at disrupting Black's development.

7	...	c6

The only other worthwhile move here is 7...♘bd7. From Black's point of view, if he can avoid playing ...c7-c6 then he may be able to play ...c7-c5 in one go saving a tempo, and he retains the possibility of recapturing on d5 with pieces. If White meets this with 8 ♘e5 then 8...c5!? is not so loosening as Black has a lead in development. Black is also happy following 8 cxd5 ♘xd5 9 ♗xe7 ♕xe7 10 ♘xd5 ♗xd5 11 ♘e5 a6! 12 ♘c6 ♕h4! threatening 13...♘c5 with good play.

However, 8 ♗xf6! is the critical move when 8...♗xf6 9 cxd5 exd5 10 g3 c5 11 ♗h3 a6 worked out well for Black in the first game in the line (12 ♖d1 b5 13 ♕c2 c4 14 0-0 0-0 15 e4 dxe4 16 ♘e5 ♘b6 with chances for both sides; Bönsch-Stohl, Brno 1993) but some recent games of the young Dutch grandmaster Loek van Wely's indicate an advantage for the first player after 12 dxc5! bxc5 13 e4 d4 14 ♘d5 ♗xd5 15 exd5 ♖a7 16 0-0 0-0 17 ♕c6.

8	♗xf6	♗xf6
9	cxd5	exd5

Karpov voluntarily gives up the bishop pair. This type of position, characterized by 'static' pawns, gives Black few immediate chances for counterplay as his only pawn-break (an early ...c6-c5) tends to be self-weakening unless thoroughly prepared. The same pawn structure is frequently obtained from the QGD Tartakower variation, a line that was thoroughly tested in the Karpov-Kasparov matches of 1985 and 1987.

10	g3	

On g2 the bishop will already bear down on the d5 pawn in case Black ever risks ...c6-c5.

10	...	0-0
11	♗g2	♘d7

Now is Black's first opportunity to try the ubiquitous 'freeing move' 11...c5(!?). After 12 0-0 ♗c6 13 ♕d1 ♘a6 14 ♕d2 ♖e8 15 ♖ad1 ♘c7 there is no obvious way for White to punish Black's expansion but the black centre will require constant protection.

12	0-0	♗e7!?

It is more conventional to bide

one's time with 12...♖e8 13 ♖fd1
g6 14 ♖ac1 ♗g7 15 e3 ♘f8 with
a manoeuvring type of game in
prospect.

13　♖fd1　　f5!?

The FIDE World Champion
was geared up to play an early
e2-e4 when (after ...dxe4 followed by ♘xe4) he has the freer
piece play. Korchnoi puts a stop
to this in radical fashion at the
risk of weakening the e6 and e5
squares.

14　e3　　　♗d6
15　♘e2

If Korchnoi really is trying to
play the opening like a Stonewall
Dutch (pawns on c6, d5 and f5)
he might have continued with the
typical 15...g5 intending ...♕f6
and ...f5-f4. There is however,
always the risk that such moves
create weaknesses in one's own
camp without causing any com-
pensating problems for his opponent.

15　...　　　♕e7
16　♘f4

This knight is heading for d3, a
useful posting, where it helps
control c5 in case Black finally
decides to lash out, but more importantly it supports its colleague's likely advance into the
hole on e5.

Korchnoi finds an alternative
way of expanding on the queenside.

16　...　　　a5
17　♘d3　　b5
18　♕c2　　a4
19　♖e1

In such a blocked position
knights are generally preferable
to bishops. In particular the
bishop on b7 is at present a so-
called 'bad' one.

19　...　　　♔h8

Slightly more accurate is
19...♖ae8 20 ♖ac1 ♘b6 but it
comes to virtually the same thing.
White will threaten to play ♘d3-
c5xb7 winning the c-pawn, so
Black must choose between exchanging on c5 (giving the first
player an enormous square on d4)
or play to block the c-file (as in
the game).

20　♖ac1　　♘b6
21　♘fe5　　♘c4
22　f4

White is well installed on e5
and Black on the slightly less important c4 square. Karpov has an
advantage if he can organize a
general liquidation on the queenside of both a- and b-pawns
(which would undermine c4) or
by timing a kingside break with
g3-g4 (using his monster on e5).

22　...　　　g5!

The only chance to introduce
some confusion into the game.

23　♕e2　　♖g8
24　♔f2

Alternatively 24 ♕h5 ♖af8 25
♘f3 also forces concessions on
the kingside.

24　...　　　♖af8
25　♘f3

Korchnoi is obliged to again
move one of his pawns. This is
sometimes a problem in chess
because of the rule which states

that they can't move backwards!

25   ...   h6

The main alternative was 25...g4 26 ♘fe5 h5!? 27 ♖h1 ♔g7 28 h3 ♖h8. I can't see an immediate breakthrough for White but he will always be better in view of the miserable bishop on b7.

26   ♘fe5

Karpov is very patient in such positions and one would generally expect him to find the right plan to keep the initiative, but he now changes his mind, so often a mistake in chess!

26   ...   ♔h7
27   ♔g1?!

White should play for g3-g4, despite the need for heavy manoeuvring, as Black can only wait and see, e.g. ♖e1-h1, ♖c1-g1, ♗g2-f3, h2-h3, ♔f2-e1-d1 (or alternatively put the rooks on g2 and h2 and king on h1) and then finally g3-g4. Karpov obviously didn't really trust such a long-winded reorganization but his plan in the game is less convincing.

27   ...   ♕e8
28   ♕c2   ♔h8
29   ♘f2   ♖g7
30   ♖e2   ♗c8
31   ♖ce1   ♖fg8

Karpov has not really achieved much over the past few moves and Korchnoi is ready to push his h-pawn. It's no longer clear who is better. Karpov decides to justify his last few moves by grabbing a pawn as otherwise he has

nothing to show for his efforts.

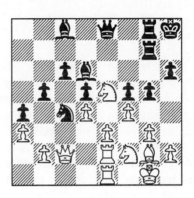

32   ♘xc4?!

For the record, 32 ♘fd3! (waiting) was stronger as 32...h5 is met by 33 ♘f3 with unclear play.

32   ...   bxc4!

Probably better than 32...dxc4 33 fxg5 hxg5 34 e4 f4 35 e5 with complications. This was best avoided as White's pieces spring to life.

33   ♕xa4   ♖b7

Korchnoi has good play on both wings and a space advantage for his pawn. He didn't necessarily need to switch plans as the more direct 33...h5!? looks interesting.

34   ♘d1   h5!
35   ♔f2   ♗d7
36   ♕c2   ♕g6
37   ♔f1

Black threatened to take twice on f4.

37   ...   h4
38   ♖f2   g4
39   ♔g1   ♖gb8

Karpov was more afraid of

39...h3! 40 &f1 &b3 and White is totally tied down.

40	&e2	h3
41	&f1	&c7
42	b4!	

Striking out for freedom. The best practical chance as the alternative would have been gradual suffocation.

| 42 | ... | cxb3 |

After 42...&a8 43 &b2 &ba7 44 e4 fxe4 45 &e3 White sets up a blockade that looks hard to break.

| 43 | &b2 | &d6 |
| 44 | a4 | &e6 |

Karpov has an unpleasant defensive task ahead of him, one which may have been harder after 44...c5! (or 45...c5) as after the capture on c5, Black's bishop will pressurize the a7-g1 diagonal right into the white camp.

| 45 | &d1 | &a7 |
| 46 | &d3 | &h7 |

Korchnoi is still rather hesitant about committing himself.

| 47 | &d1 | c5 |

Finally getting the break in but now, with the loss of the b-pawn, Karpov obtains counter chances.

48	&xb3	&xb3
49	&xb3	c4
50	&b6	&a8

More dynamic was 50...&c7 with the plan of pushing the c-pawn.

Korchnoi's nervous play has allowed Karpov back into the game. Now Karpov takes the bull by the horns with the thunderbolt...

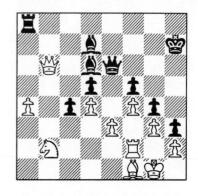

| 51 | e4! | |

Again turning the tables!

| 51 | ... | fxe4 |

Black has no shortage of alternatives but none are convincing;

a) 51...&xe4 52 &xd6 winning;

b) 51...dxe4 52 &xc4 offers White a clear advantage, he has an extra pawn and liberated pieces. Then after 52...&e7 53 a5 (53 &b7? &c6!) e3 54 &b2 Black is clearly struggling;

c) 51...&b8 52 exd5! and the complications offer White the better chances.

d) 51...&e7 52 &xe6 &xe6 53 exd5 &xd5 54 &xc4 &e4 offers drawing chances but two pawns is a lot of material to give Karpov in an ending!

| 52 | f5 | &e7 |
| 53 | &d1 | |

This knight that so successfully blockaded the b-pawn is brought across to handle the passed e-pawn.

| 53 | ... | &b8 |
| 54 | &a5 | &c6 |

55 f6

Karpov causes as much disruption as possible with his passed pawn before Black gets his own going.

55 ... ♕e6

55...♗b4 is met by 56 ♕xd5! a profitable desperado leading to an excellent ending for White after 56...♗xd5 57 fxe7 ♗xe7 58 ♘c3 as White picks up at least one pawn.

56 ♘e3 ♖b3

Korchnoi later considered 56...♔g6 superior as in the game, by abandoning the back rank, he has greater difficulties with the f-pawn.

57 ♕a7+ ♗b7

57...♖b7 58 ♕a6 is no better as Black is unable to defend the kingside.

58 a5

Threatening 59 a6 but there was a better alternative in 58 ♗e2! hitting the g-pawn; after 58...♖b1+ 59 ♖f1 ♖xf1+ 60 ♗xf1! (60 ♔xf1? fails to 60...♕xf6+ 61 ♔e1 ♗xg3+! 62 hxg3 h2 or 62 ♔d1 ♕c6) 60...♕c8 61 ♗e2 White keeps an advantage but the position is complex and Black is not without counter chances.

58 ... ♗f8

59 ♖f4?

Now 59 ♗e2 is again possible as 59...♖xe3 60 ♕xb7+ ♔g6 is countered by 61 ♕b8! and White keeps the advantage, e.g. 61...♗d6 62 ♕h8 or 61...♔f7 62 ♕f4.

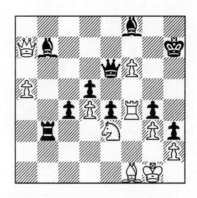

Karpov allows one of the combinations of the year.

59 ... ♗h6!

60 f7 ♗xf4!

Karpov must have overlooked this resource and, while still in shock, he fails to find the best continuation.

61 f8♕?

61 f8♘+! leads to a likely draw in an unlikely fashion.

a) 61...♔g8 62 ♘xe6 ♗xe3+ 63 ♔h1 ♖b1 64 ♕b8+ ♔f7 65 ♕c7+ ♔xe6 66 ♕e5+ and White takes the draw by perpetual check;

b) 61...♔h6 62 gxf4 (after 62 ♘xe6? ♗xe3+ 63 ♔h1 ♖b1 mates as White has no checks this time) 62...♕c8 (62...♕f7!?) 63 ♕c5 ♕xc5 64 ♘f5+ ♔h5 65 ♘g7+ drawing in original style.

61 ... ♗xe3+

62 ♔h1 ♗h6

With rook, bishop and pawn for the queen Black has nominal material equality. However, the pair of queens are impotent compared with the black pieces swarming in for the attack.

| 63 | ♕f2 | ♗g7! |

Now White's pin on the seventh rank is broken.

| 64 | a6 | ♖f3! |
| 65 | ♕e1 | |

After 65 axb7 ♖xf2 66 b8♕ White has a third queen but more importantly Black has 66...♖xf1 mate.

| 65 | ... | ♗xa6 |
| 66 | ♗e2 | ♖f7 |

The white king is forever stuck in the corner and despite both queens defending the attack rolls on.

| 67 | ♕c5 | c3! |
| 68 | ♕cxc3 | |

Equally hopeless is 68 ♗xa6 ♕xa6 69 ♕cxc3 (or 69 ♔g1 ♕a2

winning) 69...♖f1+ mating.

68	...	♗xe2
69	♕xe2	♕f6
70	♕c1	

After 70 ♔g1, lesser players may have fallen for 70...♕xd4+? 71 ♕xd4 ♗xd4+ 72 ♔h1 ♖a7 when 73 ♕xe4+! dxe4 is stalemate! However 70...♗h6! (as in the game) will win.

70	...	♗h6
71	♕b1	♕f5
72	♔g1	♖c7

White resigned as 73...♖c1+ is coming. The advantage switched back and forth in a game rich in ideas and surprises which finished with a great victory for the ever popular Korchnoi.

0-1

Game Twenty
Garry Kasparov-Vladimir Kramnik
Novgorod 1994

The six-player category XIX event in Novgorod, Russia, did not involve Karpov but most of the other top players were there; Kasparov and Ivanchuk were in impressive form to share first place.

1	e4	c5
2	♘c3	♘c6
3	♘ge2	

A move order chosen by those who like to 'play an open Sicilian, if Black prepares himself for a closed, and a closed if he prepares himself for an open!' as one specialist assured me.

| 3 | ... | ♘f6 |
| 4 | d4 | |

I really can't see Kasparov playing anything else, it's not his style to grovel around in dull sidelines.

| 4 | ... | cxd4 |
| 5 | ♘xd4 | e5 |

Kramnik does not hesitate to play his pet Sveshnikov; a sharp game is in prospect.

6	♘db5	d6
7	♗g5	a6
8	♘a3	b5
9	♘d5	♗e7
10	♗xf6	

White gives up the bishop pair to play for control of the pivotal d5 square.

10	...	♗xf6
11	c3	0-0
12	♘c2	♖b8
13	h4	

Another of their recent encounters continued as follows: 13 a3 a5 14 h4 ♘e7 15 ♘ce3 ♘xd5 16 ♘xd5 ♗e6 17 g3 ♕d7 18 ♗g2 ♗d8 19 0-0 ♗b6 20 ♕d2 and White kept a slight edge in Kasparov-Kramnik, from the Moscow (PCA) quickplay a few months earlier. Kasparov could have repeated this line, hoping that his opponent had no improvements ready, and playing for the same mini-advantage, but he is not so naive, and was obviously aware that Kramnik must have had something up his sleeve.

13	...	♘e7

Evidently 13...♗xh4?? is suicide; 14 ♕h5 g5 15 g3, etc. More reasonable is 13...♗e6 when 14 ♘ce3 a5 15 ♕f3 b4 16 ♗c4 has been played before in Yurtaev-Holmsten, Helsinki 1992, although White has a firm grip on d5 and therefore keeps some advantage.

14	♘xf6+

A new move. Kasparov decides to relinquish his control of d5 for chances against the black kingside. Previously theory recommended 14 ♘ce3, e.g. 14...♘xd5 15 ♘xd5 ♗b7 16 g3 b4 and Black had adequate counter

chances in Smagin-Gorelov, USSR 1982. He has a lead in development and queenside play to compensate for the d5 outpost.

14	...	gxf6
15	♕d2	♗b7
16	♗d3	d5

Kramnik reacts in the centre now that White has abandoned control of d5.

17	exd5	♕xd5
18	0-0-0!	

Kasparov sacrifices his a-pawn and clearly puts faith in his kingside attack, bearing in mind that his own monarch will not be particularly safe on the queenside in the long-term. Yet again Kasparov demonstrates the depth of his home preparation.

18	...	e4
19	♗e2	♕xa2!?

Kramnik probably suspected that this was all home preparation but despite this unnerving feeling he bravely plays the 'man's move'!

Alternatives play even more into White's hands: 19...♕xd2+ 20 ♖xd2 ♖fd8 21 ♖hd1 gives a clear advantage to White (who has the d-file and better pawns) and 19...♕e5, centralizing the queen, is best met by 20 ♘e3! threatening 21 ♘g4, and after 20...f5 then 21 ♕d6 again gives a superior ending.

20	♕h6	♕e6
21	♘d4	♕b6

A winning attack follows for White after 21...♕e5 22 f4 exf3 23 ♗d3.

22 ♖h3

Kasparov plays the natural move but critical is the sharp alternative 22 g4(!). Play would most likely continue 22...♔h8 23 ♘f5 ♘xf5 24 gxf5 ♖fd8! 25 ♗h5 when White has a strong initiative, but after 25...b4! 26 c4! (not 26 ♖dg1? ♖g8 27 ♗xf7 bxc3 28 bxc3 ♕c6 and Black has dangerous threats of his own, nor 26 cxb4?! e3 27 ♖hg1 ♖bc8+ 28 ♔b1 ♖xd1+ 29 ♗xd1 ♗e4+ 30 ♔a2 ♖g8 and Black is not worse) 26...e3! 27 ♖hg1 ♖xd1+ 28 ♗xd1 ♖g8 29 ♖xg8+ ♔xg8 30 ♕xe3 ♕c6! (rather than the blunder 30...♕a5?? 31 ♕g3+ winning as 32 ♕b8+ follows or 30...♕xe3+?! 31 fxe3 which is excellent for White as his king is by far the quicker to enter the fray) Black has good drawing chances.

22 ... ♔h8

23 ♗g4!

With several menacing threats, the most direct being 24 ♘f5.

23 ... ♖g8

24 ♘e6!?

A spectacular move that has been analysed by the whole chess world these past few months. Whether or not the move is objectively sound is only part of the story, in terms of creativity the move deserves '!!'.

In practical terms Kramnik has to weave his way through intricate complications to survive (and even gain an advantage), and in time trouble this is not often possible.

24 ♗e6 also requires precise defence. The consensus is that best play is 24...♖g6 25 ♕f4 fxe6 (not 25...♖f8 as 26 h5 is too strong) when after 26 ♕xb8+ ♖g8 27 ♕h2 (27 ♕f4 e5) 27...e5 Black picks up the f-pawn with adequate compensation for the exchange.

24 ... ♖g6!

Best. Others fail quickly: 24...♖xg4 is refuted by the beautiful 25 ♘g5! ♖xg5 (on 25...fxg5 then 26 ♕xb6 and White wins on material) 26 hxg5 which wins because of mate (26...♔g8 27 ♕xh7+ ♔f8 28 ♕h6+); 24...♘g6 25 h5 fxe6 26 ♖d7 also mates; and 24...fxe6 25 ♕xf6+ ♖g7 26 ♖d7 ♖e8 (after 26...♕c5 27 ♖g3 Black cannot defend) 27 ♖g3! with deadly threats.

25 ♕f4 ♖e8

Kramnik, in time trouble, had many variations to calculate. The first of which, 25...♖bg8, provokes a spectacular finish: 26 h5!! ♖xg4 27 ♕xf6+ ♖4g7 28 h6

♕xe6 (hopeless is 28...fxe6 29
hxg7+ ♖xg7 30 ♖g3 ♘g6 31
♖d7) 29 hxg7+ ♖xg7 30 ♖d8+
♘g8 31 ♖xg8+ ♔xg8 32 ♕d8+
♕e8 33 ♕xe8 mate!

The second, 25...♖a8, is better
but after 26 ♖d6 ♘d5 27 ♖xb6
♘xf4 28 ♘xf4 ♖xg4 29 ♖xf6
Black has an unpleasant ending
with the inferior minor piece and
worse pawns.

Thirdly, and best, is 25...♗d5!
which defends the rook on b8,
stops White's possible ♖d6, and
helps fend off the attack. With
more time Kramnik may have
found this move and as a result
reduced Kasparov to the unfamil-
iar role of scrambling for the
draw. After 25...♗d5 the following variation has come under
close scrutiny: 26 ♗h5 ♗xe6 27
♗xg6 ♘xg6 (possible is
27...hxg6 28 ♕xf6+ ♔g8 29
♕xe7 ♗xh3 30 gxh3 ♕xf2 31
♕xe4 when Black is slightly
better according to Kasparov, but
White would surely expect to
draw) 28 ♕xf6+ ♔g8 29 ♖g3 (or
29 h5 ♗xh3 30 ♖d6 ♕c5 31 hxg6
hxg6 32 gxh3 e3 with winning
chances only for Black) 29...b4!
30 c4 ♕c5 31 b3 ♕a5!
(Timman's move) with complications favouring Black.

26 ♖d6 ♘d5! *(D)*

The obvious move 26...♕a5
has been another topic for dis-
cussion and has provoked many
conflicting analyses in the chess
press. Giving a critical eye to
various ideas has enabled me to

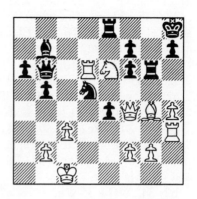

synthesize the work of others and
add some of my own. My conclusion is that White wins after
27 h5.

Now after:

a) 27...♕a1+ 28 ♔c2 ♕a4+ 29
♔b1 ♖xg4 30 ♕xf6+ ♔g8 White
has an attractive-looking move in
31 ♕xe7?! but unfortunately this
fails to win, e.g. 31...♗c6!
(31...b4? allows mate after 32
♖d8 ♗c6 33 ♕f8+! ♖xf8 34
♖xf8) 32 ♖d8 because of the
clever saving resource
32...♕d1+! and Black is okay
after 33 ♖xd1 ♖xe7. However 31
♘g5! does the trick as White
threatens 32 h6 and 32 ♕xf7+.
Now 31...♕c4 transposes to b)
(the same position that also arises
from the line starting 27...♖xg4).

b) 27...♖xg4 28 ♕xf6+ ♔g8 29
♘g5 ♕a1+ 30 ♔c2 ♕a4+ 31
♔b1 ♕c4 (worse are 31...♗d5?
32 ♖xd5 winning and 31...♕b3?
32 h6 ♖xg5 33 ♕xg5+ ♘g6 34
♕f6 ♔f8 35 ♖d7 ♖e7 36 ♕xe7+!
♘xe7 37 ♖d8 mate) with the key
position that can also arise from

a). Decisive is 32 h6! ♖xg5 (32...♘f5 33 ♕xf5 wins) 33 ♕xg5+ ♘g6 34 ♕f6 and Black cannot avoid mate for long:

b1) 34...♔f8 35 ♖d7 ♕f1+ 36 ♔a2 ♗d5+ 37 b3 ♗xb3+ 38 ♔b2! (a side-step avoiding 38 ♔xb3 ♕b1+) 38...♕e2+ 39 ♔xb3 ♕c4+ 40 ♔b2 ♕e2+ 41 ♔a3 b4+ 42 cxb4 ♖e7 43 ♕xe7+! (again this theme!) 43...♘xe7 44 ♖d8 and yes it is mate.

b2) 34...♕f1+ 35 ♔a2 (35 ♔c2 also wins) 35...♕c4+ (for 35...♗d5+ see b1) 36 b3 ♕e2+ 37 ♔a3 b4+ 38 cxb4 ♔f8 39 ♖d7 ♖e7 40 ♕xe7+! (yet again) 40...♘xe7 41 ♖d8 mate.

Rather long but convincing.

After the text move White could have settled for 27 ♖xb6 ♘xf4 28 ♘xf4 ♖xg4 29 ♖xf6 ♖e7 30 ♖e3! intending 31 g3 with a slight edge, and if 30...♖xh4 White has a strong initiative for the pawn after 31 ♖g3. However, Kasparov came up with something really rather special:

27 h5!!

One of the most surprising (and best) moves of the year. With so many pieces en prise Kasparov brings the h-pawn into the attack! Black has several defensive tries but nothing seems to work.

27 ... ♘xf4

Hopeless are 27...♖xg4 28 ♕xg4 as White wins the black queen, and 27...fxe6 28 hxg6 ♕c7 29 ♕h2 when Black can resign. Slightly more robust is 27...♖xe6

but White wins comfortably after 28 hxg6 ♘xf4 29 ♖xh7+ ♔g8 30 gxf7+ ♔f8 (or 30...♔xh7 31 ♖xb6 ♖xb6 32 f8♕ winning) 31 ♖h8+ ♔xf7 32 ♗xe6+ ♘xe6 33 ♖xb6, etc.

28 hxg6 ♕xd6

28...♖xe6 29 ♖xh7+ ♔g8 30 gxf7+ transposes to 27...♖xe6 of the previous note.

29 ♖xh7+ ♔g8
30 gxf7+ ♔xh7
31 fxe8♕

The complications have led to material equality, but not for long as the black king is under intense pressure.

31 ... ♘xe6
32 ♗f5+! ♔g7
33 ♕g6+ ♔f8
34 ♕xf6+ ♔e8
35 ♗xe6

Now if Black does nothing then 36 g4 will start a decisive advance, so Kramnik could have tried 35...e3 36 fxe3 ♗xg2 when Kasparov intended to transpose into a simply winning pawn ending after 37 ♗f7+ ♔d7 38 ♗e8+ ♔c7 39 ♕g7+ ♔d8 40 ♕xg2 ♔xe8 41 ♕e4+ ♔f7 42 ♕f4+.

35 ... ♕f8?

Now Kramnik had just enough time to resign before his time ran out and Kasparov could play 36 ♗d7+.

1-0

When I had to make a selection for this book there were just so many excellent Kasparov games to choose from but this one was top of my list. There may be some who like to criticize such games 'because the attack was not sound', but it should of course be remembered that chess is not an exact science but a practical activity (sport if you like). The strongest players are not always the most accurate but those who set the most difficult problems for their opponents.

Because of its very compli-cated nature of this game, the notes to this particular game are very detailed, but they hopefully illustrate how difficult it can be to accurately calculate in limited time. Conclusions about the worth of particular moves can take weeks to prove and shouldn't distract the reader from the most lucid conclusion of all: this was a magnificent game.

Game Twenty-One
Vassily Ivanchuk-Vladimir Kramnik
Novgorod 1994

Ivanchuk and Shirov were the two big names missing from the Candidates stage of the two World Championship cycles, so these two players had more than most to prove in tournament play during 1994. Shirov has had a reasonable year but Ivanchuk has had some major successes: first alone in both Munich and the London PCA and equal first in Novgorod. As a result Ivanchuk is now the world No.5 (on the end of September Intel world rankings). His opponent in this game, Kramnik, is still as low as ninth but is advancing fast.

1	e4	c5
2	♘f3	♘c6
3	d4	cxd4
4	♘xd4	♘f6
5	♘c3	e6

The same opening is reached with one move less per player after 5...e5 6 ♘db5 d6 7 ♗g5 (see the game position after move eight).

6	♘db5	d6
7	♗f4	e5
8	♗g5	

Black has played ...e7-e6-e5 but White has also lost a tempo by ♗c1-f4-g5. The dance of the black e-pawn and white bishop has not resulted in any gain for either side.

8	...	a6
9	♘a3	b5
10	♗xf6	gxf6
11	♘d5	f5

The Sveshnikov is one of the most popular of all opening variations, and has been a Kramnik speciality off and on in his limited career so far (see also games 5 and 20).

12	exf5	♗xf5
13	c3	♗g7
14	♘c2	♘e7

This move has become popular

of late, but Black used to prefer 14...0-0 15 ♘ce3 ♗e6 16 ♗d3 (16 g3!?) 16...f5, when White has control of d5 and hopes to use his central advantage, either to launch a kingside attack or to seek pressure against the a6 and b5 pawns. Black uses his bishop pair to obtain counterplay by pushing his f-pawn and/or organizing a queenside minority attack. One of the reasons the line has retained great popularity is the wealth of possibilities for both players.

15 ♗d3!?

The idea of challenging the bishop on the b1-h7 diagonal is known but not in this particular position.

The main alternatives consist of 15 ♘xe7 (yielding only equality after 15...♗xc2! 16 ♕xc2 ♕xe7 17 ♗e2 0-0 18 0-0 d5; Adams-Shirov, Chalikidiki 1993) and the popular 15 ♘ce3. After the latter, numerous recent games have continued 15...♗e6 16 g3 ♘xd5 17 ♘xd5 0-0 18 ♗g2 (in this line White ensures his hold on d5 but Black plays on the wings) 18...a5 19 0-0 ♖b8 20 ♕h5 f5 21 ♖ad1 ♔h8 (or 21...♕d7!? 22 ♖d2 ♕f7 23 ♕xf7+ ♖xf7 making a refreshing change from the main-line) 22 ♖d2 ♗f7 with mixed results for White (who has tried a variety of retreats as best play has yet to be resolved).

15 ... ♘xd5

If the text proves to be unsatis-

factory then 15...♗e6!? could be tried. Then after 16 ♘xe7 (on 16 ♗e4 Black has an interesting exchange sacrifice 16...f5!? 17 ♘c7+ ♕xc7 18 ♗xa8 d5 and the bishop on a8 is in great danger) 16...♕xe7 17 ♕h5?! (in order to stop Black castling kingside) is countered by 17...e4! with a good game for Black. 17 ♘e3 (instead of 17 ♕h5) looks sensible but Black has no obvious worries after 17...d5, so best is 17 ♗e4! keeping an edge as 17...0-0-0!? 18 ♗d5 ♗xd5 19 ♕xd5 ♕b7 20 ♘e3 ♗h6 21 ♕xb7+ ♔xb7 22 ♘d5 maintains control of d5.

16 ♗xf5 ♘e7
17 ♕g4

Black doesn't want to rush and play 17...♘xf5. The simplified position then favours White, who has the better pawn structure and holes on d5 and f5 to infiltrate.

17 ... 0-0
18 ♖d1 d5

Unsatisfactory is 18...♘xf5?! as 19 ♕xf5 d5 20 0-0! avoids complications and prepares to lay siege to Black's d-pawn; then 20...♖c8 21 ♕d3 ♖c5 22 ♘b4 gives a strong initiative for White.

19 ♘e3 d4
20 ♗e4!

Ivanchuk threatens 21 ♗xa8 and if 20...♖a7 21 ♘f5 ♘xf5 (21...♘g6 22 h4 also gives White a strong attack) 22 ♕xf5 ♕h4 23 ♖d3! Black is helpless against the threat of 24 ♖h3. This explains Kramnik's next move which constitutes the best practical choice.

20 ... dxe3!

With only rook and knight for the queen he hasn't quite enough material compensation, but if he can keep the initiative...

21 ♖xd8 exf2+
22 ♔xf2 ♖axd8

Threatening both 23...f5 and 23...♖d7+ hence White's next.

23 ♕e2 f5
24 ♗b7

Naturally putting the queenside under pressure. However, Ivanchuk had probably underestimated Black's idea otherwise he may have settled for 24 ♗c2 intending 25 ♖d1 exchanging a pair of rooks, followed by a probing of the light squares by a2-a4, etc.

24 ... ♖d7!

Sacrificing further material in the battle for the initiative.

Instead 24...♖d6 is passive and allows White to build pressure by 25 ♖d1 ♖fd8 26 ♖xd6 ♖xd6 27 ♕e3 ♔f7 28 ♔e1 as 29 ♕a7 is threatened.

25 ♗xa6 ♖fd8
26 ♕xb5 ♖d2+
27 ♔g3 e4

White has a substantial material advantage (queen and two pawns for rook and knight) but has problems with his king. The critical moment is at hand.

28 ♖e1!

Developing his last piece and preparing to meet 28...♖8d3+ with 29 ♕xd3! ♗e5+! (after 29...exd3 30 ♖xe7 White has excellent winning chances in the ending, e.g. 30...♖xb2 31 ♗c4+ ♔f8 32 ♖f7+ ♔e8 33 ♖xg7 d2 34 ♗e2 ♖b1 35 ♖xh7 winning) 30 ♔h3 ♖xd3+ 31 ♗xd3 exd3 32 ♖d1! picking up the d-pawn and winning (32...♘d5 is simply met by 33 g3).

28 ... ♘g6

Now Black really is threatening to win with 29...♖8d3+.

29 ♖e2!

The main point behind his previous move was this simple, but effective, construction of a shelter on f2 for the king. Instead of the text, 29 ♕xf5 is of course ridiculous: 29...♗e5+ 30 ♔h3 ♘f4+ and White's king will be battered to oblivion.

29　...　♗e5+

Kramnik could have tried 29...f4+?! but after 30 ♔f2 I can't find a convincing continuation for Black. Even 30 ♔g4 e3 31 g3! (31 ♔f3!?) looks good enough to obtain a winning game as Black's tactics don't quite work:

a) 31...♖f8 32 ♖xd2 exd2 (after 32...♘e5+ 33 ♔h3 exd2 34 ♕d5+ ♔h8 35 gxf4 White wins comfortably) 33 ♕d5+ ♔h8 34 ♕xd2! (but not 34 gxf4?! as 34...♖xf4+ 35 ♔g3 ♖d4! is unclear) 34...f3 and Black has some practical chances but should really be lost.

b) 31...♘e5+ 32 ♔xf4 ♘d3+ 33 ♔xe3 ♗h6+ 34 ♔f3 ♖f8+ 35 ♔g4 ♖xe2 36 ♕xd3 ♖xb2 37 ♗c4+ ♔h8 38 h4 gives White a winning advantage.

30　♔f2　♖d1!

Again Kramnik makes the best of his chances. Instead 30...♘f4? fails to 31 ♕xe5 ♘xe2 32 ♗xe2 ♖xb2 33 ♕e6+ and Black is lost.

Also inadequate is 30...♗xh2 31 ♖xd2 (31 g3!?) 31...♖xd2+ 32 ♔e1 e3 33 ♕e8+ ♔g7 34 ♕xe3 when Black's position is prospectless.

31　♖e1　♖8d2+?

A time trouble error. Now after the exchange of a pair of rooks Black cannot put up much resistance as his attacking chances are

gone. Better were either 31...♖1d6 (Kramnik) or 31...♖1d2+!? 32 ♔g1 (32 ♖e2 repeats) 32...♔g7! (M.Gurevich) heading for f6, where it will support the activation of the knight. Black must avoid exchanging pieces when there remain significant technical problems for White in getting the queenside going.

32　♔f1　♖xe1+

32...e3?? loses immediately to 33 ♕b3+ ♔g7 34 ♖xd1 e2+ 35 ♗xe2.

33　♔xe1　♖xg2
34　♗c8!

Suddenly this 'badly-placed' bishop becomes an important asset.

34　...　f4

34...♘f4?? would hardly test Ivanchuk, who would of course have played 35 ♕e8+ ♔g7 36 ♕xe5+ taking the bishop with check.

35　♗f5!　♗f6

Kramnik is running short of reasonable moves as 35...e3?? drops the rook after 36 ♕d5+ and 35...f3 36 ♗xg6 e3 37 ♕e8+ is also winning comfortably for White.

36　♗xe4

Black could now have resigned with a clear conscience.

36	...	♖xh2
37	a4	♘e5
38	a5	f3
39	a6	♖h1+
40	♔d2	1-0

Kramnik lost on time but there was no hope left.

Modern chess games are more combative and messy than they were a generation or so ago. Rather than defend passively in inferior positions, modern grandmasters prefer to sacrifice material to mix it and create confusion. Here Kramnik's queen sacrifice was justified in practical terms but he (again!) spoilt his chances in time trouble, another typical feature of modern chess.

Why, you may ask, are so many games decided in the tension of *zeitnot*? I think that the answer lies in that most ambitious young pretenders put tremendous effort into their games to find new ideas and difficult moves to test their opponents. This of course takes deep analysis at every stage of the game, a process that enables them to find sensational moves but is time-consuming. One ill-considered move can be fatal.

Game Twenty-Two
Evgeny Bareev-Zbynek Hracek
Pardubice 1994

Overall, the Russian grandmaster Evgeny Bareev has had a disappointing year. He did fairly well in Linares but finished last in Novgorod and Madrid. His poor form has seen him slip from an established top-ten spot in 1993 to a lowly 22nd in the September Intel rankings.

His best efforts of 1994 were second at Tilburg and sole winner of a category XV in the Czech Republic. I anticipate that he will regain ground in 1995 as he is probably the most underrated 2600+ player at present.

1	d4	♘f6
2	c4	e6
3	♘c3	

By playing the text White indicates that he is not afraid of meeting the Nimzo-Indian (after

3...♗b4), and retains more favourable options against both 3...c5 (the Benoni) and in some lines after 3...d5 (Queen's Gambit).

Some players prefer to avoid the Nimzo-Indian with 3 ♘f3, but then after 3...d5 exchange variations (an early cxd5 by White) are considered less favourable for the first player. This is essentially because, after an early ♘f3 by White, Black usually has enough time to develop his queen's bishop to f5, an important step on the road to equality.

3	...	d5
4	cxd5	♘xd5!?

More usual is 4...exd5 and after 5 ♗g5 ♗e7 6 e3 c6 (6...♗f5? loses a pawn to 7 ♗xf6 ♗xf6 8 ♕b3) 7 ♕c2 Black has not been able to develop his bishop to f5.

If instead 7 ♘f3?! (which can transpose from 3 ♘f3 d5 4 cxd5, etc.) then Black can safely develop his queen's bishop with 7...♗f5.

5	e4	♘xc3
6	bxc3	c5
7	a3!	

The routine 7 ♘f3 transposes to the main line of the Queen's Gambit Declined, Semi-Tarrasch Defence where Black can simplify with 7...cxd4 8 cxd4 ♗b4+ 9 ♗d2 ♗xd2+ 10 ♕xd2 0-0 and White has a fairly difficult task proving an opening advantage.

By preventing ...♗b4+ White retains the dark-squared bishops and thus extra attacking potential.

7	...	♗e7
8	♘f3	0-0
9	♗d3	cxd4
10	cxd4	♘c6
11	♗b2	♕a5+

Hracek again aims for exchanges. Here 12 ♕d2 ♕xd2+ 13 ♔xd2 looks marginally better for White who can put his king on the e3 square, supporting his centre, and hope to use his slight space advantage to engineer a timely d4-d5, etc. However Bareev prefers to play for the attack!

12	♔f1!?	♖d8
13	h4	

The logical follow-up to his last move. The rook will enter the fray by ♖h3 and the h-pawn can be used to force concessions. Black is behind in development, hence his desire to bring his queenside into play.

13	...	b6
14	♕e2	

White avoids the threatened 14...♗a6, exchanging bishops.

14	...	♗b7

Hracek, the present champion of the Czech Republic, develops 'naturally' but slips into a passive position. Instead 14...♘b8?! (insisting on ...♗a6) could have been considered, but 15 h5 h6 16 ♘e5 makes Black's plan look dangerously slow.

The best move was the surprising 14...♗c5(!), as after 15 dxc5? Black has 15...♖xd3! grabbing the initiative (as 16 ♕xd3?? loses to 16...♗a6). Critical is 15 d5 ♘e7 as White has been forced to advance the d-pawn prematurely and its not clear that he can maintain his centre.

15	♖d1	♗f8

Obviously 15...♗xa3?? loses to 16 ♖a1 so the a-pawn remains defended by tactical means.

16	♖h3	♖ac8

Black is now fully mobilized

but he lacks counterplay as there are no obvious targets in the white position.

17 ♔g1

An instructive move. Bareev first removes his own king from any potential checks before launching his attack.

17 ... ♘e7

Perhaps 17...♘b8!? 18 ♕e3 ♗a6 19 ♗b1 ♕b5, trying to keep White occupied, offered better chances of a successful defence.

18 h5 h6

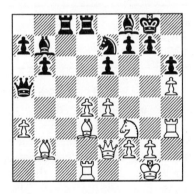

White has built up a nice-looking position but how does he progress?

19 d5! exd5
20 e5

The d-pawn blocks the influence of no less than four black pieces and is in effect a hindrance for the defender. Compare this position with that arising if Bareev had played 19 e5? where the bishop on b2 would be blocked out of play and Black would have access to the d5 square.

20 ... d4

Giving back the superfluous pawn for some breathing space. It's hard to suggest a defence against the plan of ♘f3-d4, ♖h3-g3, ♕e2-g4 and then e5-e6 or ♘d4-f5. Hracek is probably already lost!

21 ♘xd4 ♕d5
22 ♖g3 ♘c6

After 22...♔h8 I think that 23 ♖e1! (rather than 23 e6?! ♖d6! which is less clear) is strongest, first supporting the e-pawn with ideas of ♕g4 and again ♘f5 or e6.

23 ♘f5 ♔h8

23...♕e6 may have been the original intention but then 24 ♖xg7+! ♗xg7 25 ♕g4 ♔f8 26 ♕xg7+ ♔e8 leaves White with several ways to win. Perhaps the most sadistic is 27 ♕h7! with the idea that 27...♕d5 is met by the crushing 28 e6(!).

24 ♘xh6!

Picking off a pawn as the knight cannot be safely captured.

24 ... ♕e6

After 24...gxh6 25 ♕g4! is the clearest (25 e6+ also wins but unnecessarily prolongs the game), e.g. 25...f6 26 e6 ♕g5 27 ♗xf6+! concludes neatly.

After the text White can of course play 25 ♘f5, with his booty intact, but who could resist the following line?

25 ♘xf7+! ♕xf7
26 e6

White is a piece down but look at the effectiveness of his army!

26	...	♛f4

Hopeless for Black are 26...♛e7 27 ♛e4 and 26...♛g8 27 h6 ♞d4 28 hxg7+ ♝xg7 29 ♛h5+.

27	h6!	♞d4

After 27...♛xh6 White has 28 ♜h3.

28	hxg7+	♝xg7
29	♛h5+	♛h6

29...♝h6 is despatched by 30 e7 as Black cannot defend all of the squares e8, d4 and h6, e.g. 30...♜e8 31 ♝xd4+ ♛xd4 32 ♛xh6+ or 30...♜d6 31 e8♛+, etc.

30	♛xh6+	♝xh6
31	e7	♜d5

31...♜d6 was slightly more robust but after 32 ♝f5! Black's position still collapses.

32	♝e4	1-0

A good example of the power of two bishops directed at the opposing king. Note the importance of 7 a3! and 12 ♔f1 in avoiding exchanges that could blunt the power of the attack.

Game Twenty-Three
Garry Kasparov-Alexei Shirov
Horgen 1994

The Horgen (near Zurich) Masters saw Kasparov in impressive form, comfortably outclassing his closest rivals. Gelfand lost four games, Shirov was effective against the lower-ranking participants but also lost to Lautier, a game which was awarded the brilliancy prize. However, the following game involves a profound exchange sacrifice, the study of which is a must for serious students of chess. In fact it seems that Shirov's aggressive attacking style lends itself to brilliant games for both himself and his opponent!

1	e4	c5
2	♞f3	e6
3	d4	cxd4
4	♞xd4	♞f6
5	♞c3	♞c6
6	♞db5	d6
7	♝f4	e5

I have already outlined some of the typical ideas in this variation elsewhere, and this is the key move that sets the scene; Black 'weakens' d5 but stakes a claim on some central dark squares. White typically exchanges his dark-squared bishop for the king's knight in order to obtain a firm grip on d5 and then Black tries to use his bishop pair to play around White's outpost.

8	♝g5	a6
9	♞a3	b5
10	♞d5	♝e7
11	♝xf6	♝xf6
12	c3	

The knight presently sidelined on a3 will be centralized to e3 to support its colleague.

12 ... ♗b7

Kasparov has certainly been tested in the Sveshnikov variation of the Sicilian; only one month earlier in Novgorod his labours had paid off with an astonishing win against Kramnik (see game 20) who castled in this position. Shirov, who was present there, had already played this variation on several previous occasions, so who would be first to come up with a new idea?

13 ♘c2 ♘b8

At first sight a surprising retreat but Black also intends to improve the position of his knight by coming to d7 and then either b6 or f6 (to challenge White's control of d5) or even the more active c5 square, hitting e4.

Inferior is 13...♘e7 allowing White to favourably switch plans with 14 ♘xf6+ gxf6 15 ♗d3 and Black has no compensation for an inferior pawn-structure.

14 a4!

The most critical continuation. Less testing is the plan tried by Anand against Nunn from this year's Melody Amber tournament in Monaco: 14 g3 intending ♘ce3, h4, ♗h3 etc, when Black had time to get his pieces reorganized.

14 ... bxa4
15 ♖xa4

Kasparov would have known of Shirov's games in this line including Zapata-Shirov, Manila Olympiad 1992, which continued

15 ♘ce3 ♘d7 16 ♕xa4 0-0 17 ♖d1 ♗g5 18 ♕c2 ♘c5 19 ♘f5 g6 20 b4! with complications in which Black had to be careful to hold his own.

15 ... ♘d7
16 ♖b4!

An interesting new idea which sets difficult practical problems for his opponent.

16 ... ♘c5?!

Not best but a move that requires a Kasparov to show us why. After the game Shirov regretted his choice and instead proposed 16...♖a7, while Black can also consider the more conventional 16...♖b8.

17 ♖xb7!!

An astonishing exchange sacrifice that wouldn't even have crossed the mind of the vast majority of grandmasters.

17 ... ♘xb7
18 b4

A necessary move that severely restricts the black knight. In fact the black rooks and minor pieces have few prospects whilst White has a bind on the light squares in general, and d5 in particular. Kasparov is playing for the quality of his pieces compared with those of his adversary, but does he have enough long-term compensation for the exchange?

18　...　♗g5
19　♘a3

Heading for c4. The white king is not really in danger so there is no hurry to castle, but it is certainly time for the Latvian monarch to flee because it's necessary to open lines for the rooks.

19　...　0-0
20　♘c4　a5

Many players would have been tempted by 20...f5?!, but after 21 ♗d3 White has all the answers: 21...f4 22 ♕g4 and Black's f-file demonstration has not helped his rook but only further compromised the light squares; 21...g6 'maintaining the tension' is followed by 22 exf5 gxf5 23 h4! ♗h6 24 ♗xf5! only helping to generate an attack for White, and 21...fxe4 22 ♗xe4 ♗h6 gives added tactical chances but only for the first player.

21　♗d3　axb4
22　cxb4　♕b8

Black gives himself the option of ...♘b7-d8-e6. The 'long' move 22...♖a2 at least activates a piece but Black lacks any targets after, say, 23 0-0 ♕a8 24 ♘cb6 ♕a3 25 ♗c4 ♖d2 26 ♕g4 with a clear advantage for White according to Kasparov.

23　h4　♗h6

23...♗d8 will observe the h-pawn from afar but is likely to upset his own knight, which is robbed of its only square(!), and after 24 g3 followed by 25 0-0 Black will be in an even more trussed-up condition.

24　♘cb6　♖a2
25　0-0

It's rare to see grandmasters castle so late in such a combative opening, but White's king has had few worries until now and the extra tempo has been more usefully spent reinforcing the bind.

Of course 25 ♘d7? fails to win back material after 25...♕a7.

25　...　♖d2
26　♕f3　♕a7

Preparing to finally centralize with ...♘d8-e6.

27　♘d7

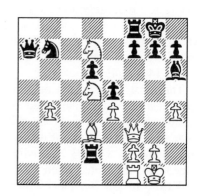

Later analysis suggested that Kasparov should have played 27 ♗b5 when Black's best could be the paradoxical 27...♖xd5!? 28 ♘xd5 ♘d8 followed by 29...♘e6 with a reasonable game (although

White's b-pawn still enables him to claim an edge, e.g. 29 ♕g4 ♘e6 30 ♗d7! followed by 31 b5; here the bishop cannot be taken as 30...♕xd7 is met by 31 ♘f6+).

27...♖d8 is worse because 28 ♗c6! (28 ♘e7+?! would be less accurate as after 28...♔f8 29 ♗c4 d5! 30 ♗xd5 ♘d6 White's knights lose their harmony) keeps Black tied up and threatens 29 ♘e7+ ♔f8 30 ♗d5.

Another try is 27...♘d8 28 ♘d7 ♘e6 29 ♘e7+ ♔h8 30 ♘xf8 ♕xe7 31 ♘xe6 ♕xe6 32 ♗c6 when Black is still on the defensive but the presence of opposite-coloured bishops guarantees reasonable drawing chances. Kasparov judges this as only slightly better for White.

27 ... ♘d8?

It is out of character for Alexei Shirov to play so passively.

27...♖a8! was best as 28 ♘e7+?! ♔h8 29 ♕xf7 is unsound after 29...♖xd3 30 ♘f8 ♕a2! (the rook has to be on a8 to permit this clever defence). Then White is worse after 31 ♘eg6+ hxg6 32 ♘xg6+ ♔h7 33 ♘f8+ ♖xf8! (33...♔h8 is equal) 34 ♕xa2 ♖d2 35 ♕a7 ♖f7! (when I prefer Black despite the miserable knight) or 31 ♕f5 g6 32 ♘fxg6+ ♔g7! (Gavrikov's move).

Instead 28 ♗c4! (28 ♘7b6?! is best met by 28...♕a3! as 29 ♘xa8 ♖xd3 favours Black) looks the best to me when 28...♘d8 29 ♘5b6 ♖d4! allows White to win back the exchange but in the process allows Black to activate his remaining pieces with good play.

28 ♘xf8 ♔xf8
29 b5 ♕a3?!

White keeps good winning chances even after the more accurate 29...♕d4 30 ♖d1 ♖xd1+ 31 ♕xd1 ♘e6 32 ♕b1! ♘c5 33 ♗c2 and the b-pawn is a menace to Shirov.

Centralizing the knight is too slow: 29...♘e6 30 b6 ♕b7 because of 31 ♖a1 ♘d4 32 ♕h5 with the threat of 33 ♖a7.

30 ♕f5! ♔e8

Capturing the rook allows a forced mate after 31 ♕d7.

31 ♗c4 ♖c2

After 31...♕c5 White can calmly capture on h7 for the same reason.

32 ♕xh7! ♖xc4
33 ♕g8+ ♔d7
34 ♘b6+

The fork yields a decisive gain of material.

34 ... ♔e7
35 ♘xc4 ♕c5
36 ♖a1 ♕d4

36...♕xc4 is met by 37 ♖a7+ ♔e6 38 ♕e8+ ♔f6 39 ♕xd8+, etc.

37 ♖a3 ♗c1
38 ♘e3! 1-0

An elegant finish. Now if 38...♗xa3 then 39 ♘f5+ picks up the queen and 38...g6 can be dealt with by 39 ♘d5+ ♔d7 40 ♖a8 with a quick mate. Vintage Kasparov.

6   Open Tournaments

Nowadays, there are of course hundreds of international open tournaments each year, particularly in Europe where the travel infrastructure is so sophisticated. Here I have concentrated on the results of the top 36 opens with more or less a conventional (rather than rapidplay) 'slow' time limit. This is a subjective choice based on the number of participating grandmasters, each star indicating ten or more GMs, e.g. no star tournaments aren't featured, Linares open had at least ten but not as many as twenty, Seville twenty-odd, etc.

I don't claim the list to be complete as the reporting of results from some countries is poor, so I should apologize to disappointed organizers and sponsors but do suggest that they better publicize their events. I also believe that all international opens should be classified according to my star system and therefore be allowed to advertize as a one-star open if the previous year they had, say, twelve GMs. This system immediately indicates the approximate strength of a tournament (without having to go into detail) and (ideally, from a personal point of view!) may encourage organizers to invite more grandmasters to get into the next star-category.

* Linares (Spain), January
7½/9   P.Svidler

The start of a good year for Peter Svidler who went on to win the Russian championship and later represented his country in the Moscow Olympiad.

** Seville (Spain), January
7½/9   K.Spraggett, M.Suba, A.Miles

Kevin Spraggett is the Canadian No.1 but he now lives in Portugal as he has a Portuguese wife. After flirting with the delights of Lewisham and Sunderland (in England), Mihai Suba now lives in Palma de Mallorca in the Spanish Balleric islands. Tony Miles from Birmingham (England's most widely-travelled player) registered excellent results all over the world in 1994.

* Geneva (Switzerland), January
7/9   I.Khenkin

Khenkin is an ex-Soviet now resident in Israel.

** Reykjavik (Iceland), February
7/9   V.Zviaginsev, H.Stefansson, E.Pigusov

At first sight, slightly surprising winners in such a strong open but Zviaginsev represented the successful Russia II team in Moscow (on board two) and is not yet twenty!

** Swiss Volksbank, Bern (Switzerland), February
7½/9   B.Gulko

7   M.Wahls, I.Novikov, A.Sokolov, V.Milov, V.Eingorn, K.Lerner, O.Cvitan, J.Hodgson, S.Dolmatov

A victory for experience and the favourite. The following group included three Ukrainians, which had more than passing significance in Bern, as there were extra prizes for teams of four from the same country.

* Cannes (France), February
7/9   O.Renet

After Lautier and Spassky, Olivier Renet is the French No.3. This was an excellent result for the tall Parisian who became a father for the first time shortly afterwards.

*** Cappelle la Grande (France), February
7/9   V.Chuchelov, A.Miles, G.Kuzmin, M.Hebden

The strongest French open is noted for its excellent hospitality. Chuchelov even lost in the last round to Hebden but still won on 'buchholz'. He is an ex-Soviet IM now playing under Belgian colours.

* Bad Worishofen (Germany), March
8/9   E.Magerramov

A big winning score for the Azerbaijani.

* Bled (Slovenia), March
7½/9   M.Cebalo, I.Lempert

Away from the war zone Slovenia is starting to organize some interesting tournaments. In fact the tradition for chess organization continues despite austere economic conditions in much of the former Yugoslavia.

** Petroff Memorial, Saint Petersburg (Russia), Feb/March
6½/9   V.Zviaginsev, V.Akopian, G.Serper, P.Svidler, J.Ehlvest

All ex-Soviets who participated for five different teams in the Moscow Olympiad! (respectively Russia II, Armenia, Uzbekistan, Russia I, Estonia).

* Oslo (Norway), April
7/9   I.Smirin, G.Serper

Another equal first for the Uzbeki Serper. Smirin, who vies with Yudasin as the top Israeli player, had a particularly good year in the Intel Grand Prix (see Chapter 4).

*** New York (USA), April
7½/9   J.Ehlvest, L.Oll
7/9   J.Benjamin, Y.Grunfeld, A.Ivanov, G.Kaidanov,
       E.Lobron, A.Shabalov, P.Wolff

The Estonian duo picked up the mega-bucks in the first of the two American super-tournaments.

* Ibercajo, Zaragoza (Spain), April
7½/9   R.Pogorelov

At 2415 Pogorelov was the year's lowest rated player to win a nine round * tournament outright.

* National Open, Las Vegas (USA), April/May
5½/6   W.Browne, G.Kaidanov, V.Akopian, J.Ehlvest,
       A.Mortazavi

A career-best result for the British chess journalist Ali Mortazavi who was born in Iran.

* Two Rivers, Passau (Germany), April
6/7   A.Kovalev, P.Schlosser, O.Vasilchenko, G.Siegel,
       N.Vlassov

These last two results suggest that in an open, six or seven games aren't enough! The smaller the number of rounds (and the larger the field) the more likely the smaller fry can wriggle through to the lead.

* Arnold Cup, Gausdal (Norway), April
7½/9   E.Schmittdiel

The Dortmunder recently obtained the grandmaster title after many years trying for elusive norms.

** Neptune Trophy, Cattolica (Italy), May
7½/9   V.Malaniuk, A.Onischuk
A Ukrainian double-act.

* Ljubljana (Slovenia), June
7½/9   E.Sveshnikov, S.Zagrebelny, P.Tregubov
Evgeny Sveshnikov is something of a living legend, having given his name to one of the most critical lines of the Sicilian. The other two winners are less well known, but hail from Uzbekistan and Russia respectively.

**** World Open, Philadelphia, (USA), June/July
7½/9   L.van Wely, A. Minasian
The strongest (non-rapidplay) open of the year is appropriately named, as it is the only **** event in my ranking system. The Americans finished well down the field this year enabling "Lucky Loek" van Wely from the Netherlands and the debonair Armenian Minasian to take the honours.

* Oberwart (Austria), July
8/9   K.Landa
Another Russian victory!

* Dresden (Germany), July
7½/9   K.Chernyshov
And another!!

* Benasque (Spain), July
7½/9   L.Psakhis, B.Lalic
A good year for the Croat Lalic who became a father for the first time in February 1994.

* Bismarck Open, Pardubice (Czech Republic), July
7½/9   M.Krasenkov, S.Kiselev
The farther east one goes, the more likely the Soviet school of chess is to dominate.

** Biel (Switzerland), July
8½/11   U.Adianto
8   A.Chernin, U.Andersson, V.Tkachiev, L.Gutman
It was surprising to see Ulf Andersson playing in some open tour-

naments this year, after many years of almost exclusive attention to top-level round-robins, but obviously his 'let's play the ending' style works well enough even there. Adianto had a purple patch this summer, following up this victory with a high placing (and qualification for the London Intel Grand Prix) in London's Lloyds Bank open one month later.

* Leeuwarden (Netherlands), July/August
7/9 A.Kharlov, Y.Yakovich

The Russian duet finished ahead of many well-known and higher-rated grandmasters.

* Kstovo (Russia), August
7½/9 V.Loginov

Another Uzbeki success.

* Mondariz (Spain), July/August
7/9 G.Georgadze, V.Dimitrov

This is the young Georgadze who played in the Georgian team in Moscow. The elder T.Georgadze (responsible for the Georgadze system in the Modern Defence) is now inactive in chess but a successful businessman.

* Porto San Giorgio (Italy), August
7/9 V.Malaniuk, G.Sax

Sax has dropped down the rating list and out of the limelight in recent years but is still active.

* Lost Boys, Antwerp (Belgium), August
7½/9 van der Sterren

In the first round Paul van der Sterren was the only grandmaster not to win, but after that there was no stopping the mild-mannered Dutchman who works on the editorial staff of the highly-respected *New In Chess* magazine.

* Dutch Open, Amsterdam (Netherlands), August
7½/9 A.Huzman

Another Ukrainian victory, the second most successful nation in open tournaments (after Russia) in 1994.

*** Lloyds Bank, London (England), August

9½/10	A.Morozevich
8	R.Mainka
7½	U.Adianto, R.Akesson, T.Markowski, A.Miles, D.Norwood, J.Nunn, V.Tkachiev, P.Wells

The best individual performance of the year from the 'young' Russia team (Moscow Olympiad) board one.

** Berlin (Germany), August

7½/9	G.Kuzmin, M.Wahls, V.Mikhalevski, V.Komliakov, V.Chuchelov, O.Nikolenko,V.Eingorn, A.Kharlov

The least decisive result of the year!

* Pula (Croatia), October

7/9	V.Tukmakov

The experienced Ukrainian is particularly active in the stronger opens.

** Cap D'Agde (France), October/November

7/9	L.Gofshtein
6½	A.Nenashev, L.Oll, I.Smirin, I.Novikov, A.Vyzmanavin, L.Psakhis, N.Rashkovsky, G.Georgadze, M.Palac

Gofshtein (yet another Israeli!) had a winning streak at the end to overtake a fistful of heavyweight names.

* Vienna (Austria), November

7½/9	S.Kindermann, P.Blatny

Kindermann is in most respects German but he has an Austrian passport. Blatny is Czech and has made progress with good results in several opens this year.

* Madrid (Spain), November

7½/9	E.Ubilava

The Georgian grandmaster is resident in Spain and is Anand's trainer.

The countries that hosted the most star tournaments were as follows:

6	Spain
4	Germany
3	USA, Switzerland, France

The most successful countries were (giving one point for an outright victory, half for a two-way tie, a third for a three-way, etc.) as follows:

1st   Russia
2nd   Ukraine
3rd   Israel
4th   Uzbekistan
5th   Germany

The ex-Soviet players obtained about three-quarters of the first places in this year's star opens, a remarkably high percentage.

Game Twenty-Four
Anthony Miles-Nino Kirov
Cappelle la Grande 1994

Tony Miles has been both very active and very successful in opens throughout the world over the past couple of decades and has shown even renewed enthusiasm this year. His style is flexible and he adapts well to different circumstances. I would summarize his qualities as:

a) he avoids lines where his opponent will feel comfortable;

b) he picks the appropriate type of position depending upon the style of his opponent;

and c) he has an iron will to win.

These are the necessary qualities to win opens.

Miles often uses offbeat openings and ideas to destabilize his opponents (a few years ago he won with Black against Karpov after meeting 1 e4 with 1...a6) but he quite frequently switches to positional grinding mode as here in our main game.

1	d4	d5
2	c4	c6
3	♘f3	♘f6
4	♘c3	dxc4
5	a4	

The main line of the Slav Defence. The text move deters ...b7-b5 and enables White to win back the c-pawn. The drawback is the weakening of the b4 square.

5	...	♗f5
6	♘e5	

Most common is 6 e3, intending to capture on c4 with the bishop, when play typically continues as follows: 6...e6 7 ♗xc4 ♗b4 8 0-0 ♘bd7 when Black has active piece play and access to b4 but White has potential in the centre with a well-timed e3-e4, etc.

6	...	♘bd7
7	♘xc4	♘b6?!

The Bulgarian has in fact played this suspect move before and is evidently not keen on entering the normal variations following 7...♕c7 8 g3 e5 9 dxe5 ♘xe5 10 ♗f4 ♘fd7.

8   ♘e5   a5

The two most active practitioners of this line are father and son, Nino Kirov and Kiro Ninov (Bulgarians and Icelanders change surnames to a derivative of their fathers Christian name!) Here they used to play 8...e6 but there is always the danger of a timely a-pawn advance, for instance 9 a5!? ♘bd7 10 a6 destabilizing the Black queenside pawns.

9   f3

In a more recent game 9 g3 e6 10 ♗g2 ♗b4 11 0-0 0-0 12 e3 h6 13 ♕e2 ♗h7 14 ♖d1 gave White a pleasant edge in Kramnik - Short, Novgorod 1994.

9   ...   ♘fd7
10   ♘xd7

10 ♘d3!? makes sense, keeping the tension. Miles instead plays to restrict the bishop on f8.

10   ...   ♘xd7
11   e4   ♗g6
12   d5!?

After a routine move like 12 ♗e3 Black can play 12...e6 followed by the comfortable development of the king's bishop. After the text, Black can move his e-pawn only at the cost of obtaining an isolated pawn.

12   ...   e5
13   dxe6   fxe6
14   ♗e3

The move that first catches the eye is 14 ♕b3, hitting two pawns.

This was in fact successfully played by Kozul against Kirov in Novi Sad 1992: 14...♘c5 15 ♕c2 e5? (too slow; 15...♕h4+ 16 g3 ♕f6 is playable) 16 ♗e3 ♗f7 17 ♖d1 ♕b6 (17...♕f6 18 ♘b5!) 18 ♘b5! ♖c8 19 ♖d6! ♗b3 20 ♕c3 and Black resigned.

14   ...   ♗c5

The exchange of dark-squared bishops would seem to take the sting out of the position, but if we concentrate on the respective pawn structures, Black has three pawn islands (against White's two) and the solid structure e4, f3, g2 keeps Black's bishop out of play. Miles therefore happily accepts simplification because he is able to maintain a structural advantage.

15   ♗xc5   ♘xc5
16   ♗c4   ♕xd1+
17   ♔xd1!

The king is well-placed on c2, covering the queenside.

17   ...   ♖d8+
18   ♔c2   ♔e7
19   ♖hd1   e5

White would like to probe the black pawn structure by putting pressure on e5 and a5, and this can be best achieved by bringing his knight to the c4 square hitting both weak pawns and some other sensitive squares, b6 and d6. Miles now goes about achieving this plan in a single-minded manner.

20   ♖xd8

The text liberates the d1 square ready for the manoeuvre ♘c3-d1-e3-c4, but Miles keeps one pair of rooks as this enhances his winning chances.

20	...	♖xd8
21	♘d1!	♗f7
22	♘e3	♗e6
23	♗xe6	♔xe6
24	♘c4	

Now that the black rook has to take up a passive role Miles takes control of the d-file.

24	...	♖a8
25	b3	♘d7
26	♖d1	

Kirov covers all the weak points except one (the d6 square) but one chink is all that Miles needs to get inside the Bulgarian's armour.

26   ...   ♖a7

Not 26...g6? as 27 ♖d6+ ♔e7 28 ♖xd7+! wins a piece after 28...♔xd7 29 ♘b6+.

27   ♘d6   b6

Again 27...g6? is not possible: 28 ♘c8 ♖a8 29 ♖d6+ ♔f7 30 ♖xd7+ ♔e8 31 ♘b6 winning.

28   ♘f5   g6

Hanging on for dear life!

29	♖d6+	♔f7
30	♘h6+	♔g7
31	♘g4	♖c7
32	h4!	

Bringing up the reserves.

32   ...   ♔f8

After 32...h5 33 ♘f2! (on 33 ♘e3 the combative 33...b5 keeps White out of c4) 32...♔f7 34 ♘d3 ♔g7 35 ♔b1! and Black is in zugzwang: 35...♔f7 allows the simplifying 36 ♖xd7+! ♖xd7 37 ♘xe5+ and 35...c5 fails to 36 ♘b2! coming to c4 (this is why the king side-stepped to b1 rather than b2). Otherwise 35...b5 36 axb5 cxb5 37 ♖d5 allows White to win at least a pawn.

Another plan (after 32...h5) is to play ♘g4-f2-h3-g5 with unpleasant threats.

33   h5!   ♔e7

After 33...gxh5 then 34 ♘h6 heading for f5. With the knight on this square Black's three isolated kingside pawns are all in danger.

Has Kirov finally been able to force Miles's pieces to retreat?

34 hxg6!

It seems not!

34 ... ♔xd6

Hopeless is 34...hxg6 after 35 ♖xg6, etc.

35 gxh7 ♖c8

36 ♘h6

There are two threats: 37 ♘g8 followed by queening and variations based on 37 h8♕ ♖xh8 38 ♘f7+; Black cannot defend against both.

36 ... ♘f6

The best practical chance.

37 h8♕ ♖xh8

38 ♘f7+ ♔e6

39 ♘xh8

The combination has resulted in the winning of a pawn, quite enough to win in the long term in such an ending. A logical continuation such as 39...♘h5 40 ♘g6 ♔f6 41 ♘h4 ♘f4 42 ♔d2 ♔g5 43 g3 ♘e6 44 ♘f5 allows White to consolidate. In order to then win he must time a knight sally on the queenside, e.g. 44...♔f6 45 ♔d3 ♔g5 46 ♔c3 ♔f6 47 ♘d6!? ♘d4 48 ♘c4 ♘xf3 49 ♘xb6 ♘g5 50 ♘c4 ♘xe4+ 51 ♔c2 ♘xg3 52 ♘xa5 c5 53 ♘b7 and the a-pawn yields a decisive advantage for the first player.

39 ... ♘xe4?

This wins back the lost pawn but is too slow.

40 fxe4 ♔f6

41 ♔c3

1-0

Now that the time control has been reached Kirov calculated that further resistance was hopeless, e.g. 41...♔g7 42 b4! axb4+ 43 ♔xb4 ♔xh8 44 a5 bxa5+ 45 ♔xa5 ♔g7 46 ♔b6 ♔f6 47 ♔xc6 ♔g5 48 ♔d6 ♔f4 49 ♔d5 and White wins. A fine example of top grandmaster technique.

Game Twenty-Five
Sergei Tiviakov-Gyozo Forintos
Porto San Giorgio 1994

The next game entails a clash of generations. Tiviakov, one of the best of the new generation with recent experience of the PCA Candidates, against Forintos, who was a leading member of the Hungarian team before his younger opponent was even born.

1 e4 e5

2 ♘f3 ♘f6

The Petroff Defence, which has the reputation of being a rather drawish opening. It's true that if White is not in fighting mood then this isn't the most aggressive way of seeking to complicate the game.

Gyozo Forintos (who is incidentally the father-in-law of English grandmaster Tony Kosten) resides in Budapest, Hungary. Apart from his experiences over the board and as Hungary's captain he has written several books, the most notable being on the Petroff Defence!

3   d4

One of the reasons that the Petroff is not in the repertoire of many attacking players is the continuation 3 ♘xe5 d6 4 ♘f3 ♘xe4 5 ♕e2 ♕e7 6 d3 ♘f6 with a symmetrical position and dull equality.

3   ...   ♘xe4
4   ♗d3   ♘c6!?

This astounding move cannot be found in any of the traditional books on the Petroff. I was there when Jacob Murey unleashed it against Timman in a French League game, Strasbourg 1993. He was so proud of his remarkable novelty that he was inviting people to look at his board whilst Timman was deep in thought, contemplating the consequences of his temporary piece sacrifice! Unfortunately (for the eccentric genius Murey) Timman kept his cool and steered the game into a favourable ending which he won. Despite the result, yet another of Murey's ideas had found its way onto the chess scene. During tournaments, Murey 'who breathes, eats and sleeps chess', can be found analysing chess non-stop for hours with anyone at any hour! He is in effect, 'married' to chess, the love of his life!

5   ♗xe4   d5

The principal point behind Murey's idea is that after 6 ♗d3 then 6...e4 enables Black to win back his piece without any problems. Critical is 6 ♗g5 ♕d6 (Murey played the less active 6...♕d7 against Timman) 7 dxe5! (7 ♗d3 e4 8 ♘c3 exd3 9 0-0 a6 10 ♕xd3 f6 has been shown to only yield equal chances) 7...♕b4+ 8 ♘c3 dxe4 9 a3 ♕a5 and now following either 10 ♘d2 or 10 ♘d4 Black has to be very careful.

6   ♗xh7!?

Grabbing a pawn but permitting the veteran Hungarian a strong initiative.

6   ...   ♖xh7
7   dxe5   ♗g4
8   ♗f4   ♕d7

Black has adequate compensation due to his bishop pair, free piece play and the semi-open h-file. The question arises as to how and where the white king will seek a safe haven.

9   ♘bd2   ♕f5
10   ♗g3   0-0-0
11   0-0

White has little choice. Despite the risks on the kingside there is no other way of developing satisfactorily.

11   ...   ♗c5
12   a3   ♗b6
13   b4   ♕h5

Forintos, for all his activity, has yet to achieve anything concrete for the pawn. However most players, given the choice, would prefer to play with the black pieces as the initiative persists.

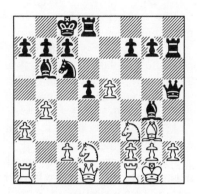

14 ♖e1?!

Evidently not 14 h3?? due to 14...♗xh3 15 gxh3 ♕xh3 16 ♘h2 ♕xg3+ and mates. However, I prefer 14 c3! to the text, preventing 14...d4 because of 15 c4 and stopping the black knight coming to the d4 square. This move also prepares queenside expansion with a3-a4-a5 and ♕b3 or ♕a4.

14 ... ♘d4
15 a4 a6
16 ♖a3

Defending along the third rank.

16 ... ♘f5
17 ♘f1

White cannot preserve his bishop and hope for a comfortable life: 17 ♗f4 g5! 18 ♗xg5 ♖g8 19 ♗f4 (19 h4?? loses immediately to 19...♖xg5) 19...♗h3 20 g3 (20 ♗g3? fails to 20...♘xg3 21 hxg3 ♗xg2! 22 ♘h4 ♕xh4! 23 gxh4 ♖xh4) 20...♗g4 and the attack is ferocious.

17 ... ♘xg3

The simplest, winning back the pawn and retaining some initiative despite the simplifying exchanges.

18 ♘xg3 ♗xf3
19 ♖xf3

Tiviakov could equally have played 19 ♕xf3 but not 19 ♘xh5? ♗xd1 20 ♖xd1 ♖xh5 and Black has an extra piece. The Hungarian finally wins back the gambit pawn.

19 ... ♕xh2+
20 ♔f1 g6

A cautious move, defending the f7 pawn and controlling the f5 square. Black has the better minor piece and the safer king.

21 ♖d3

White has two reasonable alternatives: 21 e6, opening lines for the white rooks, and 21 ♖f4!?, intending 22 ♕f3, which (with the inevitable benefit of hindsight) may well be tougher to crack.

21 ... ♕h4
22 ♖xd5

After 22 c3 Black can pin with 22...♕c4! intending to double on the h-file and 23 e6?! fxe6 24 ♖xe6 ♖f8 then leaves Black with a strong attack. The plan with e5-e6 is less effective when White's rook has already left the f-file.

22 ... ♕c4+
23 ♖d3 ♖xd3
24 ♕xd3 ♕xb4
25 e6?!

Following 25 ♖d1 ♔b8 26 ♕e4 Black does best to keep the queens, as 26...♖h4 27 ♕xb4 ♖xb4 is unclear after 28 ♖d7. So best is 26...♕c5! keeping the pressure up.

25	...	♕f4
26	♖e2?	

An error but the alternative 26 ♕f3 enables Black to win a pawn by 26...♕xf3 27 gxf3 ♖h2! as 28 ♖e2 (neither 28 exf7 ♖xf2+ 29 ♔g1 ♖xf3+ 30 ♔g2 ♖xf7 nor 28 e7 ♖xf2+ 29 ♔g1 ♖e2+ 30 ♔f1 ♖xe1+ 31 ♔xe1 ♔d7 give any hope) 28...fxe6 29 ♔g1 ♖h4 30 ♖xe6 ♖xa4 31 ♖xg6 ♖c4 gives the second player a winning ending.

26	...	♕xg3!

Now either capture allows mate in one.

27	♖e3	♖h1+

White's last hope was 27...♗xe3?? in view of 28 fxg3.

28	♔e2	♕g4+
	0-1	

After 29 ♖f3 ♕xe6+ White must shed further material.

I have an opinion that grandmasters of all strengths have a certain responsibility to participate in at least one open tournament a year. This gives lesser players the opportunity to play, and create upsets against, the top stars. Playing mixed opposition in a competitive environment is actually a healthy training exercise, even for the world's leading players, so my idea isn't quite so balmy! Perhaps one day it will be an obligation for the top echelon, who in this way would be made to give something back to the chess world!

Game Twenty-Six
Alexander Morozevich-Margeir Petursson
London (Lloyds Bank) 1994

The best open tournament performance of the year was achieved by the young Russian Alexander Morozevich, who achieved an astonishing 2900+ result in London. At the time, the 17-year-old's outstanding victory in the final Lloyds Bank surprised the world, but in fact a string of tournament victories in 1994 and selection as first board for young Russia (in the Moscow Olympiad) suggest that he is no flash-in-the-pan. His opponent in this game is an experienced lawyer from the country where there is the biggest concentration of grandmasters, Iceland (six for a population of 200,000).

1	e4	c5
2	♘f3	♘c6
3	♗b5	d6
4	0-0	♗d7

This move is more trustworthy than the 4...♗g4 that was unsuccessfully employed by Tiviakov against Adams (see Chapter 2).

5	♖e1	♘f6
6	c3	a6

Putting the question to the bishop now that Black has avoided any question of doubled pawns.

7 ♗f1

The best move as the two main alternatives are less testing: the other retreat 7 ♗a4 c4!? 8 d4 cxd3 9 ♗g5 e6 10 ♕xd3 ♘e5 11 ♘xe5 ♗xa4 12 ♘c4 ♗c6 13 ♘bd2 b5 yields equal chances, as in Bronstein-Timman, USSR 1979, and 7 ♗xc6 ♗xc6 8 d4!? ♗xe4 9 ♗g5 is a speculative gambit that no longer causes problems. The safest Black defence is then 9...♗d5 10 ♘bd2 e6 11 c4 ♗xf3 12 ♕xf3 cxd4 13 ♕xb7 ♕c8 and White has adequate play, but after 14 ♕b6 (14 ♕f3 ♗e7 15 ♘b3 h6 and it was White who was fighting for equality in Pedersen-Sher, Farum 1993) 14...♕c5 15 ♕b7 ♕c8 it is dead equal; Timoschenko-Kupreichik, Ashkabad 1978.

7	...	♗g4
8	d4	cxd4
9	cxd4	d5

After 9...♗xf3 White's pawn structure is slightly damaged but he maintains the advantage in the centre: 10 gxf3 e5 11 d5 ♘d4 12 ♗e3 g6 13 f4 and White successfully undermines the knight (Kotronias-Kuijf, Wijk aan Zee 1992). Instead of 10...e5 Black could try 10...d5 intending 11 ♘c3 (11 e5 ♘d7 12 e6!? is interesting) 11...e6 12 ♗g5 dxe4.

10	e5	♘g8
11	♗e3	e6
12	a3	

Taking away the b4 square from Black and preparing a later space-gaining advance b2-b4. Petursson has achieved a type of French Defence position with his light-squared bishop outside the pawn chain but he suffers from a distinct disadvantage in space.

12	...	♘ge7
13	♘bd2	♘f5
14	♗d3	♗e7

The blunder 14...♘fxd4? loses a piece to 15 ♗xd4 ♘xd4 16 ♕a4+ when 16...♘c6 is met by 17 ♕xg4.

15	♕b1	♕d7

Keeping the tension by overprotecting the f5 square. Instead, capturing the bishop on e3, now or later, fails to solve Black's problems: he exchanges off White's least effective bishop, enables White to consolidate the centre (after the reply fxe3) and White has attacking potential on the semi-open f-file and b1-h7 diagonal.

16	b4	♗h5

White would like to play ♘d2-b3-c5 but if the queen's knight moves then Black would be able to break-up the white pawn structure with ...♗xf3. Therefore, White should first play 17 h3! toying with the idea of g2-g4 and stopping his opponent from kingside castling, e.g. 17...0-0? 18 g4! ♘xe3 and White wins a pawn with the intermediate 19 ♗xh7+ ♔h8 20 fxe3. After 17 h3 White is better, as it's hard to find a reasonable plan for Black.

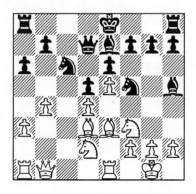

17 ♖a2?!

Not the most precise, but the idea behind Morozevich's alternative plan will become apparent later.

17	...	0-0
18	h3	

Too late in the sense that Black feels much more comfortable after he has succeeded in castling.

| 18 | ... | ♔h8! |
| 19 | ♖f1 | |

A paradoxical undeveloping move. Morozevich is in fact preparing g2-g4 when after Black captures on e3 (and White retakes with fxe3) the rook will be on a semi-open file.

19	...	♖ac8
20	g4	♘xe3
21	fxe3	♗g6
22	♗xg6	hxg6
23	♘b3	

Now the idea behind 17 ♖a2 becomes clear: the rook will arrive quickly on the kingside via the second rank.

23 ... ♘a7?!

If 23...a5? 24 b5 a4? 25 bxc6 wins as the queen is attacked, so first 23...♕c7!? intending 24...a5 is worth considering. Another idea is to play 23...b6 first of all, stopping the white knight blocking the c-file as in the game, then 24 h4 ♘a7 25 g5 (25 a4!? ♘c6 26 ♖h2 ♘xb4 27 g5 is an alternative method of pursuing the attack) 25...♘b5 26 ♖h2 gives Black counter chances but White's attack remains dangerous.

24 ♘c5!

Blocking the c-file.

24 ... ♕c6

Unappetizing is 24...♗xc5?! 25 bxc5 as Black exchanges off his best defensive piece and opens the b-file for White's use.

25 a4

Keeping the knight out of action. Now Black's counterplay comes too slowly and without the help of the sidelined knight.

25 ... b6

26 ♘d3

A more sensible move than taking the a-pawn, which would leave the knight trapped out of play. In any case, the queenside is a distraction, the young Russian is really interested in attacking the Icelander's king.

	26	...	♔g8
	27	h4	♕d7
	28	g5	♖c3

29 h5!

Petursson's had prepared to meet 29 ♖h2 by 29...♕xa4 30 ♘f4 ♖xe3, when Black arrives quickly and it is no longer clear that White has time to pursue the attack. The text is more incisive.

	29	...	gxh5
	30	♘f4	♖xe3

Obviously after 30...g6? White has 31 ♘xg6 leading to a swift

mate.

	31	♘xh5	♕c6
	32	♘f6+!	

Natural and strong as Black can hardly play 32...gxf6 as after 33 gxf6 his king is fatally denuded.

	32	...	♗xf6
	33	gxf6	g6
	34	♖c2	

A novel way of building a bridge, e.g. 34...♖c3 35 ♕c1 ♖xc2 36 ♕h6 mating. The most testing defence is 34...♕xa4 (in order to meet 35 ♕c1 with 35...♕a3) when White should continue with 35 ♖g2! as the threat to capture on g6 is very strong. Black can struggle on with 35...♖c8 36 ♖xg6+! ♔f8 37 ♖h6 ♔e8 38 ♖h8+ ♔d7 39 ♖xc8 ♘xc8 (39...♔xc8? 40 ♕c1+ picks up the rook) 40 ♕h7 and the loss of the f-pawn spells the end for Black.

	34	...	♕d7?

Losing immediately.

	35	♕c1	1-0

Black resigned as the rook on e3 is attacked and dare not move because of 36 ♕h6 mating.

Game Twenty-Seven
Julian Hodgson-Ferdinand Hellers
Leeuwarden 1994

Julian Hodgson has made enormous strides in the past few years and has established himself in the England Olympiad team. He was always considered talented but rather lazy, and now that he works harder at the game his FIDE rating has risen sharply. He used to play exclusively offbeat openings but now switches more often to mainstream variations. As White he is best known for his success in revitalizing the hitherto dull Trompowsky into a dangerous weapon.

Ferdinand Hellers was a rising star in the mid-eighties but significantly reduced his chess-playing activities due to his studies and has now sought employment outside of chess. Scandinavia is relatively expensive which makes the task of being a professional chess-player particularly difficult.

1	d4	♘f6
2	♗g5	♘e4
3	♗f4	

Julian promoted the outlandish 3 h4!? for a while, a move scorned by many commentators, but one which garnered him numerous points. Typical after 3 h4 is 3...c5!? 4 d5 g6 5 ♕d3 ♕a5+ 6 ♘d2 ♘xg5 7 hxg5 ♗g7 8 c3 d6 9 e4 ♘d7 10 a4 ♖b8 11 ♘c4 ♕c7 12 f4 and White has a space advantage as well as the semi-open h-file, as in the last of three(!) victories by Julian over the strong English international master John Emms.

The reason Julian gave up on 3 h4 was probably his unfortunate experience at the hands of Salov: 3...d5 4 ♘d2 ♗f5 5 ♘xe4 ♗xe4 6 f3 h6! (Black already has a comfortable game) 7 fxe4 hxg5 8 ♕d3 e6 9 ♕b5+?! ♘c6 10 ♕xb7 ♘b4 11 ♕b5+ ♕d7 12 ♕b7 ♕c8 13 ♕b5+ ♕d7 14 ♕b7 ♕c8 15 ♕b5+ c6 with advantage to

Black; Hodgson-Salov, Wijk aan Zee 1993.

3	...	d5
4	f3	♘f6
5	♘c3	

Similar to the game is 5 e4 when after 5...dxe4 6 ♘c3 exf3 7 ♘xf3 g6 8 ♗c4 ♗g7 9 ♕e2 0-0 10 0-0-0 c6 11 d5 cxd5 12 ♘xd5 ♘xd5 13 ♖xd5 White has a strong initiative for the pawn.

| 5 | ... | c5 |
| 6 | e4! | |

The most energetic continuation, exploiting his lead in development to open the centre quickly.

| 6 | ... | dxe4 |

Here 6...cxd4! 7 ♕xd4 ♘c6 8 ♗b5 ♗d7! 9 ♗xc6 ♗xc6 10 e5 ♘d7 11 0-0-0 e6 represents a more solid method of defence.

| 7 | d5 | |

A real gambit as Julian expects to remain a pawn down until well into the middlegame. However, he hopes that his advantage in development will permit his active army to use the open lines to create inroads into the black camp. The position on the board is analogous to a Blackmar-Diemer gambit (1 d4 d5 2 ♘c3 ♘f6 3 e4 dxe4 4 f3 c5 5 d5) except that White has the extra move ♗c1-f4 which enables him to envisage speedy queenside castling.

7	...	exf3
8	♘xf3	g6
9	♘b5	♘a6
10	♕e2!?	

A dangerous move. More natural, but slower to make contact is 10 ♗c4 as 10...♗g7 11 ♕e2 0-0 allows Black to develop more or less harmoniously. In this case, White still has irritating pressure for the pawn.

10   ...   e6?

Losing his sense of danger! The Swedish tactician could have tried 10...♗g7 when after 11 d6 ♘d5! (rather than 11...♗e6?! 12 dxe7 ♕xe7 13 ♗d6 which looks unpleasant for Black) I can't find a convincing continuation for White. Instead of 11 d6, Julian should misplace his opponent's king with 11 ♘d6+! ♔f8 12 ♘xc8 ♖xc8 13 0-0-0; White has nothing concrete but Black has the awkward task of trying to 'castle by hand' on the kingside. Perhaps he should then continue with 13...♘e8!? to resist the advance of White's d-pawn.

The text only open lines for his opponent's attack.

11   0-0-0   ♕b6

After 11...♘xd5 White wins a

piece with 12 c4.

12   dxe6   ♕xe6

Natural is 12...♗xe6 but 13 ♘d6+ ♗xd6 14 ♖xd6 ♕a5 15 ♕e5 wins for White. Black is already struggling to defend.

13   ♕d2   ♗e7

After 13...♗d7 14 ♗e5 ♖d8 15 ♗c4! Black's defences collapse.

14   ♖e1   ♘e4

Hellers must have underestimated the following combination, which keeps the black king marooned in the centre.

15   ♖xe4!   ♕xe4
16   ♘d6+   ♗xd6
17   ♕xd6

Black's only problem is that it is illegal to castle in this position!

White threatens 18 ♗b5+ hence Black's next trying to restrict the white king's bishop, as otherwise 17...♗d7 loses the queen after 18 ♗xa6 bxa6 19 ♖e1.

17   ...   c4

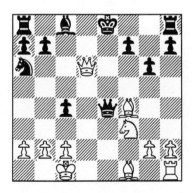

18   ♗xc4!

Julian isn't counting material, his pieces just head for Black's helpless king.

| | 18 | ... | ♛xc4 |
| | 19 | ♗g5 | ♛c7 |

After 19...♛e6 the game comes to an abrupt end: 20 ♛d8 mate!

| | 20 | ♖e1+ | ♗e6 |
| | 21 | ♖xe6+! | 1-0 |

Hellers, who is in his youth was noted for playing attacks of similar ferocity, didn't bother to wait for 21...fxe6 22 ♛xe6+ ♚f8 23 ♗h6+ ♛g7 24 ♛f6+ ♚e8 25 ♗xg7 before resigning. The attack was irresistible after the imprudent 10...e6.

7 Women in 1994

The Women's Olympiad is covered in Chapter 9 covering team events and although Judit Polgar's rise and rise is mentioned elsewhere, two games from her record-breaking success in Madrid can be found below.

The most important non-championship event was held in embargo-hit Belgrade. Despite the dire economic situation in the former Yugoslavia their enthusiasm for hosting important tournaments is not diminished. Some players choose not to participate in view of the volatile political situation but some of the world's elite are tempted to play despite frowns from some quarters.

Belgrade (Yugoslavia), March

6½/9	A.Galliamova
5½	A.Maric, S.Matveeva
4½	I.Madl, N.Bojkovic, Peng Zhaoqin, A.Sofieva
4	A.Botsari
3½	A.Stefanova
2	K.Arakhamia

Even stronger was the van Oosterom-inspired match between the world's elite of yesteryear and the premier women. Xie Jun rather impressively scored as well as Judit Polgar, but Arakhamia seemed to be out of form this year, perhaps affected by problems at home in Georgia.

Women vs Veterans, Monte Carlo (Monaco), June

Women 37
7½ Xie Jun and J.Polgar, 7 Zsu.Polgar, 6½ N.Ioseliani, 5½ M.Chiburdanidze, 3 K.Arakhamia

Veterans 35
8 V.Smyslov, 7½ V.Hort, 6 B.Spassky, 5½ L.Portisch, 4½ B.Ivkov, 3½ B.Larsen

Merlo, April/May
P.Cramling (4) v C.Amura (2)
A training match for the Argentinian Amura went rather as expected.

Candidates final, Tilburg (Netherlands), November

10½/16	M.Chiburdanidze, Zsu.Polgar
8½	P.Cramling
8	A.Galliamova, A.Maric
7½	Peng Zhaoqin
7	C.Foisor, N.Ioseliani
5	K.Arakhamia

The most important event in the women's calendar was the Tilburg Candidates tournament. This double-round nine-player all-play-all was a real test of endurance, but in the end there was no doubt about the qualifiers for the Candidates final, Maia Chiburdanidze and Zsusza Polgar finishing well clear of the chasing pack. These two will now play a match to decide the challenger to Xie Jun for the World Championship.

Game Twenty-Eight
Alexei Shirov-Judit Polgar
Madrid 1994

No female player had ever come close to winning a category XVI event before, so Judit Polgar's outright victory in Madrid (see Chapter 5 for the full result) was all the more notable. Here is Judit in great form, introducing a new idea and then outplaying Shirov with the black pieces.

Judit was the only woman playing in the 'mixed' Olympiad, where she was top board for Hungary.

1	d4	♘f6
2	c4	g6
3	♘c3	♗g7
4	e4	d6
5	♗e2	0-0
6	♘f3	e5
7	d5	

The most common move is 7 0-0, when Black's most active reply is 7...♘c6. Kramnik has been playing the text move recently, intending to follow-up with the annoying pin 8 ♗g5.

| 7 | ... | a5 |

Kasparov preferred the traditional 7...♘bd7 recently in his game against Kramnik from Linares (see Chapter 5, game 12). Judit plays the more modern line as she had an interesting idea prepared.

8	♗g5	h6
9	♗h4	♘a6
10	0-0	♕e8

Unpinning the knight without playing the weakening ...g7-g5.

11	♘d2	♘h7
12	a3	

In many lines of the King's Indian White tries to expand with b2-b4 and c4-c5, but in this variation the plan is often delayed in order to first negate any black activity on the kingside.

12	...	♗d7
13	♔h1	

A few years ago Garry Kasparov showed the downside of 13 b3 (avoiding any ...a5-a4 ideas, fixing the queenside), which imperceptibly weakens the long diagonal: 13...f5! 14 exf5 gxf5 15 ♗h5 ♕c8 16 ♗e7 ♖e8 17 ♗xe8 ♕xe8 18 ♗h4 e4 with excellent play for the exchange; Yusupov - Kasparov, Barcelona 1989.

| 13 | ... | h5 |

The alternative method of activating the 'King's Indian' bishop.

14	f3	♗h6
15	b3	♕b8

Judit's new idea, which is reminiscent of a game of Rubinstein's in which Black also employed the ...♕d8-b8-a7 manoeuvre to take the initiative on the queenside.

16	♕c2	♗e3
17	♗f2	♕a7

Judit's idea is to use the queen to maintain a dark-square presence after the exchange of bishops.

| 18 | ♗xe3 | ♕xe3 |

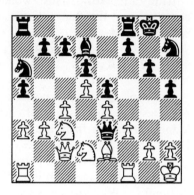

| 19 | f4?! |

The Latvian typically looks for tactical play but in the process creates strategic problems for himself. More logical is 19 ♖ae1 ♕g5 20 ♕b2 preparing to push the b-pawn. Note that then 20...f5 21 exf5 gxf5 22 b4 axb4 23 axb4 ♘xb4? fails to 24 f4 cutting the communication between the queen and the d2 knight. Black could instead try 23...c5 but 24 dxc6 bxc6 25 c5! favours White. The opening up of the whole board leaves the black king devoid of cover.

A better plan is introduced by 20...♘c5 (rather than let the knight be locked out of play, Black prepares to exchange it) 21 b4 axb4 22 axb4 ♘a4 23 ♘xa4 ♖xa4 and Black has a reasonable game. The critical 24 c5 ♖fa8 25 ♗c4 ♕e7 looks unclear; White has gained space but Black is not without counterplay.

19	...	exf4
20	♖ae1	♕c5
21	♕c1	

After 21 ♕b2 Black would compete for the long diagonal with 21...♕d4.

21	...	♕d4
22	♖xf4	♖ae8
23	♖ff1	

The rook is rather exposed on f4. Despite the fact that her knights are away from the action Black has long-term pressure against the e4 pawn, and because it requires constant attention, it's difficult for White to get going on the queenside.

| 23 | ... | ♕g7 |
| 24 | ♕c2 | |

On 24 ♕b2 Black can even play 24...♘c5 threatening the e-pawn in view of the pin on the long diagonal.

| 24 | ... | h4?! |

Not a bad plan, but Black should first prepare to double rooks on the e-file with 24...♖e7, keeping White occupied in the defence of e4. Black can then push her h-pawn or play ...♘c5 or ...♘g5 depending on circumstances. Judit looks for a tactical solution where patience was more appropriate! So best was 24...♖e7.

| 25 | ♘f3 | h3!? |

Complicating the struggle. Now the patient(!) 25...♕h6 can be met by 26 b4! (with counterplay) 26...axb4 27 axb4 and if

27...♘xb4 then 28 ♕b1 wins back the pawn.

| 26 | gxh3 | |

Too passive would be 26 g3?! as the presence of the pawn on h3 would allow additional mating possibilities.

| 26 | ... | ♗xh3 |
| 27 | ♖g1 | ♕h6 |

On 27...f5? the open lines are dangerous only for Black's king after 28 ♘h4.

| 28 | ♖g3 | ♔g7 |

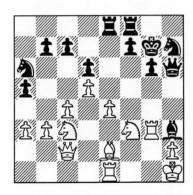

Judit hopes for play on the h-file.

| 29 | ♕b2 | |

A natural move, aiming for both b3-b4 and tricks on the diagonal, but this proves to be too slow. Interesting is 29 ♘d1!? ♘f6 30 ♘f2 ♗c8 and Black will proceed with ...♖h8 with either ...♘c5 or ...♘h5, when the bishop is evicted but the other black pieces come to life.

Shirov could have introduced complications with 29 ♖eg1 (playing for tricks against g6). However, after 29...♖h8 30 e5

dxe5 31 ♗d3 ♘f8 32 ♘g5 ♗d7
33 ♘xf7 ♔xf7 34 ♗xg6+ Black
refutes the attack with 34...♘xg6!
35 ♖xg6 ♕xh2+! 36 ♕xh2
♖xh2+ 37 ♔xh2 ♖h8+ and wins.

29	...	♘f6
30	b4	axb4
31	axb4	

The black knight on a6 is de-
prived the use of the c5 square,
but is not really out of play as
White must now constantly defend the b4 pawn.

31	...	♗g4
32	♘d1!?	

Black's hold on the dark
squares will increase after the
exchange of her bishop for the
white knight. So perhaps 32 ♘d4
should have been tried. Instead
Shirov sacrifices the e-pawn for
tricky play.

32 ... ♗xf3+

32...♖xe4 was in fact possible.
After 33 ♘f2 ♗xf3+ 34 ♖xf3
♖f4 35 ♖f1 (35 ♘g4? loses
spectacularly to 35...♖xg4 36
♖xf6? ♕xh2+! and mate follows)
looks dangerous, but it safely diffused by 35...♖xf3 36 ♗xf3 ♕h4
37 ♘g4 ♖e8. Judit prefers to
keep the initiative, fully aware
that if Shirov offers you a pawn
you should be naturally suspi-
cious!

33	♗xf3	♖h8
34	♘e3	

A crude threat allowing Black
to release the pin. 34 ♖e2 was
possible but 34...♕h4! (34...♖e5
is met by 35 c5) threatens the
rook and after, say, 35 ♔g1,

permits 35...♔f8 anyway.

34	...	♔f8
35	♘g4	

The text avoids the loss of the
e-pawn but leaves White with
static weaknesses. Instead 35 ♖f1
(looking for play on the f-file)
allows 35...♘xb4! (35...♕xe3 is
well met by 36 ♕xf6). Shirov
was probably not attracted by 35
♘f1 ♕h4 36 ♔g1 ♖h7 when the
e-pawn is attacked and 37 ♕b1
(37 e5? dxe5 38 ♖xe5 allows the
demolition of the queenside by
38...♕xc4) is rather passive. Perhaps 37...♘d7 intending ...♘e5 is
the best way of keeping up the
pressure.

35	...	♘xg4
36	♗xg4	♕g7
37	♕f2?	

The exchange of queens is fatal
for White: 37 ♕xg7+ ♔xg7 38
♖b3 f5 39 ♗f3 ♖e5 and ...♖he8
wins material. However White
can try to defend with 37 ♕d2
♕e5 38 ♔g1. Black has no immediate breakthrough and if
White can stop the knight from
participating then it will be tough
to progress.

37 ... ♘xb4! (D)

Now is a good moment to grab
the pawn. It has been twenty-
eight moves since this knight
moved but its role in holding the
queenside has been crucial and
now this piece will win the game
for the Hungarian star.

38 ♖b1?

I'm surprised that Shirov
didn't try 38 ♗e6! as it was his

only hope. Black must find

38...♔g8! (38...♔e7 allows a dangerous piece sacrifice: 39 e5! fxe6 40 exd6+ ♔xd6 41 dxe6

with tremendous complications) when 39 ♖xg6 ♕xg6 40 ♖g1 wins the queen but after 40...♕xg1+ 41 ♕xg1+ ♔f8 Black should win comfortably enough, e.g. 42 ♕f2 ♖h7 43 ♗f5 ♖g7 44 ♕d2 ♖a8 45 ♕c3 ♘d3 46 h4 ♘f2+ 47 ♔h2 ♖a2.

38	...	♘a6
39	♖xb7	♘c5
40	♖xc7	♘xe4

Black wins the exchange, and with his king totally open to the winds Shirov decided to call it a day.

0-1

Game Twenty-Nine
Judit Polgar-Sergei Tiviakov
Madrid 1994

Standard isolated queen's pawn (IQP) positions can arise from several openings. These positions are often difficult to evaluate as White has a potentially weak pawn compensated by an active piece deployment. In general, the early stage favours White who has attacking chances whereas quiet endings are Black's domain. Here we see a tense middlegame in which Black is left under constant nagging pressure, despite having full development. Judit Polgar handles the white pieces with skill and imagination, developing her attack slowly but surely!

| 1 | e4 | c5 |

| 2 | c3 |

Judit has previously suffered on the black side of this variation (see Karpov-J.Polgar, Chapter 5, game 10), so she decides to venture it with White. One of the opening developments of the year was how fashionable the text has become at the top level, as it used to be seen only in games from open tournaments.

2	...	d5
3	exd5	♕xd5
4	d4	♘f6
5	♘f3	♘c6
6	♗e2

This, the main line, leads us into an IQP game. 6 ♘a3!?, with ideas of ♘b5, tends to lead to a different type of position.

6	...	cxd4
7	cxd4	e6
8	0-0	♗e7
9	♘c3	♕d6

It's generally a matter of taste whether the queen retreats to d6 or d8. The text is perhaps more provocative.

10	♘b5	♕d8
11	♗f4	♘d5
12	♗g3	a6

Judit (playing Black) against Lautier in Linares 1994 preferred 12...0-0 first and only after 13 ♗c4 did she play 13...a6. She soon drifted into a poor position: 14 ♗xd5 exd5 (14...axb5 15 ♗e4 b4 may offer better chance of equality) 15 ♘c7 ♖a7 16 ♕b3 ♗d6 17 ♗xd6 ♕xd6 18 ♕b6 and Black was tangled up.

It's surprising how many top grandmasters are willing to play the same opening with both colours, whereas lesser players tend to have strong opinions on whether a variation is 'good' or 'bad' and consequently are only willing to play a line with one colour.

13	♘c3	0-0

White seems ill-prepared to organize the thematic battery (♕d3 and ♗b1 or ♗c2) but Judit, in her own time, arranges it anyway.

14	♖c1	♘f6

A cautious retreat. 14...♘xc3 seems natural but Tiviakov prefers to keep this knight for the defence of the kingside.

15	h3

Cautious indeed! This avoids any problems with ...♘h5, exchanging the bishop, and makes a bolt-hole for the king.

15	...	b6

As ...a7-a6 has been played the Russian should have seriously considered 15...b5 as the tactical line 16 ♘xb5 axb5 17 ♖xc6 ♖xa2 18 ♕b3 is well met by 18...♕d5. The text more or less loses a tempo.

16	a3	♗b7
17	♗d3	♖c8
18	♗b1	b5

Quite!

19	♕d3

White has finally engineered her battery. The idea is to force ...g7-g6, which weakens the dark squares around the black king.

19	...	♘a5

Seeking counterplay.

20	♘e5	♘c4
21	♖c2

Slightly clumsy-looking but the rook will come to the e-file where it will defend b2 from a more active square. There is still latent pressure on the diagonal and sooner or later Black will be obliged to play ...g7-g6.

21 ... ♞d6

Aiming to play 21...♞f5 hitting d4 and g3 or even 21...♞de4, hence White's next move.

22 f3 g6

Inevitably if Black tries to play for tactics without this move he has problems: 22...♞f5 23 ♗f2 ♞h5 is best met by 24 ♞e2! (threatening 25 g4) rather than 24 g4 ♞f4 25 ♕d2 because of 25...♗g5. Naturally 23...♞d5 (instead of 23...♞h5) is punished by 24 ♞xd5 ♗xd5 25 g4.

23 ♗f2 ♖e8
24 ♗a2

The bishop now switches back to a more useful diagonal. Before combinations appear its important to improve the position of inactive pieces.

24 ... ♗f8
25 ♖e2 ♗g7
26 ♖fe1

Judit has patiently built-up her position. Tiviakov has all his pieces in play but cannot fully combat the persistent pressure. For another IQP game with a similar theme see Kamsky-Short, Chapter 2, game four.

26 ... ♞d5?!

Probably a mistake as from now White's initiative becomes clear. After 26...♞d7 interesting would be 27 ♞xf7 ♞xf7 28 ♗xe6 ♖xe6 29 ♖xe6 ♞f8 when rook and two central pawns are worth

at least two pieces.

27 ♞xd5 exd5

An ugly positional move but Tiviakov had probably seen that the natural 27...♗xd5 fails tactically after 28 ♗xd5 exd5 29 ♕b3! ♞c4 (the best chance is 29...♗xe5 30 dxe5 ♞c4 31 ♗d4 ♕h4 but the threats on the dark squares give White a clear advantage) White has 30 ♞xf7! leading to a better ending after 30...♖xe2 31 ♞xd8 ♖xe1+ 32 ♗xe1 ♗xd4+ 33 ♗f2 ♗xf2+ 34 ♔xf2 ♖xd8.

28 ♕d1! a5

Hoping for play with ...♗a6 but this never materializes.

29 h4!

Judit has an excellent sense of the attack and likes very much to push her h-pawn (see game thirty)!

29 ... ♕c7?!

Oblivious to the danger, the young Russian starts to drift. Either the consistent 29...b4 or the careful 29...♖f8 were better.

30 h5 ♞c4?

A tactical error as the rook on

e8 is inadequately defended.

31 h6! ♗xh6

The alternatives were all equally miserable: 31...♗h8 allows mate after 32 ♘xc4 ♖xe2 33 ♕xe2 dxc4 34 ♕e8+ and both 31...♗f8 32 ♘g4 ♖xe2 33 ♕xe2 and 31...♗xe5 32 dxe5 leave Black chronically weak on the dark squares around the king.

32 ♘g4 ♖xe2
33 ♘xh6+ ♔g7
34 ♖xe2

Also good was 34 ♘f5+ forcing doubled (and weak) pawns. However, Judit senses that mate is near!

34 ... ♔xh6
35 ♕e1

Intending 36 ♖e7. The natural 35...♖d8 fails to 36 ♕c1+ ♔g7 37 b3 exploiting the pin to win a piece. Black's pieces do not contribute to the defence of his king.

35 ... ♔g7
36 ♖e7 ♕b6

36...♕c6 loses in more or less the same way: 37 ♗xc4 dxc4 38 ♕e5+ ♔g8 39 ♗e3 ♕d5 40 ♕f6 ♖d8 41 ♗h6 with mate to follow.

37 ♗xc4 bxc4
38 ♕e5+ ♔g8
39 ♗e3 f6
40 ♕f4

Or 40 ♕h2 h5 41 ♕g3 g5 (41...f5 42 ♕e5) 42 ♗xg5 and mate again follows shortly.

40 ... ♔f8
41 ♖xh7 ♔e8
42 ♕h6 1-0

A model example of patiently building up before launching the attack.

Game Thirty
Xie Jun-Lajos Portisch
Women vs Veterans, Monaco 1994

This chapter would not be complete without a game from the World Champion. In the 'veterans' against 'women' match in Monaco she achieved an excellent score for the women's team, including this victory over Portisch. In the middlegame complications the veteran Hungarian was no match for the young Chinese star, who is at present consistently increasing her rating. Portisch, who is noted for practising his singing in his hotel room during tournaments(!), has been one of the top players in the world for over thirty years. Only recently did he slip below the 2600 barrier for the first time.

1 e4 c5
2 ♘f3 e6
3 d4 cxd4
4 ♘xd4 a6
5 ♗d3 ♘c6
6 ♘xc6 bxc6
7 0-0 ♕c7!?

An unusual move in this posi-

tion; in which Black usually reacts immediately in the centre
with 7...d5. Then, after 8 c4 ♘f6,
White has a choice between 9
♘d2 keeping the tension or 9
cxd5 cxd5 10 exd5 opening up
the position.

| 8 | f4 | d5 |
| 9 | c4 | |

The thematic way of undermining the centre, but White has the
extra move f2-f4 and Black ♕c7,
compared with the normal position.

9	...	dxe4
10	♗xe4	♘f6
11	♗c2	

11 ♗f3 would probably lead to
the exchange of this piece after
the logical plan of ...♗b7, ...♗e7,
...0-0 and ...c6-c5.

11	...	♗e7
12	♘c3	0-0
13	♕e2	♖e8
14	♔h1	c5

Both sides complete their respective developments independ-
ently. Black has a comfortable
game and the new idea 7...♕c7
has paid off.

15	b3	♗b7
16	♗b2	♕c6
17	♖ad1	♖ad8

With the white pawn on f4, so
useful in many Sicilian variations, the World Champion has a
problem with her g2 square. Portisch's next few moves suggest
that he may already be seeking
the initiative; if White's activity
is negated then f4 may become a
serious weakness.

| 18 | ♖xd8 | ♗xd8 |

The more natural 18...♖xd8?!
allows 19 f5! e5 20 ♖e1! (20
♘d5?! is not really any good after 20...♘xd5 21 cxd5 ♕xd5 22
♖d1 ♕c6 23 ♖xd8+ ♗xd8 24
♗xe5 h6 with easy equality) and
White has annoying pressure on
the e-pawn, which has become
dislocated from the rest of the
chain. If the knight on f6 moves
then White occupies e4 and d5
and if the pawn is pushed then
White blockades with ♘c3-d1-e3.

| 19 | ♘d1 | ♗e7!? |

A critical stage. White is better
after the rash 19...♘e4 20 ♕g4
(20 ♖e1?! is well met by 20...f5)
20...♘f6 21 ♕h3 ♘e4 22 ♖e1 but
Portisch could completely equalize with 19...♘d7! (intending
20...♗f6) as 20 f5 ♗f6 21 ♗xf6
(21 ♗c1 ♗d4) ♘xf6 22 fxe6
♖xe6 gives Black no problems at
all.

| 20 | ♘e3 | ♘d7 |
| 21 | ♘g4 | |

Now ...♗f6 is prevented and
White retains the more active
pieces.

| 21 | ... | f6 |

Portisch was aiming for this
move; cutting out any ideas of
♘e5 by White and reducing the
effect of the bishop on b2. Ar-
guably 21...f6 is a concession as
now both e6 and h7 are sensitive
points but Portisch's idea is to
defend everything with a knight
on f8 and further hit f4 with his
bishop on d6. If Xie Jun's kingside ambitions come to nought

then it may be difficult to protect this pawn as even ...♘g6 then becomes an option.

22	♖f3	♗d6
23	♘f2	♕c7

Not a bad move but unfortunately preparing an oversight! Better was the immediate 23...♘f8 24 ♘e4 (24 ♗e4 leads nowhere: 24...♕c7 25 ♗xb7 ♕xb7 26 ♘e4 ♗e7 27 ♖d3 ♘g6 28 ♕f3 ♕c7 29 g3 ♖d8) 24...♗e7 25 ♖g3 ♔h8 although 26 ♕h5 keeps some pressure.

24	♖h3	♘f8?

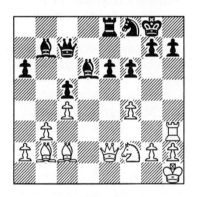

With hindsight we can conclude that 24...h6! was absolutely necessary. Then 25 f5! is best when after 25...♗e5 the ambitious 26 ♗c1! keeps some vague attacking chances (26 ♗xe5 is only equal after 26...♕xe5). Many players would be tempted by the more direct 25 ♕g4? but after 25...♗xf4 26 ♕g6 White fails to deliver the knock-out blow, e.g. 26...♔f8! 27 ♕h7 ♘e5 and as a result Black takes control. White can win the exchange

but after 28 ♗xe5 ♕xe5 29 ♕h8+ ♔f7 30 ♗g6+ ♔xg6 31 ♕xe8+ ♔h7 she would be mated as the back rank is too weak.

25	♗xh7+!

A novel way of introducing the 'Greek gift' sacrifice. Here the tactical weakness of the rook on e8 allows the combination.

25	...	♘xh7
26	♕h5	♔f8

Naturally 26...♘f8 is met by 27 ♕xe8.

27	♕xh7	♕f7

27...♗xf4 is the main alternative seeking material parity. The obvious 28 ♗xf6? gxf6 29 ♕h8+ ♔e7 30 ♖h7+ is frustrated by 30...♔d6! 31 ♖xc7 ♗xg2+! 32 ♔xg2 ♖xh8) and 29 ♕g6 is even worse after 29...♕g7. White does in fact have a spectacular refutation in 28 ♕g6! ♕f7 29 ♖h8+ ♔e7 and only now 30 ♗xf6+! gxf6 31 ♖h7 with a win.

28	♗a3!

Rather than defend the sickly f-pawn Xie Jun prefers to keep Black tied to the isolated c-pawn.

28	...	e5!

A good practical try; Black must liberate his pieces and seek complications before White gets her pieces totally organized.

29	♕d3 (D)
29	...	exf4?

Portisch doesn't give up without a fight, and he gives a piece for tactical play against the white back rank. Unfortunately this fails so 29...♔g8! was better (avoiding the possibility of 30 h8+) and White cannot then take as 30 ♕xd6? loses to 30 ...exf4 (see the next note).

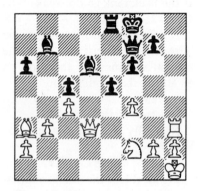

After 29...♔g8! perhaps 30 f5!, taking the opportunity to close the centre, is best as 30 fxe5?! ♖xe5 31 ♖e3 ♕h5 is dangerous.

30   ♖h8+!

Quite rightly continuing her own attack.

30 ♕xd6+ is obvious but bad, e.g. 30...♔g8 when Black wins after both 31 ♕d1 ♕g6 32 ♖f3 ♕c2! 33 ♕f1 ♕d2 34 ♘d3 (34 ♖d3 ♖e1 35 ♔g1 ♕e2) 34...♗xf3 35 gxf3 ♖e2 or 31 ♘d3 ♕g6 32 ♖f3 ♗xf3 33 gxf3 ♖e2. These lines could have arisen from 29...♔g8! 30 ♕xd6? exf4!, etc.

30   ...   ♔e7
31   ♘e4!   ♗xe4

Black has no choice as 31...♖xh8 is crushed by 32 ♕xd6+ ♔e8 33 ♕b8+ mating or winning the black queen.

32   ♕xe4+   ♔d7
33   ♕b7+   ♗c7

Another try was 33...♔e6!? 34 ♖xe8+ ♕xe8 35 ♗xc5! (35 ♕xg7 ♔f5 looks too dangerous and White is virtually obliged to bail out with a perpetual) 35...♗xc5 36 ♕d5+ ♔e7 37 ♕xc5+ when Black can avoid the exchange of queens by 37...♔f7. White has a difficult technical win after 38 ♕f2 followed by 39 h3 and the queenside pawns will roll.

34   ♖xe8   ♕xe8
35   ♗xc5!

Surprisingly there is now nothing to be gained against White's back rank.

35   ...   ♕e2
36   ♗b6!   ♕d1+
37   ♗g1   a5
38   c5

White has tucked his king away in an impenetrable box and she now pushes her pawns at will.

38   ...   ♕d2
39   a3   g5
40   b4   axb4
41   axb4   1-0

After 41...g4 42 b5 Black cannot counter the threat of b6.

Game Thirty-One
Alisa Maric-Zsuzsa Polgar
Women's Candidates final, Tilburg 1994

The Women's World Champion-   ship cycle reached the Candidates stage this year. Two players dominated and will play a match to determine Xie Jun's challenger. Zsuzsa Polgar (Judit's eldest sister) and Maia Chiburdanidze (the previous World Champion), showing a return to good form, were very convincing qualifiers. Here is a game from each, firstly Zsuzsa who is generally considered the second strongest woman in the world (after her sister) at the moment.

1	d4	d5
2	c4	c6
3	♘f3	e6

Zsuzsa employs a type of Semi-Slav which I think should be called the 'Triangle Defence'.

4 e3

One of the typical ideas is that after the natural 4 ♘c3 Black can capture on c4 and obtain certain concessions from White if she wishes to win back the pawn. 4 g3, hoping for a type of Catalan, and 4 ♕c2 are also good moves here.

| 4 | ... | f5!? |

Switching to a Stonewall Dutch set-up now that White cannot develop her queen's bishop outside the pawn chain.

| 5 | ♗d3 | ♗d6 |
| 6 | 0-0 | |

A slightly committal move. The plan of 6 ♘c3 followed by ♕c2, b3, ♗b2, 0-0-0, and h3 followed by g4 was more aggressive. In fact Alisa Maric plays to exchange the dark-squared bishops but after that is

rather stuck for a constructive plan.

6	...	♘f6
7	b3	♕e7
8	a4	a5!

A good move stopping White gaining space with the further a4-a5 and even a5-a6. Black can sometimes profit from the hole on b4.

9	♗a3	♗xa3
10	♘xa3	0-0
11	♕b1	

White has a positional threat of playing 12 cxd5 and Black cannot retake with the desired e-pawn because the f-pawn would be hanging. In some Stonewall positions Black is happy to take back with the c-pawn if she can be quick on the queenside. Here White has ♘b5 and ♖c1 and would take the initiative, and this explains why the Yugoslav preferred the b1 square to c2 for her queen, so as not to be exposed along the c-file.

11	...	♘e4
12	♕b2	♘d7
13	♘c2?!	

Here the plan of getting this knight to d3 to exert influence on c5, e5 and f4 is too slow. More to the point was 13 ♖ae1 b6 14 ♗xe4 fxe4 15 ♘d2 followed by f2-f3.

| 13 | ... | b6 |
| 14 | ♖fc1 | |

White's moves at this point are very unconvincing.

| 14 | ... | ♗b7 |
| 15 | ♗f1 | |

15 ... f4!

After 15...c5 White would be happy to play 16 ♘a3 eyeing b5. Zsuzsa immediately plays for the initiative on the kingside as her opponent has been rather lacklustre with her manoeuvring.

16 ♖e1 c5
17 cxd5 exd5
18 exf4?!

The active moves 18 ♗b5 and 18 ♖ad1 put more pressure on the black centre. The text only helps Black's attack to get rolling.

18 ... ♖xf4
19 ♘d2?

White has a difficult position but she could have limited the damage by 19 ♖ad1. Black is to be preferred after 19...♖af8 20 dxc5 bxc5 21 ♘e3 d4 22 ♗c4+ ♔h8 23 ♘d5 ♗xd5 24 ♗xd5 ♘df6 but by exchanging some pieces the defence is eased considerably.

19 ... ♕f6
20 ♘xe4 dxe4
21 ♗c4+ ♔h8
22 ♖e2 ♖f8

23 ♖f1 cxd4

Maric manages to hold onto the sensitive f2 point just in time but now she has to face further threats as Zsuzsa brings up the reserves.

24 ♘xd4

After 24 ♕xd4 then 24...♘e5 is even stronger.

24 ... ♘e5!
25 ♘e6

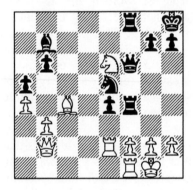

The best chance. At least by grabbing material the defender can sometimes stave off an attack by offering back something.

25 ... ♖g4?

Going for glory Zsuzsa loses her objectivity. Correct was 25...♘f3+! transposing to a good ending after the following forced sequence: 26 ♔h1 ♖h4 27 h3 ♕h6 28 ♕xg7+ (the only move) 28...♕xg7 29 ♘xg7 ♔xg7 30 gxf3 ♖xf3 31 ♔g2 ♖fxh3 32 ♖g1. White can put up some resistance but should lose.

26 ♘xf8?

Over the board it is almost impossible to decide between the three possible defences. Unfortunately for Maric she chose a losing one.

Also inferior is 26 h3 but not because of the tempting 26...♖xg2+?! which only leads to a draw after 27 ♔xg2 ♕f3+ 28 ♔h2 e3 29 fxe3 ♕xf1 30 ♘xf8 ♕h1+ 31 ♔g3 ♕f3+. Instead, critical is the line 26...♘f3+! 27 ♔h1 ♕h6 28 ♘xf8 ♕f4 29 g3 ♕h6 30 ♔g2 ♘g5 31 ♖h1! e3+ 32 ♔f1 ♗xh1. Black has a strong attack but the game is not yet won: 33 hxg4?? loses immediately to 33...♗g2+! but 33 h4 ♕c6 34 ♖xe3 ♕g2+ 35 ♔e2 ♘e4 36 ♔e1 ♖xg3 (36...♕g1+ leads nowhere after 37 ♗f1 ♗g2 38 ♕e2) 37 ♖xg3 ♘xg3 38 ♕d4 may survive. Also 33 ♖xe3 ♕xh3+ 34 ♔e1 looks playable. So after 26 h3 by very accurate play White can keep in the game.

Best is however 26 f3!! an astonishing move that may turn the tables. After 26...exf3 (26...♘xf3+ 27 ♔h1 ♕h4 is countered by 28 ♕e5!! and the other attacking try 26...♖f7 27 ♖d2 ♘xf3+ 28 ♔h1 ♘xd2 29 ♖xf6 e3 soon runs out of steam: 30 h3 ♖xg2 31 ♖xf7 ♖f2+ 32 ♖xb7 and wins) 27 ♖xe5 f2+ 28 ♕xf2! ♗xg2 29 ♕xg2 ♖xg2+ 30 ♔xg2 ♕g6+ favours White because of 31 ♘g5! when 31...♖xf1 32 ♗xf1 h6 is met by 33 ♗d3.

In mutual time trouble the defender has to be the most accurate because one mistake and it is mate!

| 26 | ... | ♘f3+ |
| 27 | ♔h1 | ♕f4 |

Now the attack crashes through.

| 28 | g3 | ♕h6 |

Just as good is the pretty 28...♖h4.

0-1

Game Thirty-Two
Maia Chiburdanidze-Alisa Maric
Women's Candidates final, Tilburg 1994

Maia Chiburdanidze, the ebullient ex-World Champion, has seemingly overcome a period of mixed results and is again showing the determination necessary to win back the title. She has shown great interest in Georgian culture and even been involved in politics. Despite the distractions and uncertainties of a civil war and disastrous economic situation, Maia was able to lead the proud Georgian team to gold in the Moscow Olympiad including an excellent personal performance.

| 1 | c4 | e5 |

This variation of the English opening is analogous to a Sicilian Defence with reversed colours.

| 2 | g3 | ♘f6 |
| 3 | ♗g2 | d5 |

Ambitiously taking on a reversed "open" Sicilian.

4	cxd5	♘xd5
5	♘f3	♘c6
6	0-0	♘b6
7	b3	♗e7

More accurate is 7...♗d6 to follow 8 ♗b2 with 8...♕e7 9 d3 0-0 and ...♗g4. The text necessitates 8...f6, a move that Black can do without.

8	♗b2	f6
9	♘c3	0-0
10	♖c1	f5

Played only two moves after having played 8...f6! Of course aggressive intentions are commendable but what about the development of the queenside? Alisa soon suffers from this important loss of tempo.

11	d3	♗e6
12	♘d2	♗f6
13	a3	

White intends to expand on the queenside with 14 b4 which Black immediately avoids.

In this type of position (an open Sicilian with reverse colours) it is much harder for Black to obtain kingside attacking chances using the e5, f5 pawns (than for the first player with colours reversed) and if White grasps the initiative they will become targets rather than trumps.

| 13 | ... | a5 |
| 14 | ♘c4 | |

Black has more space but White's pieces are bearing down on the Yugoslav centre.

| 14 | ... | ♖e8 |

| 15 | ♘b5 | ♘d5 |

After 15...♘xc4 White can recapture with either pawn but Maia would have certainly played 16 bxc4 and retained excellent piece play. Note how effective White's minor pieces are.

On 15...♗d5?? 16 ♘xc7 ♗xg2 17 ♘xe8 ♗xf1 18 ♘xf6+, or 18 ♘xb6 etc., leads to a gain in material.

| 16 | e4! | |

Well-judged! White seemingly weakens her own pawn structure but Maia decides it is time to hit back. The black centre doesn't collapse immediately but needs plenty of attention to keep it defended.

16	...	♘de7
17	♕c2	♘g6
18	♘e3	

Forcing a decision about the f5 pawn. If now 18...f4 then 19 ♘d5! with tremendous play.

Note that the squares d3 and d4 cannot be attacked by Black, so 16 e4 wasn't weakening but a positive way of attacking the centre.

| 18 | ... | fxe4 |
| 19 | dxe4 | ♘d4 |

Otherwise the Georgian would have followed-up with 20 ♖fd1 and 21 ♘d5.

Maric takes her chance to release the threats against her c7 pawn as 20 ♕xc7?? allows 20...♘e2+.

| 20 | ♘xd4 | exd4 |
| 21 | ♘d5 | ♗e5 |

After 21...♗xd5 22 exd5 it is

hard to see how both c7 and d4 will last for long, and if 22...d3? then naturally 23 ♗xf6.

22   ♖fd1

One can note the success of White's strategy simply in regarding the harmony of the white pieces and the difficulty Black has in repulsing the pressure.

Chiburdanidze had the option here of chasing a pawn by 22 ♘xc7 ♖c8 (22...d3 is simply met by 23 ♘xe6 ♖xe6 24 ♕d2) 23 ♘xe6 ♖xc2 24 ♘xd8 ♖xb2 25 ♘xb7 ♖xb3 26 ♘xa5 ♖xa3 27 ♘c4 ♖a2. She would have seen that she could emerge with an extra pawn but that it allows drawing chances, either because of opposite-coloured bishops or after 28 ♘xe5 ♘xe5 because of Black's active pieces and the advanced d-pawn. An experienced grandmaster such as Maia Chiburdanidze also probably took into account the fact that h8 is a dark square and so her bishop is known as the 'wrong' bishop (because the ending of king, bishop and h-pawn against lone king is a draw if Black can get to the corner square).

Grandmasters prefer to keep the initiative rather than hand it over to their opponent for a small material gain.

22   ...   c6
23   ♘e3   ♗f6

Black's most active try 23...♕b6 is met by 24 ♘c4.

24   ♘f5

The remnant of the centre (the d4 pawn) is certainly having a hard time!

24   ...   ♕b6

Finally threatening something. The b3 pawn at least enables Maric to keep on level terms materially but the queen soon finds herself a long way from the black king. If instead 24...♗xf5 25 exf5 ♘e7 White wins a clear pawn after 26 ♗xd4 ♗xd4 27 ♕c4+ ♔h8 28 ♖xd4.

25   ♘xd4   ♗xd4
26   ♖xd4   ♕xb3

The ending after 27 ♕xb3 ♗xb3 28 ♖d7 ♖e7 favours White

because of the bishop pair but the ex-World Champion had prepared a nasty surprise!

27   ♜d7!   ♜e7

Hopeless is 27...♕xc2 28 ♜xg7+ ♚f8 29 ♜xc2 as Black is a pawn down and has an exposed king.

28   ♜xe7   ♞xe7
29   ♕d2!

The black pieces are awkwardly placed to defend g7. Of course the ending gives an edge but a mating attack gives so much more pleasure!

29   ...   ♚h8
30   ♕d4   ♜g8
31   h4!

White's intention is clear. Now Black rushes back to defend the home front.

31   ...   ♗f7
32   ♜c5   ♕b6
33   ♕c3

Unpinning with gain of time and winning a pawn by force.

33   ...   a4?

33...h6 had to be played when

White can first take the a-pawn and then try and mate.

34   ♜g5

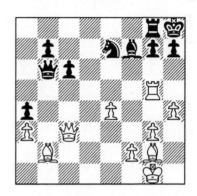

A good position to illustrate pressure on the long diagonal!

34   ...   ♞g6
35   h5   ♕d8
36   h6!   1-0

A pretty finish. Obviously 36...♕xg5 37 hxg7+ ♜xg7 38 ♕xg7 is mate and on 36...♕f8 37 f4! would be more sadistic than taking the exchange with 37 hxg7+, etc.

8   National Championships

This is simply a roll-call of national championship winners. Nowadays most national championships seem to be disappointingly short of their top players, probably due to financial reasons or prior commitments; grandmaster involvement is often limited.

The Russian, USA and Israeli championships were the strongest in view of the high numbers of ex-Soviet participants.

Australia, December/January
8½/11   J.P.Wallace

Filettino, Italy, January
9/11   M.Godena, B.Belotti

Hyderabad, India, January
13½/19   P.Thipsay

Rosario, Argentina, February
7/9   H.Spangenberg

Tivat, Yugoslavia
7½/12   M.Vukic, B.Ivanovic, D.Kosic

Lithuania
10/13   S.Sulskis

Bulgaria
9½/13   A.Delchev

Usti nad Labem, Czech Republic
8/11   Z.Hracek, V.Jansa
(Hracek won the play-off match)

Amsterdam, the Netherlands, June
8½/11   J.Piket

Minsk, Belarussia, June
9/11   J.Schulman

Lucerne, Switzerland, July
7/11   L.Brunner, B.Zuger
(Brunner won the play-off 1½-½)

Aalborg, Denmark, July
6½/9   C.Hansen, L.B.Hansen
(Curt Hansen won the play-off 3-1)

Haparanda, Sweden
10/13   R.Wessman
Norwich, Great Britain, August
9/11   W.Watson
Because of financial limitations only three grandmasters participated.

Chambery, France, August
11/15   M.Santo-Roman, M.Apicella
The title was decided by two 20 minute games; 2-0 to Santo-Roman.

Iceland
8½/11   H.Stefansson, H.Olafsson, J.Hjartarson

Hamilton, Canada, September
11½/15   K.Spraggett

Elista, Russia, September/October
8/11   P.Svidler
This result earned the young Leningrad player the honour of playing in the gold-medal winning Russian team in the Moscow Olympiad.

Israel, October
9/11   L.Yudasin

Portugal, October
10/11   L.Galego

USA, October
9½/13   B.Gulko
By an impressive one and a half point margin in a strong (category XIII) round-robin with only Kamsky missing amongst the top active players.

Germany, November
7/9   P.Enders

Bucharest, Romania, November
9½/13   M.Marin

9 Team Chess

Chess is really an individual game, one against one. The very nature of the game means that 'team chess' is really a rather artificial invention, and in fact it represents only a small part of the chess activity of most grandmasters.

National Team Championships

Whereas local leagues are essentially social affairs, grandmasters play in national leagues mainly as imported mercenaries. Most countries do have a cup and a league (sometimes with several divisions), but the number of places available for foreigners is usually limited to one or two per team and only the top clubs can afford to pay top stars. So the degree of professionalism is limited but enables pros, leading amateurs and juniors to compete side-by-side with a common interest. Interesting is the compulsory inclusion of at least one female player (France, UK) or two (former Yugoslav countries), which must be a positive step for women's chess.

Many players worldwide feel a strong bond with their club and enjoy the camaraderie and excitement involved, but there are unfortunately very few non-championship tournaments for teams, even at amateur level. This is in area that future sponsors could investigate, particularly if they are looking for new ideas.

Sponsorship is the key. Building a successful team usually takes several years and requires a faithful sponsor. To win their respective leagues all these clubs have had to court the favour of enough of the top domestic players plus some foreign grandmasters and this can be expensive.

Austria - Inter Schweppes, Salzburg
Belgium - Rochade Eupen
British Isles - Invicta Knights, Maidstone
France - Lyon-Oyannax

Germany - SG Cologne-Porz
Hungary - Honved Budapest
Netherlands - De Variant Breda
Romania - R.A.T. Bucharest
Spain - Goya, Las Palmas
Switzerland - Allschwil
Yugoslavia - Insa, Belgrade

European Club Cup

As many as 57 teams took part in the European Club Cup: seven groups of eight and the previous winners Lyon-Oyannax. Each group played a three-day (usually knock-out) tournament to find one qualifier for the grand final weekend, which was held in Lyon.

Some of the qualification rounds enjoyed less than full participation due to the tremendous cost of sending seven people (six players and a captain/substitute) to the far end of Europe and paying them a fee as well. Not all teams could convince their sponsors of the benefits.

Here are some of the details of the venues and the top two (or finalists) for each group.

Eupen (Belgium) Reykjavik   **3-3**   Bayern Munchen (Germany)
Pula (Croatia) Donbass   **4½-1½** Zalaegerseg (Hungary)
Strasbourg (France) Sarajevo   **4-2**   Breda (Netherlands)
Budapest (Hungary) Honved   **3½-2½** Djakovo (Croatia)
Asiago (Italy) Novosibirsk   **4-2**   Clichy (France)
Gorzow (Poland) 1st Kaise Vilnius
Calarasi (Romania) 1st Beersheva, 2nd Riga (Latvia)

Thirty-five grandmasters were present for the finals in Lyon, a good indication of the importance of this competition.

Novotronika Lugansk
Donbass (Ukraine)   **5½-½**   Reykjavik (Iceland)
Beersheva (Israel)   **3½-2½** Novosibirsk (Russia)
Honved Budapest (Hungary)   **3-3**   Sarajevo (Bosnia)
Kaise Vilnius (Lithuania)   **1½-4½** Lyon-Oyannax (France)
Lyon Oyannax   **3-3**   Beersheva
Novotronika   **1½-4½** Sarajevo

(Kasparov surprisingly lost to A.Shneider, a Ukrainian grandmaster who is approximately 180th in the world rankings.)

The Final

Sarajevo, Bosnia	**3 - 3**	**Lyon-Oyannax, France**
G.Kasparov	½ - ½	J.Lautier
I.Sokolov	1 - 0	V.Anand
Pr.Nikolic	0 - 1	E.Bareev
Z.Azmaiparashvili	½ - ½	J.Dorfman
B.Kurajica	1 - 0	A.Vaiser
E.Dizdarevic	0 - 1	M.Sharif

Both teams advanced during the weekend by winning a match on board count, an indication of how even in strength were the group winners. The final further enforced that view.

There was talk of organizing a quickplay play-off between the teams, as according to the rules board count shouldn't be used to decide the final. An agreement couldn't be reached and so the title is shared in 1994. (Sarajevo would have been sole champions on board count.)

Moscow Olympiad

The best known, and for many, the most important event in the 1994 chess calendar was the Moscow Olympiad. A grand total of 124 teams participated in the 'mixed' event and 81 in the women's. The mixed is often incorrectly known as the 'men's', but in fact it is open to women, although Judit Polgar, the Hungarian top board, was the only member of the fairer sex to take part in this event.

There was a significant increase in the number of teams entered this time, but this was entirely due to the large number of ex-Soviet, ex-Yugoslav and ex-Czechoslovak splinter states: fifteen, five and two respectively in both the mixed and women's except for the absence of a women's team from Tajikistan.

Several different teams held the lead at various stages of the main event (Yugoslavia, Netherlands, Bosnia, England and Russia II), but it was the favourites, Russia I, led by Garry Kasparov, that had the best second week and finally won. Kasparov and his team looked out of sorts at first but fourteen rounds permits the occasional setback. War-torn Bosnia-Herzegovina earned the silver medal despite relying almost entirely on their top four boards. Russia, the host country, were entitled to two teams and the second team was a junior squad that pipped England for third place on buchholz. There was talk before the event that the FIDE World Champion, Anatoly Karpov, would head the 'second team' with Salov, etc., but as it was, Kasparov and Makarov (who organized the FIDE Olympiad) scuppered any chance of the participation of an alternative (pro-Karpov) team.

One remarkable event was the re-election of Florencio Campomanes as FIDE President after some bizarre behind the scenes activity to change the electoral rules. Makarov, the Russian lawyer, politician and head of the pro-Kasparov pro-PCA Russian Chess Federation (the alternative RCF is pro-Karpov and headed by Bebchuk but has financial problems), and Bachar Kouatly the French-Lebanese grandmaster (who was the main alternative to another Campomanes term) were offered positions in the next Campomanes administration. In the world of chess politics shifting alliances and unconvincing democracy is the norm. Kasparov, who only a year ago was public enemy No.1 in FIDE's eyes, has now has been accepted back as the main power-broker. Karpov, the official FIDE World Champion has been rather sidelined.

If Campomanes and Kasparov are again friends does this mean an eventual reunification of the two World Championship cycles, and if so, what does Karpov make of that?

Mixed

1	Russia I	37½	
(Kasparov, Kramnik, Bareev, Dreev, Tiviakov, Svidler)
| 2 | Bosnia | 35 | |
(P.Nikolic, I.Sokolov, Kurajica, Dizdarevic, N.Nikolic, Milovanovic)
| 3 | Russia II (young Russia) | 34½ | |
(Morozevich, Zviaginsev, Ulibin, Rublevsky, Sakaev, Yemelin)
| 4 | England | 34½ | |
(Short, Adams, Speelman, Nunn, Miles, Hodgson)

5	Bulgaria	34	(Topalov, etc.)
6	Netherlands	34	(Timman, etc.)
7	USA	34	(Gulko, etc.)
8	Belarussia	33½	(Gelfand, etc.)
9	China	33½	(Ye Rongguang, etc.)
10	Georgia	33½	(Azmaiparashvili, etc.)
11	Hungary	33½	(J.Polgar, etc.)
12	Ukraine	33½	(Ivanchuk, etc.)

The teams are of six players, four of whom participate in each particular match. Both events are fourteen rounds long. Board Prizes are awarded to those players scoring the best percentages. Only three of the winners were of grandmaster strength as it is easier to score high percentages playing for lesser teams against weaker opposition. The gold medal winners were

1   Campora $7\frac{1}{2}/9$
2   Davila $10\frac{1}{2}/13$
3   Arlandi $7\frac{1}{2}/9$
4   Seirawan $8\frac{1}{2}/10$
5   Didishko $9/11$ and Williams $6/7$ (after a protest and only 26 hours later!)
6   Kelly $5\frac{1}{2}/7$

Women

1 **Georgia 32**   (Chiburdanidze, Ioseliani, Arakhamia, Gurieli)
2 Hungary 31   (Zsu.Polgar, Zso.Polgar, Madl, Csonkics)
3 China   27   (Xie Jun, Peng Zhaoqin, Qin Kanying, Zhu Chen)
4 Romania 27   (C.Foisor, Radu, Peptan, Nutu-Gajic)
5 Ukraine 25   (Galliamova-Ivanchuk, etc.)
6 England $24\frac{1}{2}$ (S.Lalic, etc.)
7 Estonia $24\frac{1}{2}$ (Tsiganova, etc.)
8 Germany $24\frac{1}{2}$ (Kachiani-Gersinska, etc.)

Amongst the female board gold medal-winners there is only one familiar name:

1   Zhitsova $10\frac{1}{2}/13$
2   Zso.Polgar $12\frac{1}{2}/14$
3   Hernandez $8\frac{1}{2}/9$
4   Sedina $10\frac{1}{2}/12$

In the women's event the teams are of four, three playing each time. There was little suspense in this contest as Georgia comfortably outpaced, Hungary who scored indifferently on board three. Third seed China never competed for first but always seemed a reasonable bet for the bronze which they earned on tie-break over an in-form Romania.

Game Thirty-Three
Eduard Rosentalis-Predrag Nikolic
Lithuania-Bosnia, Moscow Olympiad 1994

At the Novi Sad Olympiad in 1990, no-one could have envisaged that only four years later there would be so many splinter states emanating from Eastern Europe. This game was played by representatives of two of them: Eduard Rosentalis from Lithuania, the country that most challenged for independence from the then USSR, and Predrag Nikolic from Bosnia, where a clash of ideologies and cultures has had tragic consequences. This was in fact a second Olympiad (in recent times) for both, but neither achieved particularly dramatic results in Manila. Here, Lithuania finished in an unremarkable 24th position, but the surprise team of the 'mixed' Olympiad was Bosnia, pleasing many neutrals by achieving the silver medal. The top four boards, who played virtually all the games, had representatives from all three ethnic communities, something that the politicians could learn from.

These two players have calm placid personalities, but whereas Nikolic plays in a style true to his nature, Rosentalis is willing to take risks for the attack. Overall, Nikolic was impressive on board one but he did lose the following brilliancy in round four.

1   e4   e6

Nikolic tends to stick closely to a fairly narrow repertoire and the French Defence would have been anticipated by Rosentalis.

2   d4   d5
3   ♘d2   a6!?

Black prepares for 4...c5 without allowing an early ♗b5. Although this move spends a tempo ...a7-a6 can be useful in other ways: allowing the retreat ...♗c5-a7 or even preparing ...b7-b5.

4   ♘gf3   c5
5   dxc5   ♗xc5
6   ♗d3   ♘e7
7   0-0   ♘bc6
8   c3   0-0
9   ♕e2

In a game against Topalov earlier this year, Kotronias preferred c2 for his queen. The game continued 9 ♕c2 h6 10 ♖e1 ♗a7 11 ♘b3 e5 12 exd5 ♕xd5 13 ♗e3 ♗xe3 14 ♖xe3 ♕d6 15 ♖ae1 f6 16 h3 and Black's kingside pawn structure looks ugly but White could not prove any advantage.

9   ...   ♘g6
10   ♘b3   dxe4

Avoiding the pitfalls of having an isolated queen's pawn but conceding ground in the centre.

Kholmov-Dolmatov, Volgadonsk 1983 suggested that Black fails to equalize by 10...♗d6 11 ♗g5 ♕c7 12 exd5 exd5 13 h3 ♘f4 14 ♗xf4 ♗xf4

15 ♖ad1 ♗e6 16 ♘bd4. The bishop pair is not so effective in this position and White has the initiative due to his central bind.

11	♗xe4	♗d6
12	♗e3	♕c7
13	♖ad1	♖d8
14	♕c4!	

Directed against the liberation of Black's queen's bishop as 14...b5?? fails to 15 ♕xc6 and 14...e5 to 15 ♘g5 ♕e7 16 ♗xg6 hxg6 17 ♕h4.

| 14 | ... | ♗d7 |

Rosentalis now exploits his opponent's passive opening by immediately switching to an attack against the king.

15	♗xg6!	hxg6
16	♘g5	♗e7
17	♘c5!	

Introducing a clever piece sacrifice, distracting Black's dark-squared bishop away from his king. The more direct 17 ♕h4 ♗xg5 18 ♗xg5 f6 (possible is 18...♖f8!? 19 ♖d3 f6 20 ♖h3 ♔f7!) 19 ♗xf6 gxf6 20 ♕xf6 ♗e8 21 ♕xe6+ ♗f7 doesn't really give White enough for the piece.

| 17 | ... | ♘e5 |

Inadequate is 17...♗xg5 18 ♗xg5 ♘e5 in view of 19 ♗xd8 winning material.

| 18 | ♕h4 | ♗xc5 |
| 19 | ♗d4! | ♗e8 |

Despite the extra piece, Black is strangely helpless against White's slow but powerful build-up. His problem stems from the fact that his knight on e5 cannot move, else White crashes through with a capture on e6. For instance, after 19...♗b5 20 ♖fe1 (the impatient 20 ♕h7+ ♔f8 21 ♕h8+ is not appropriate: 21...♔e7 22 ♕xg7 ♗xd4 23 cxd4 ♖g8 24 ♕xe5 ♕xe5 25 dxe5 ♗xf1) 20...♗xd4 21 cxd4 ♘c6 22 ♕h7+ ♔f8 23 ♖xe6! Black is defenceless.

| 20 | ♖fe1 | ♖d5 |
| 21 | f4 | ♖ad8 |

Black has to give back the piece. He dare not do otherwise: 21...♗xd4+ 22 cxd4 ♘c6 (22...♖xd4?? fails to 23 ♖xd4 ♕c5 24 fxe5 and 22...♘d7 again loses to 23 ♕h7+ ♔f8 24 ♖xe6! as 24...♘f6 25 ♕h8+ ♘g8 26 ♘h7 is mate) 23 ♕h7+ ♔f8 24 ♖xe6! fxe6 25 ♕h8+! ♔e7 26 ♕xg7+ ♔d8 27 ♘xe6+ mating.

| 22 | fxe5 | ♖8d7 |

The text is a tacit admission of defeat, but does give his king a flight square in some lines. Unfortunately for the Bosnian No.1, 22...♖xe5 exposes the e6 square to a tactical blow after 23 ♕h7+

♔f8 24 ♘xe6+! when both captures lose:

a) 24...fxe6? 25 ♕h8+ ♔e7 (25...♔f7 26 ♖f1+ ♔e7 27 ♕xg7+, etc.) 26 ♕xg7+ ♗f7 27 ♕xe5 winning easily; and

b) 24...♖xe6 25 ♕xg7+ ♔e7 26 ♕f6+! ♔d7 27 ♖xe6 fxe6 28 ♗xc5+ ♔c8 when White comes out two clear pawns ahead.

23 ♔h1!

An excellent preparatory move emphasizing the hopelessness of Black's defensive task. The crude 23 ♖f1? is less clear in view of 23...♖xe5! 24 ♕h7+ ♔f8 25 ♕h8+ ♔e7 26 ♕xg7 ♔d8! (the point behind 22...♖8d7).

23	...	♗xd4
24	cxd4	♕b6
25	♖e4	

Holding onto the d-pawn long enough to prepare the decisive doubling of his rooks on the f-file.

| 25 | ... | ♖c7 |

25...♕xb2 26 ♖f1 ♕b6 loses in the same way as the game.

26	♖f1	♖cd7
27	♖ef4	♖xd4

White to play and mate in six!

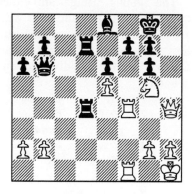

28	♕h7+	♔f8
29	♕h8+	♔e7
30	♖xf7+	♔d8
31	♕xe8+!	1-0

Black resigned rather than allowing 31...♔xe8 32 ♖f8+ ♔e7 33 ♖1f7 mate.

Game Thirty-Four
Vaselin Topalov-Garry Kasparov
Bulgaria-Russia I, Moscow Olympiad 1994

The next game is one that will live on in people's memories long after the details of the Olympiad are forgotten. Kasparov is brutally mated in 31 moves!

The conditions of play were not ideal in Moscow and Kasparov had a poor first week whilst he adjusted to the noisy and cramped environment. Was he distracted by this and his penchant for politicking? However, he recovered from this loss with excellent form in the second half of the event as Russia I moved into overdrive to take the gold.

Topalov is one of the world's most improved players; on the July 1st 1992 FIDE list he was

2520 (approximately 230th) whereas on the July 1st 1994 list, two years later, he was 2645 (a top twenty spot).

1   e4

The young Bulgarian either opens with the text move or with 1 c4. In Linares, ten months earlier, 1 c4 led to a King's Indian Defence in their individual encounter.

1	...	c5
2	♘f3	d6
3	d4	cxd4
4	♘xd4	♘f6
5	♘c3	a6
6	♗e3	e6
7	g4	

Vaselin is clearly in the mood for a sharp game.

7	...	h6
8	f4!?	♘c6
9	♗e2	e5!

Kasparov correctly reacts actively in the centre before White fully organizes his kingside play.

10   ♘f5

The alternative 10 ♘xc6 bxc6 11 fxe5 can be met by the shot 11...♘xg4! (11...dxe5 12 ♕xd8+ ♔xd8 13 0-0-0+ ♔c7 is also playable) when the complications following 12 ♗xg4 ♕h4+ 13 ♗f2 ♕xg4 14 exd6 ♕g2 15 ♖g1 ♕xh2 are rather unclear.

10	...	g6
11	♘g3	exf4
12	♗xf4	

As both kings are still in the centre, such an open position lends itself to tactical play. Each side has various pawn weak-nesses but the crucial question revolves around the fate of the d6 pawn. Kasparov's main problem is what to do with this liability, as ...♗g7 preparing to castle is met by the awkward ♗xd6, winning a pawn and keeping the black king in the centre.

| 12 | ... | ♗e6 |

Preparing general liquidation with ...d6-d5.

13   ♖f1

White cannot seriously envisage castling kingside and he therefore decides to centralize the rook.

| 13 | ... | ♖c8 |
| 14 | h3 | ♕b6!? |

Kasparov rejects the simple equality on offer after 14...d5 15 exd5 ♘xd5 16 ♘xd5 ♕xd5 17 ♕xd5 or 16...♗xd5 17 ♗f3 and tries for more.

| 15 | ♕d2 | ♗g7? |

The pawn-grabbing 15...♕xb2 gives White a strong initiative after 16 ♖b1 ♕a3 17 ♖f3. Topalov instead suggests 15...♘d7! when he even prefers Black after 16 0-0-0 ♘de5 17 a3 ♘a5. Instead 16 ♘f5!? is tempting but inadequate after 16...♘de5 17 ♘xd6+ ♗xd6 18 ♕xd6 ♕xb2 e.g. 19 ♗xe5 ♘xe5 20 ♕xe5 ♕xa1+ 21 ♔d2 ♕xc3+ 22 ♕xc3 ♖xc3 23 ♔xc3 ♗xa2.

16   ♗xd6

Kasparov has given the d-pawn and cannot get his king to safety. He must try to act quickly before White can consolidate and make use of the extra pawn.

16 ... ♘xg4?!

Spectacular but not sound. To-palov again suggests 16...♘d7 just to free the dark-squared bishop, but after 17 ♘f5! ♗xf5 18 exf5 ♘b4 19 fxg6 fxg6 20 ♕f4 White's attack gets there first.

17 ♗xg4

There is no great merit in not taking on g4 as 17 ♘a4 is met by 17...♕e3 (or even 17...♕d4 18 ♕xd4 ♘xd4 19 hxg4 ♘xc2+ 20 ♔f2 ♘xa1 21 ♖xa1 ♖c2) 18 hxg4 ♕xd2+ 19 ♔xd2 ♖d8 and Black is better.

17 ... ♕xb2
18 e5?

The Bulgarian complicates his task as 18 ♘ge2! seems to win after either 18...♕xa1+ 19 ♔f2 ♕b2 20 ♖b1 or 18...♘d4 19 ♖b1 ♘xc2+ 20 ♔d1.

18 ... ♘xe5

Again taking the rook leads to the loss of Black's queen. The other capture on e5, 18...♗xe5, is best met by the active 19 ♘ge4! (rather than 19 ♘ge2?! due to

19...♕xa1+ 20 ♔f2 ♕b2 21 ♖b1 ♕xb1 22 ♘xb1 ♖d8 with enough for the queen) with the important difference that following 19...♕xa1+ 20 ♔f2 ♕b2 21 ♖b1 ♕xb1 22 ♘xb1 ♖d8 can now be met by the spectacular 20 ♕f4! winning, as 20...♗xf4 21 ♘f6 is mate!

Kasparov is now forced to take refuge a dubious ending.

19 ♖b1 ♕xc3

After 19...♘c4 20 ♖xb2 ♘xd2 21 ♗xe6 fxe6 22 ♔xd2 ♗xc3+ 23 ♔c1 ♗xb2+ 24 ♔xb2 Black has adequate material but has little play for the rooks which are dominated by the active white pieces.

20 ♕xc3 ♖xc3
21 ♗xe6 fxe6
22 ♖xb7

General simplification has not eased the plight of the black king stuck in the centre. The extra pawn is not really a factor as Black has insurmountable problems in bringing his king's rook into play.

22 ... ♘c4

After 22...♖xg3 23 ♖xg7 ♖xh3 White doesn't play 24 ♗xe5? because of 24...♖e3+ with drawing chances nor with 24 ♔f2?? (threatening 25 ♗xe5 and 25 ♖b1) due to 24...♖f3+ when Black is better, but rather 24 ♖f4 with many threats. White must surely be winning.

23 ♗b4 ♖e3+
24 ♘e2 ♗e5
25 ♖ff7

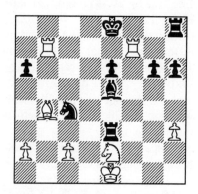

Can Black defend?

25 ... ♖xh3?

After this, surely not. Possible was 25...♗d6 but 26 ♖g7! seems clearly winning to me, e.g. 26...♔f8 27 ♖gc7! ♗xb4+ 28 ♖xb4 ♘d6 29 ♖b8+ ♘e8 30

♔f2! ♖xh3 (30...♖e5 31 ♖xe8+, etc.) 31 ♘f4 mating. The counterattack 26...♗g3+ falls short after 27 ♔f1. So it looks as if the position in the last diagram is already lost for Kasparov.

26 ♘d4!

As the knight cannot be taken (because of 27 ♖fe7+ ♔d8 28 ♖b8 mate) this fourth piece contributes to a mating net around Kasparov's king.

26	...	♖e3+
27	♔f1	♖e4
28	♖fe7+	♔d8
29	♘c6+	1-0

Rather than allow mate by 29...♔c8 30 ♘a7+ ♔d8 31 ♖bd7 Kasparov resigned.

Game Thirty-Five
Rune Djurhuus-Alexei Yermolinsky
Norway-USA, Moscow Olympiad 1994

The United States team was struggling way down the field for much of the event, but they managed to put in an impressive spurt in the latter part to finish a rather undeserved seventh. Yermolinsky was one of four ex-Soviets in the six-man team that was expected to be more competitive for the medal placings.

1	d4	♘f6
2	♘f3	e6
3	e3	

The Norwegian has shown a liking for this system before. This apparently quiet continuation generates many transpositional possibilities and can be a good way to play against those players who specialize in forcing main line openings.

3	...	d5
4	c4	c5
5	♘c3	a6!?

The symmetrical 5...♘c6 is usual but the American tries to make his opponent show his hand. The text is a multi-purpose move preparing a timely ...dxc4 followed by ...b7-b5, avoiding the pin with ♗b5 and often allowing the dark-squared bishop to drop back to a7 (see move 13).

6	cxd5	exd5
7	♗e2	♗d6
8	dxc5	♗xc5

Black accepts an isolated pawn but hopes to get active piece deployment in compensation.

9	0-0	0-0
10	♕d3!?	

More conventional is 10 b3 ♘c6 11 ♗b2 ♗a7 12 ♖c1 ♕d6 13 ♕c2 ♖d8 14 ♖fd1 as in Spasov-Ftacnik, Malta Olympiad 1980. Judging such positions comes down to a matter of taste and each player has his own feelings about the strengths and weaknesses of isolated pawns. Here Black was probably not too unhappy about his opening.

10	...	♘c6
11	♖d1	♗e6

White's tenth virtually forces this move. Aggression with 11...♘b4? 12 ♕d2 ♗f5 13 a3 ♘c2 14 ♖a2 is misplaced and would be soon regretted.

12	b3	♕e7
13	♗b2	♗a7
14	♖ac1	♖ac8
15	♕b1 *(D)*	

Completing the manoeuvre started by 10 ♕d3.

15	...	♖fd8

I think that Black has achieved equality as none of White's continuations seem to offer anything.

16	♗d3?!	

Also ambitious is 16 ♘g5!? but this is well met by 16...d4 17 ♘xe6 ♕xe6! (not 17...dxc3? 18 ♘xd8 cxb2 19 ♘xc6 winning) 18

exd4 ♗xd4 when Black has the initiative after:

a) 19 ♗f3 ♘e5! 20 ♗xb7 ♖b8 (or even 20...♗xf2+ 21 ♔f1 ♖b8) 21 ♗e4 ♘eg4; and

b) 19 ♗c4 ♕g4 20 h3 ♕f4.

If this is the case, and if the plan introduced by the text is unconvincing, then White should settle for 16 h3 d4 17 exd4 ♘xd4 18 ♘xd4 ♗xd4 19 ♗f3 with equal chances.

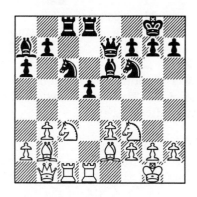

16	...	♗g4!
17	♗f5?!	

Djurhuus persists with his plan but pawn weaknesses on the kingside turn out to be more significant than the bishop pair. 17 ♗e2 is playable but it is very hard to bring yourself to play such a move!

17	...	♗xf3
18	gxf3	♖c7
19	♔h1	

Natural seems 19 ♘e2 aiming for control of the d4 square. Then 19...♘e5 20 ♗xe5 ♕xe5 21 f4! ♕e7 22 ♖xc7 ♕xc7 23 ♖c1 ♕e7 24 ♕d3 looks satisfactory for

White, however 19...♗xe3! 20 fxe3 ♕xe3+ 21 ♔f1 ♕xf3+ would give Black plenty of pawns and obvious attacking chances for the piece.

19	...	g6
20	♗d3	♖cd7
21	♘e2	

To obtain an advantage White needs only to play 22 ♕a1 followed by 23 ♘d4. Alas, it is of course Black to move.

| 21 | ... | d4! |
| 22 | e4 | |

Simplifying into a miserable ending with 22 ♘xd4 ♘xd4 23 ♗xd4 ♗xd4 24 exd4 ♖xd4 25 ♗f1 is not really an option, while after 22 ♕a1 Black has all the play after 22...♘h5.

| 22 | ... | ♘e5 |
| 23 | ♘g1 | |

A sign that things have gone sour, but 23 ♔g2 ♘h5 24 f4 ♘xf4+! 25 ♘xf4 ♕g5+ is no better.

23	...	♘h5
24	♗f1	♘f4
25	♖d2	d3!

The black pieces are perfectly placed whereas the white army has retreated in total disarray.

26 ♖cd1

If instead 26 ♕a1 then the same combination works as in the game. Otherwise 26 ♗xe5 ♕xe5 27 ♘h3 ♘xh3 28 ♗xh3 ♗b8 offers White no hope.

26 ... ♘xf3!

White's whole structure caves in. The Norwegian couldn't see any point in continuing with 27 ♘xf3 ♕xe4 28 ♗g2 ♘xg2 29 ♔xg2 (or 29 ♘g5 ♕c6 30 ♖c1 ♕d5 and wins) 29...♕g4+ 30 ♔f1 ♕xf3 31 ♔g1 ♖d5, etc.

0-1

A smooth performance by the 1993 co-American Champion.

Game Thirty-Six
Predrag Nikolic-Jan Timman
Bosnia-Netherlands, Moscow Olympiad 1994

The Dutch team were sole leaders of the tournament at one stage and had a fairly good Olympiad overall. Only a 3½-½ loss to England marred their performance. Jan Timman, who was the top non-Soviet player for many years, has had a slightly below par year and here his brave efforts to take on Nikolic in one of the Bosnian's pet lines were to no avail.

1	d4	♘f6
2	c4	g6
3	♘f3	♗g7
4	g3	

Nikolic frequently fianchettoes this bishop. It is generally considered as White's most solid variation against the King's Indian/Grünfeld Defence.

4	...	0-0
5	♗g2	c6
6	0-0	d5
7	b3	

Games one and three from the Karpov-Kasparov, World Championship match, Seville 1987, tested the main alternative 7 cxd5 cxd5 8 ♘e5 e6 9 ♘c3 ♘fd7 10 f4 ♘c6 11 ♗e3 ♘b6. The game starts from a symmetrical position but within only a few moves the position becomes quite tense.

7	...	♘e4
8	♗b2	♗f5
9	e3	

Nikolic has recently showed a preference for this simple move as earlier attempts to immediately undermine the Black minor pieces are not convincing: 9 ♘c3 can be met by 9...dxc4 10 bxc4 c5!? and 9 ♘h4 by 9...dxc4 10 ♘xf5 gxf5 11 ♗xe4 fxe4 12 bxc4 c5 13 ♘d2 (Malaniuk-Marinkovic, Vrnjacka Banja 1991) when 13...cxd4! 14 ♘xe4 ♘c6 may even be slightly preferable for Black.

Critical is 9 ♘e5 ♘d7 10 ♘d3 preparing g4 and f3, but this is well countered by the active continuation 10...dxc4 11 bxc4 ♘b6 12 g4!? (less risky is 12 ♘a3) 12...♘xc4! 13 gxf5 ♘xb2 14 ♘xb2 ♕xd4 15 ♕xd4 ♗xd4 16 ♗xe4 ♗xb2 17 ♘d2 ♗xa1 18 ♖xa1 (P.Nikolic-I.Sokolov, Belgrade 1991) with dynamic equality.

| 9 | ... | ♘d7 |
| 10 | ♕e2 | ♕a5 |

In yet another of Nikolic's games in this line, 10...a5 11 ♘h4 ♗e6 12 f3 ♘d6 13 c5 ♘b5 14 a4 ♘c7 15 f4 gave Smirin, as Black, a seriously constricted game.

| 11 | ♖c1 | ♖fe8 |
| 12 | ♘c3 | |

True to his nature Nikolic chooses the most solid continuation. 12 ♘h4!? is ineffective after 12...♗e6 13 f3 ♘f6 14 ♗f1 g5! 15 ♘g2 ♗f5 when it is the white pieces that have been displaced.

12	...	♘xc3
13	♗xc3	♕a6
14	♗f1!	

Threatening to simplify with advantage, e.g. 14...♖ac8 15 cxd5 ♕xe2 16 ♗xe2 cxd5 17 ♗b4 intending the awkward ♗b5.

| 14 | ... | dxc4 |

Bad is 14...e5? 15 cxd5 ♕xe2 16 ♗xe2 e4 17 dxc6! (17 ♘h4 only gives an edge) 17...exf3 18 cxd7 fxe2 19 dxe8♕+ ♖xe8 20 ♗b4 and White will win.

| 15 | e4 | |

Expanding in the centre now that Black's d-pawn has quit its defensive post.

| 15 | ... | ♗g4 |

16   h3

Taking the bishop pair.

16   ...   ♗xf3

17   ♕xf3   e6

With the text Timman admits that his opening has not really been a success as White maintains a solid edge. Even worse is 17...b5 18 a4! cxb3 19 axb5 ♕b7 20 ♗c4 e6 21 bxc6 ♕xc6 22 ♗xb3 with a clear advantage as the two bishops support the central majority, and furthermore Black's a-pawn is weak.

18   a4!   ♕b6

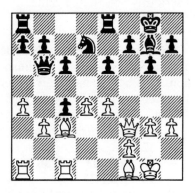

19   a5!

Forcing Black to retreat as 19...♕xb3 20 ♖cb1 ♕c2 21 ♖b2 loses the queen.

19   ...   ♕d8

20   ♗xc4   b5

Timman is fighting for space. Otherwise after 21 b4 White could retreat along the a2-g8 diagonal and stop any ideas of ...c6-c5.

21   axb6   axb6

22   e5   ♖xa1

23   ♗xa1   ♗h6

The impatient 23...c5 just loses a pawn after 24 ♗b5 ♕c7 (24...cxd4 25 ♕c6 ♖e7 26 ♕c8 ♕xc8 27 ♖xc8+ ♗f8 28 ♗xd4 will cost Black his b-pawn) 25 ♗xd7 ♕xd7 26 dxc5 bxc5 27 ♖xc5.

24   ♖c2   ♕a8

Gaining time for the defence of c6.

25   ♗b2   ♖c8

26   ♔g2

A cautious move typical of Nikolic. His philosophy can be summarized as 'when in doubt improve your worst placed piece'. The queen is defended and he avoids checks on the eighth rank.

26   ...   b5

Finally Timman can activate his knight which now heads for d5 via b6.

27   ♗d3   ♘b6

28   ♗e4   ♘d5

29   h4!   ♘b4

The white rook has to leave the c-file and Black can now prepare counterplay with a timely ...c6-c5, but Nikolic has earned enough time to start thinking about Timman's hitherto neglected king!

30   ♖e2   ♕a7

31   h5!*(D)*

Slowly but surely the attack gains momentum.

31   ...   c5?!

It looks as if Black doesn't have enough time for this move. Objectively best is 31...♘d5! but staying passive is not a pleasant decision to make. Then 32 hxg6 (or 32 ♕g4 ♔g7! 33 ♖e1 ♕a2! frustrating White's plans for the attack) 32...hxg6 33 ♕g4 ♔g7 (33...♕d7?! is too defensive, especially as White can play 34 ♖e1 ♔g7 35 ♖h1 ♖h8 36 ♕h3 ♔g8 37 ♖a1) 34 ♖c2 ♕d7 might be tenable.

| 32 | hxg6 | hxg6 |
| 33 | ♕g4 | c4 |

On 33...♕e7 34 dxc5 (34 d5!?) 34...♖xc5 35 ♗xg6 fxg6 36 ♕xb4 Black doesn't have 36...♖c1 'check' as Nikolic has already removed his king to g2. One just never knows when a variation will depend on a safe king, for instance at move 26

there was no concrete reason for the king move. Grandmasters know, however, that as soon as the tactics start counter checks can spoil all the good work, so it is typical of GM chess to see such 'time outs' for an unexpected side-step with the king.

After 33...♔g7 then 34 d5 with a crushing attack and on 33...♖c7 then 34 ♗xg6 fxg6 35 ♕xg6+ ♗g7 36 ♕xe6+ ♖f7 37 d5; White has excellent compensation for the piece, perhaps after 37...♕b7 Black is alive but White is a strong favourite.

| 34 | ♗xg6! |

Crashing through as 34...fxg6 35 ♕xe6+ costs Black his rook.

| 34 | ... | c3 |
| 35 | ♗e4+ | ♔f8 |

Equally hopeless is 35...♗g7 36 ♗c1 ♔f8 (36...♕xd4? 37 ♗h7+ and the queen is lost) 37 d5 etc.

| 36 | ♕h4 | ♗g7 |
| 37 | ♗xc3 | 1-0 |

As 37...♖xc3 allows mate by 38 ♕d8 Black is two pawns down. Therefore Timman resigned.

Game Thirty-Seven
Cruz-Yasser Seirawan
Peru-USA, Moscow Olympiad 1994

What is the difference between a grandmaster and a lesser master? Murray Chandler, himself a grandmaster and the English team

captain in Moscow, once explained to me his view that the difference is not dramatic. However, the stronger player has a very small superiority in each aspect of the game. Of course, in an individual encounter it's not always possible to prove that one is superior to one's opponent, but on other occasions, such as this one, patience is necessary and only late into the game does the grandmaster's talent get a chance to shine through.

Yasser Seirawan is one of the few top American's with no links to the ex-USSR. His immediate family is from Syria and England. He was the top US player for many years but is more active in chess journalism and less in practical play these days. Playing on a lower board this time he scored heavily, including this beautiful endgame win out of nothing.

The early stages of the game reflected an even tussle and analysis of the first thirty-five moves would not add to our appreciation of this endgame masterpiece, so I have exclusively concentrated on the latter stages of the game.

1 d4 ♘f6 2 ♘f3 e6 3 c4 b6 4 g3 ♗b7 5 ♗g2 c6 6 0-0 d5 7 ♘c3 ♘bd7 8 cxd5 cxd5 9 ♗f4 a6 10 ♖c1 ♖c8 11 ♕b3 ♗e7 12 ♖fd1 0-0 13 a4 ♘h5 14 ♗d2 ♗d6 15 ♘a2 ♕e7 16 ♗b4 ♘hf6 17 ♘e5 ♗xb4 18 ♘xd7 ♘xd7 19 ♘xb4 a5 20 ♘d3 ♗a6 21 e3 ♖c4 22 ♗f1 ♖fc8 23 ♖c3 ♖xc3 24 bxc3 ♗c4 25 ♕b2 ♕d6 26 ♘e5 ♘xe5 27 dxe5 ♕b8 28 ♗xc4 ♖xc4 29 ♖d4 ♖c5 30 e4 dxe4 31 ♕d2 ♖c8

32 ♖d7 ♖f8 33 ♕d4 b5 34 axb5 ♕xb5 35 c4 ♕b1+ 36 ♔g2

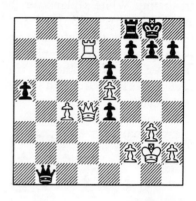

36 ... ♕d3

Yasser heads for the ending. Instead, attempts to win with 36...a4 will more than likely rebound after 37 ♖a7! (rather than 37 c5?! a3 38 ♖a7 a2 39 c6 h6 40 c7 ♔h7 41 ♕a4 ♖c8 or in this 39 ♕a4 ♕c1 40 ♖a5 ♕c3 41 ♕xa2 ♕xe5 when White has some problems) 37...♕c2 38 c5 and it is White who has the winning chances.

37 ♕xd3 exd3
38 ♖xd3 ♖c8
39 ♔f3 g5!

Why this move? Black wishes to free his rook from the defence of the back rank, naturally, but he uses his g-pawn to restrain the white kingside.

40 ♖c3 a4
41 ♔e3 a3
42 ♔d4?!

The Peruvian didn't want the irritating defensive task that 42 ♖xa3 ♖xc4 43 h3 h5 would have presented. But this would almost certainly have been drawn, given enough patience!

42	...	♖a8
43	♖c1	g4!

Definitively fixing the white kingside.

44	♖a1	♚f8
45	♖a2	♚e7
46	♚c3	♖a5
47	♚b4	♖xe5

Now 48 ♖xa3 would lose a pawn after 48...♖e2.

48	♚xa3	♖a5+!

Cruz was probably anticipating 48...♖h5 49 ♚b4 ♖xh2 50 ♚b5 and the c-pawn gives adequate counterplay.

Most players would be surprised by the text, surely he can't play the pure king and pawn ending, hasn't White an outside passed pawn? At this point Seirawan calculated the rest of the game with great accuracy and saw that in fact it is Black who wins by one tempo. A demonstration of the depth that a top-level player, given the right circumstances, is able to analyse.

49	♚b3	♖xa2
50	♚xa2 *(D)*	
50	...	♚d6
51	♚b3	♚c5
52	♚c3	

Material is equal and White has the so-called outside passed pawn. However Black can advance his kingside majority without hindrance as White, with no pawn moves, can only wait with his king. Note that White has no time to jettison his c-pawn to get

at the black pawns.

52	...	e5
53	♚d3	f5
54	♚c3	e4!

Taking away the d3 square from the white king who must now defend his c-pawn from c3 and b3.

55	♚b3	h6!

An important tempo loss so that his intended breakthrough takes place with the white king on the inferior b3.

56	♚c3	h5
57	♚b3	f4!

The moment of truth! Inferior is 57... h4? 58 gxh4 f4 59 h5 e3 60 fxe3 f3 61 h6 f2 62 h7 f1♕ 63 h8♕ ♕xc4+ with a certain draw.

58	gxf4	

Black queens after 58 ♚c3 e3 59 fxe3 fxg3 60 hxg3 h4, etc.

58	...	e3!
59	fxe3	h4
60	f5	

White is too far away to stop Black queening with one of the h- or g-pawns. So now the question arises as to how quick the white pawns are.

60 ... ♔d6!

The cleverest stage of the game, which had to be foreseen at least as early as move 48. Not 60... g3 61 hxg3 hxg3 62 f6 ♔d6 (62...g2? 63 f7 g1♕ 64 f8♕+ favours White) 63 c5+ ♔e6 64 c6 g2 65 c7 g1♕ 66 c8♕+ and White queens in time to make a draw.

61 ♔b4 ♔e5!

Again 61...g3 fails as 62 hxg3

hxg3 63 c5+ ♔d7 64 f6 g2 65 c6+! also enables White to save the game.

0-1

White resigned as he could see no improvement on 62 c5 ♔xf5 63 c6 ♔e6 64 ♔c5 g3 65 hxg3 h3! 66 ♔b6 h2 67 c7 ♔d7 68 ♔b7 and Black queens with check 68...h1♕+. A magnificent display of endgame and analytical technique.

10 Other Significant Events

Not every chess tournament fits neatly into the previous chapter headings, so here are the odds and ends that I think deserve a mention. They consist mainly of unusual formats, non-championship matches and knock-out events.

The strongest knock-out tournament, that is, at the traditional time limit is Tilburg (Interpolis) in the Netherlands. A two-game minimatch is followed, if necessary, by a series of more rapid games played in pairs. The tie-breaks, however, use the so-called 'Fischer clock' (20 minutes plus 10 seconds per move per player, and if that doesn't decide then two games at 10 minutes plus 10 seconds, etc.). For most players, who have little or no experience with the clock, it is hard to visualize how this compares with ordinary quickplay but a 30-move game would give each player 20 plus five minutes and a 60-move game 20 plus ten. The big advantage of the Fischer clock is that in a long game a player can better exercise his skill as some precious time is still available. This compares favourably with typical rapidplay chess which sometimes degenerates into instantaneous blitz play!

The first round saw 112 of the world's finest players start the tournament. The victors were joined by eight seeded players in the second round.

The problem for the sponsors has been the almost total domination by the Soviet school of chess. The last sixteen consisted of fourteen ex-Soviets and two East Europeans. This tends to dampen the enthusiasm of the Western media!

Next year Tilburg will be changing the formula of the event and I suspect that this may be the reason. Knock-out chess is excellent for quickplays of the highest calibre because of television and spectator interest but not ideal for a long drawn-out event with the conventional time-limit. There are complications for hotels, visas, travel arrangements, clashes with other events and inevitably not many of the 120 participants are still there at the closing ceremony! For 'cup-style' competitions to be successful there really need to be side events, as in Wijk aan Zee 1993 and again in 1995. The Dutch experiment with knock-outs is not yet finished.

Throughout Tilburg 1994 Salov remained unbeaten despite poor health at the start at the event. His semi-final opponent, Ivanchuk, required extra time to advance at the expense of Smyslov, Azmaiparashvili and Khalifman. So it was not surprising that another quickplay play-off was required to decide the encounter, but Ivanchuk's quickplay run was brought to an end by the eventual tournament winner.

In the other half of the draw, Bareev was another specialist at edging out his early opponents in the play-offs, but took his chances in the semi-final against Karpov, winning 1½-½. Karpov lost one embarrassing quickplay game to Kurajica in the second round, but after scraping through he scored an impressive 6/6 before his sudden loss of form against Bareev.

4th round	5th round	Semi-Final	Final
V.Salov 1 =			
G.Serper	**V.Salov** 1 =		
	V.Akopian		
V.Akopian 1 =			
E.Pigusov		**V.Salov** = = (1 =)	
		V.Ivanchuk	
V.Ivanchuk 1 0 (= 1)			
Z.Azmaiparashvili			
	V.Ivanchuk = = (1 0 1 1)		
A.Khalifman 1 =	A.Khalifman		
L.Yudasin			
			V.Salov 1 =
			E.Bareev
A.Karpov 1 1			
A.Shabalov	**A.Karpov** 1 1		
	Kir.Georgiev		
I.Sokolov			
Kir.Georgiev = = (1 0 = 1)			
		A.Karpov	
A.Dreev 1 =		**E.Bareev** 1 =	
Z.Almasi			
	A.Dreev		
V.Tukmakov	**E.Bareev** 1 =		
E.Bareev = = (1 =)			

By now in good health and good form it was the Spanish-based Salov, who won a double-edged Réti Opening in the first game of the final, which together with a draw in the second game, was enough to take the first prize of 100,000 guilders.

Non-Championship Matches

Some of the leading players have shown interest in playing training matches. There are different factors involved in preparing for one opponent over several games, and this is seen as useful in the process of graduating from being a successful tournament player to Candidate standard. It is not surprising then that it is the younger generation (with little experience in, but great hopes for, future involvement in the candidates matches) who indulge in these exhibition matches. The main ones of the year were as follows:

Aruba (Netherlands Antilles), February
J.Piket 4½-3½ L.Polugayevsky

Las Palmas (Spain), February
A.Karpov 5-1 I.Morovic

Oslo (Norway), March
M.Adams 2-2 S.Agdestein

Monte Carlo (Monaco), April
J.Piket 6-2 L.Ljubojevic

Buenos Aires (Argentina), October (25-minute)
A.Karpov 3-1 H.Spangenberg

Ubeda (Spain), November
A.Karpov 4-2 J.Lautier

Alcobendas (Spain), November
V.Topalov 4-2 M.Illescas

The following events feature the next generation of grandmasters!

World Junior Championships (under 20), Brazil, September
9½/13   H.Gretarsson (Iceland)

9	Zso.Polgar (Hungary)
8½	G.Vescovi (Brazil), N.Mariano (Philippines), D.Kumaran (England), H.Spangenberg (Argentina), C.Gabriel (Germany)

European Junior Championships (under 18), Chania (Greece), November

Boys: 7/9	R.Kempinski
Girls: 6½/9	M.Grabics

Sponsors sometimes look for something different. Here teams are invited (or contrived) to generate extra interest to individual performances.

Glendale (USA), May
USA 10-10 Armenia

The Hague (Netherlands), May
Humans 114-114 Computers
Best scorers: 5½/6 L.Christiansen, J.Nunn

Boston (USA), October (25-minute)
Humans 29½-18½ Computers
Best Score: 6½/8 J.Benjamin

Buenos Aires (Argentina), April
Rest of the World 56-44 Argentina
Best Scorers: ROW 7½/10 S.Conquest
Argentina 7½/10 D.Campora

The Argentinian metropolis of Buenos Aires is definitely the main chess centre in the southern hemisphere, the legendary Argentinian grandmaster Miguel Najdorf has seen to that. The main event there this year was dedicated to Lev Polugayevsky who is recovering from a brain operation and wasn't quite fit enough to play himself.

Sicilian theme tournament, Buenos Aires (Argentina), October

9/14	V.Salov
8½	V.Anand
7	V.Ivanchuk, J.Polgar
6½	G.Kamsky, A.Karpov

| 6 | A.Shirov |
| 5½ | L.Ljubojevic |

Cap d'Agde (France), October

4/5	B.Gelfand
3	M.Adams (5/6), B.Alterman (3½), H.Hamdouchi (3), Xie Jun (½)
2½	J.Lautier (1½/2), C.Lutz (½)
1½	V.Topalov (1½), P.Leko (½)
1	M.Apicella

Scores in brackets are quickplay play-off scores for final placings.

A ten-player, five-round, swiss of 'Young Masters', the winner to play match against Karpov.

B.Gelfand   0 1 = = (1 1)   A.Karpov

Karpov was doing most of the pressing in this mini-match against the slightly fortunate winner.

Game Thirty-Eight
Anatoly Karpov-Kiril Georgiev
Tilburg 1994

Kiril Georgiev recently ceded the first board of the Bulgarian team to the rising star Vaselin Topalov, but has maintained a steady 2600+ rating ensuring himself a top thirty world ranking. In the late-eighties he was particularly renowned for his prowess in blitz and quickplay chess.

1	d4	♘f6
2	c4	e6
3	♘f3	d5

Georgiev heads for the Orthodox Queen's Gambit Declined, one of Black's most solid defences to the queen's pawn.

| 4 | ♘c3 | ♗e7 |

5	♗g5	h6
6	♗h4	0-0
7	e3	b6

Tartakower's Defence, in which Black aims to fianchetto his queen's bishop, the problem piece in the Orthodox variation. The drawback of the line is an imperceptible weakening of Black's light squares on the queenside.

| 8 | ♗e2 | ♗b7 |
| 9 | ♗xf6 | |

To the uninitiated, a surprising move: three moves earlier White replied to 5...h6 with 6 ♗h4 and now he changes his mind and exchanges on f6 after all! White's strategy is in fact to give the game a static pawn structure whereupon his opponent's bishops have a limited role, and he commits himself to this gameplan only now that his opponent has chosen to move his b-pawn, as the Black queenside can be pressurized.

9	...	♗xf6
10	cxd5	exd5
11	b4!	

Hoping to restrain any ideas of queenside expansion by Black.

| 11 | ... | c6 |

This is cautious but more passive than the critical move 11...c5(!?) whereby Black immediately tries to break open the game for his bishops. Karpov himself preferred 11...c5 in several encounters with Kasparov in the marathon World Championship match in Moscow 1984/5. Their 42nd game continued 12 bxc5 bxc5 13 ♖b1 ♗c6 14 0-0 ♘d7 15 ♗b5 ♕c7 16 ♕c2 ♖fc8, Black has a potential weakness on d5 that offers White slightly the better chances.

After the text, the battle goes through a quiet phase as both camps organize their weaponry.

| 12 | 0-0 | ♕d6 |
| 13 | ♕b3 | ♘d7 |

If Black can organize the ...c6-c5 advance, he liberates his pieces at the cost of an inferior pawn structure. More typically, from the diagram position, Black sits and waits. White then has two plans of significance: playing for e4, when (after ...dxe4) Black's bishop on b7 sits passively behind the backward pawn on c6, or alternatively, he can advance on the queenside with b4-b5 or a2-a4-a5 to expose weaknesses.

| 14 | ♖fe1 |

An example of White playing solely on the queenside was 14 a4 ♖fe8 15 a5 ♖ad8 16 axb6 axb6 17 ♖a7 ♕b8 18 ♖a2 b5 (cutting out b4-b5 by White at the cost of being lumbered with sterile pawns) 19 ♘e1 ♗e7 20 ♘d3 ♗d6 21 g3 ♘b6 22 ♗f3 ♗c8 23 ♖fa1 ♗f5 24 ♘c5; Nikolic-Short, Manila Interzonal 1990. White has fine-looking pieces but its not clear that he can engineer a breakthrough. Black, as so typical of this line, must be patient.

Another queenside-oriented plan is, 'after due preparation', to play b4-b5 to loosen Black's grip on the d5 square. If Black ignores White's b5, then after the further bxc6 the d5 pawn is isolated and will require constant defence.

White then creates further problems in the black camp by advancing his a-pawn to fracture the remaining black queenside pawns.

Bearing this in mind, Black tends to arrange his pieces in order to meet White's b5 advance with the by-passing ...c6-c5. White therefore builds-up latent pressure on the d5 pawn (such as doubling on the d-file) to meet any ideas of ...c6-c5 with the exchange dxc5 followed by capturing the d5 pawn.

14   ...   ♝e7
15   ♜ab1   a5

Black gains some breathing space, not waiting for White to take total control.

16   bxa5   ♜xa5
17   a4!

The white pawns on a4 and d4 shepherd the pawns on b6 and c6 into passivity. White's isolated a-pawn is well defended and less of a defensive chore than Black's couplet.

17   ...   ♜e8
18   ♝f1

Karpov has already had this position before, when his opponent chose to exchange his inferior bishop with 18...♝a6, but after 19 ♝xa6 ♜xa6 20 e4 dxe4 21 ♞xe4 ♛g6 22 ♜e3 ♜b8 23 ♞c3 ♝d6 24 ♛c4 his c6 pawn came under pressure; Karpov - Bönsch, Baden-Baden 1992.

18   ...   ♝f8
19   ♛c2

Interesting is the immediate 19 e4!? dxe4 20 ♞xe4 as here Black doesn't have a satisfactory square for his queen on the kingside: 20...♛f4 21 g3 is unpleasant as is 20...♛g6 21 ♝d3 again hounding the queen.

19   ...   g6?!

Played in order to redeploy the king's bishop to the more active g7 square. However, 19...♜aa8, linking rooks was more prudent, the text is apparently self-weakening as Karpov is able to show.

20   e4!   dxe4
21   ♞xe4   ♛f4
22   ♝c4

White already takes up a threatening stance and combinations based on the weak light squares e8, f7 and g6 are in the air.

22   ...   ♝g7

White has a wide choice against 22...c5(?):

a) 23 d5 as in the game.

b) 23 ♞g3?! ♜xe1+ 24 ♜xe1 ♚h7! (better than 24...♝xf3 25 ♛xg6+ etc.) 25 d5 ♞f6 26 ♛b3 ♛d6 with counterplay, as White is tied down to the d5-pawn.

c) 23 ♞f6?!+ is not convincing as 23...♛xf6! (23...♞xf6? is bad after 24 ♛xg6+ ♚h8 25 ♛xf7) 24 ♜xe8 ♝xf3 25 gxf3 cxd4 26 ♝b5 ♞e5 gives the second player strong counterplay.

d) 23 ♞eg5! introduces complications that seem to leave Black in a sorry state: 23...♜xe1+ 24 ♜xe1 hxg5 25 ♛xg6+ ♚h8 (worse is 25...♝g7 due to 26

♘xg5) 26 ♕h5+ ♔g7 27 ♘xg5 ♕f5 28 ♗d3! (28 ♗xf7?! is inferior as after 28...cxd4 29 ♘e6+ ♔f6 30 ♕xf5+ ♖xf5 31 ♗e8 ♗b4 32 ♘xd4 ♗xe1 33 ♘xf5 ♗c6 Black is favourite) 28...♕xd3 29 ♕xf7+ ♔h8 (29...♔h6 30 ♖e6+ ♔xg5 31 h4+ wins) 30 ♕xd7 with more than adequate compensation with three pawns and the attack for the piece.

23   ♖e2   c5

With two minor pieces tied down to defending the queenside, the Bulgarian cannot just sit there while White turns the screw ever tighter. Black's queen bishop gains in influence but Karpov now has a passed d-pawn.

24   d5   ♖aa8
25   ♖be1   ♖ad8

Exchanges suit Black so 25...♘e5!? should be considered. However, this leaves the b6 square without its natural defender: 26 ♘xe5 ♖xe5 (after 26...♗xe5 27 g3 ♕f5 28 ♕b3 threatens 29 ♕xb6 and 29 ♘d6) 27 ♕b3 ♖ae8 28 f3! wins material as 28...f5 is refuted by 29 g3.

26   ♕b3

The direct threat of 27 a5 is easily parried but the mounting pressure against f7 is not so easily met.

26   ...   ♗a8
27   g3

Black's most active piece is forced to retreat.

27   ...   ♕b8

On 27...♕g4? then 28 h3!

when after 28...♕xh3 White forks with 29 ♘eg5 winning material by threatening both the queen and the rook on e8.

28   d6!   ♖f8

The text is natural but not satisfactory. A better chance was 28...♖xe4! 29 ♗xf7+ ♔h7 30 ♖xe4 ♗xe4 31 ♖xe4 ♘f8! (31...♘f6 loses to 32 ♗xg6+! ♔xg6 33 ♖e7 ♔h7 34 ♕f7 and White wins easily) 32 h4! (rather than 32 ♘e5?! ♗xe5! 33 ♖xe5 ♕xd6 and Black holds firm) 32...♕xd6 33 ♔g2! with the positional threat of h4-h5 loosening the Black king's protective cover. White keeps an edge despite the simplifications.

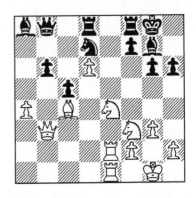

Karpov certainly goes for his combinations against Bulgarians (see game 11, Karpov-Topalov, Linares 1994)! Here the breakthrough is equally spectacular.

29   ♗xf7+!!

Chess books tend to describe such a move as a 'bolt from the blue'!

29   ...   ♖xf7

30	♘eg5!	hxg5
31	♘xg5	

Once a beginner has played only a few games of chess he learns that in the opening the f7 square is the 'Achilles' heel' of the black position. Karpov made no direct threats against the square until the 28th move but his rook sacrifice hinges on Black's difficulties in its defence.

31	...	♖df8

Hopeless is 31...♕xd6 32 ♕xf7+ ♔h8 33 ♖e7 ♕f6 34 ♖xd7 ♖f8 in view of 35 ♕xg7+! ♕xg7 36 ♖xg7 ♔xg7 37 ♘e6+ ♔g8 38 ♘xf8 ♔xf8 39 ♖e6 winning easily.

32	♖e8!

Stronger and certainly more attractive than 32 ♘xf7? because of 32...♘f6 when 33 ♘e5+ can be met by 33...♗d5.

32	...	♕xd6

This loses immediately but the alternatives offered no salvation:

a) 32...♖xe8 33 ♕xf7+ ♔h8 34 ♖xe8+ winning.

b) 32...♕b7 (with a serious counter threat!) is refuted by 33 ♕xf7+ ♔h8 34 ♖1e4 forcing 34...♕xe4 35 ♘xe4 ♗xe4 36 ♕xd7 and wins.

c) 32...c4 33 ♕xc4 ♘e5 34 ♖1xe5! ♕b7 35 ♕xf7+! ♕xf7 36 ♘xf7 ♔xf7 37 ♖5e7+ ♔f6 38 d7 and queens.

33	♕xf7+	♔h8
34	♘e6	1-0

Mate on g7 is unavoidable.

Game Thirty-Nine
Vladimir Akopian-Igor Khenkin
Tilburg 1994

Igor Khenkin is one of a new generation of émigrés from the ex-Soviet Union who now live in Israel. He is fairly active on the European circuit and was the sole winner in the Geneva open last January. Akopian is one of the top two Armenians (with Vaganian) and had a couple of equal firsts in strong internationals in 1994. He was eighteenth on the Intel (end of September 1994) ranking list.

1	e4	c5
2	♘f3	e6
3	b3	

Akopian is a hard man to prepare for due to his wide opening repertoire. He would generally play 3 d4 here, although he has in fact played the text before.

3	...	a6

Khenkin prefers to avoid the simplifying 4 ♗b5+. Instead, Vaiser continued 3...d6 in a 1993 encounter with Akopian, when 4 ♗b5+ ♗d7 5 ♗xd7+ ♘xd7 6 0-0 ♘gf6 7 ♖e1 ♗e7 8 ♗b2 0-0 9 c4 a6 10 d4 cxd4 11 ♘xd4 ♕c7 12 ♘c3 ♖fe8 13 ♕d2 yielded a slight space advantage for White although Black's position remained rock solid.

4 ♗b2 ♘c6
5 c4

An unusual position has arisen, White still retains the option of keeping the game closed or playing an early d4.

5 ... f6

Building a barricade along the long diagonal at the risk of upsetting the harmony of his own development. More conservative was 5...d6 intending ...♘f6, ...♗e7 and ...0-0.

6 ♗e2 ♘h6
7 0-0 e5

Putting the final bricks in the wall, now White must break up the structure before the cement dries!

8 ♘h4! ♗d6

Black is certainly coming up with an eccentric series of developing moves, this one is directed at restraining White's programmed f2-f4.

9 ♗h5+ g6

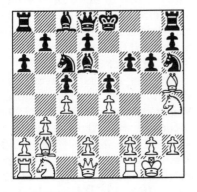

10 ♗xg6+!

The Armenian 'goes for gold'.

There is nothing immediate for White but the black queenside pieces cannot contribute to the defence of the other wing.

10 ... hxg6
11 ♘xg6 ♖g8
12 ♕h5 ♘f7
13 f4!

White must act swiftly as slower plans allow 13...♘e7 significantly easing the defensive task.

13 ... exf4
14 ♘c3 ♗e5

Playable is 14...♘e7 but after 15 ♘xe7 ♗xe7 16 ♘d5 d6 17 ♖xf4 ♗e6 18 ♖af1 ♗xd5 19 ♕xd5 ♖g6 20 ♕xb7 White has fantastic play for the piece.

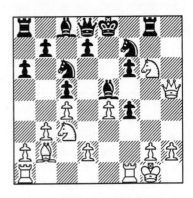

Everything is held together by the dark-squared bishop, the key to Black's defence.

15 ♖xf4!!

Aiming to blast open Black's king at all costs. At first sight it's difficult to believe that this audacious sacrifice can be sound but in a practical game the defence is hard to handle.

15 ... ♗xf4

There are two other tries but the text is best:

a) 15...d6 but White keeps up the pressure e.g. 16 ♖af1 ♗e6 17 ♘xe5 ♘cxe5 18 ♖xf6 ♕d7 19 ♘d5 ♗xd5 20 exd5 ♖g5 21 ♕h4 ♖g4 22 ♕h7 0-0-0 23 ♖xf7!, etc.

b) 15...♖xg6!? (eliminating a White attacker) deserves attention, but after 16 ♕xg6 the defence 16...♘e7 is unsatisfactory as following 17 ♕g7 ♗xf4 18 ♘d5 ♘xd5 19 exd5 ♗e5 20 d6! White crashes through. No better is 16...♗xf4 due to 17 ♘d5 with threats of mate and general butchery, e.g. 17...♔f8 18 ♗xf6 ♕xf6 19 ♘xf6 ♗e5 (19...♘e7 goes down to 20 ♘h7+ ♔e8 21 ♕g7 etc.) 20 ♕g8+ ♔e7 21 ♘d5+ and it is all over.

16 ♘d5!

Black has an extra rook and piece but the storm clouds are gathering!

16 ... ♘ce5!

Giving back some material to try and get developed.

Critical is the alternative 16...♗e5 (after 16...♗g5 17 h4 the defences to the f6 square are breached) when after 17 ♗xe5 there are two ways to recapture:

a) 17...fxe5 works well against 18 ♖f1? because of 18...♕g5! exchanging queens, but instead Akopian intended 18 h4! (it's amazing that despite being so much material down he can take his time) and there is no defence to the follow up 19 ♖f1 and 20

♘f6+, winning the queen and continuing the attack.

b) 17...♘cxe5 18 ♘xe5 fxe5 19 ♖f1 ♖f8 20 ♖xf7! ♖xf7 21 ♕xe5+ ♕e7 22 ♘xe7 ♖xe7 23 ♕xc5 (or 23 ♕h8+ ♔f7 24 e5) with a complicated game where White probably retains the advantage.

17 ♘dxf4 d6

18 ♖f1

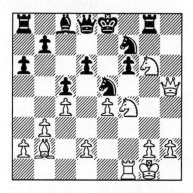

White has mobilized his whole army. Can Black defend?

18 ... ♖g7?

Tempting is 18...♗g4? but after 19 ♕h7 ♖xg6 20 ♘xg6 (the threat is 21 ♗xe5 and then 22 ♕g8+) Black has nothing better than 20...♗e6 losing a tempo over the variation below.

Best is 18...♖xg6! 19 ♘xg6 ♗e6 20 ♕h7 b5!? with unclear complications. White is always a piece down but should pick up the weak f6 pawn with enough material compensation.

19 ♗xe5 fxe5

After the other capture (19...dxe5) then 20 ♘d5 followed

by capturing on f6 is decisive.

20 ♘d5 ♔d7?!

More robust is 20...♕g5 21 ♕xg5 ♘xg5 22 ♖f8+ ♔d7 when White (with 23 ♘b6+ ♔c6 24 ♘xa8) wins back a rook leaving him two pawns ahead. Black can struggle on in view of the opposing knight temporarily stuck in the corner although Akopian believes that White is winning after 24...♗d7 25 ♖g8!, etc.

21 ♕f5+ ♔e8

Following 21...♔c6, the routine 22 ♘ge7+ forces the win of Black's queen.

22 ♘f6+ 1-0

Game Forty
Hicham Hamdouchi-Joel Lautier
Cap d'Agde 1994

Hicham Hamdouchi, the top African player of all time, is temporarily resident in Montpellier, France where he is completing his studies. He was the second African player to be awarded the grandmaster title (the first was Slim Bouaziz of Tunisia) and showed good form on top board for Morocco in the recent Moscow Olympiad.

1 e4 c5
2 ♘f3 e6
3 d4 cxd4
4 ♘xd4 ♘c6
5 ♘c3 ♕c7
6 g3

Hicham regularly adopts this safe method of developing the king's bishop to avoid any nasty surprises in the Sicilian Defence.

6 ... a6

Black's move-order is very flexible; we have reverted to the so-called Paulsen variation but after the moves that follow most commentators would probably call the game a Schevenigen.

7 ♗g2 ♘f6
8 0-0 ♗e7
9 ♗e3 0-0
10 f4

Another plan is to play 10 ♕e2 and 11 ♖ad1 before committing any pawns.

10 ... d6
11 ♔h1!? ♖b8
12 a4

A prophylactic move as Black was ready to play 12...♘xd4 13 ♘xd4 b5.

12 ... ♖e8

This precise position is known but not that common. One recent example was 13 ♕e2 ♗d7 14 ♘b3 ♘a5 15 g4!? (15 ♘xa5 ♕xa5 16 g4 ♗c6 17 g5 is more conventional, and offers equally good chances for an attack) 15...♘xb3 16 cxb3 ♗c6 17 g5 ♘d7 18 b4! and White took the initiative on both wings in Topalov-Lautier, Las Palmas 1994. White has a potentially weak pawn structure so if Black can ride out the storm he has good prospects in an ending.

12...♖d8!? could be better. The rook has a role to play on e8 if White intends putting his queen on e2 but Hamdouchi's next makes the text look out of place.

13 e5!

An inspired pawn sacrifice to take the leading French player (who is known for the quality of his preparation) out of the book and set some unexpected problems.

13 ... ♘xd4

Joel had a difficult choice. White has strong attacking chances for the pawn after the critical 13...dxe5, e.g. 14 fxe5 (14 ♘xc6 is possible, settling for an edge after 14...bxc6 15 fxe5 ♘d5 16 ♗d4) 14...♘xe5 15 ♗f4 ♘fd7 16 h4 (stopping 16...g5 releasing the pin) which is unpleasant for Black who has great difficulty completing his development.

14 ♗xd4 ♘d7
15 ♕g4 dxe5

After 15...g6 16 exd6?! ♗xd6 17 ♘e4? f5! Black wins, so 16 ♘e4 heading towards Black's weakened kingside should be tried. Closing the centre with 15...d5?! is met with 16 ♖ae1 followed by a quick f4-f5 giving White a strong attack, Black should really try to open lines so that White's king will also feel insecure.

16 fxe5 ♗c5

The best chance. After 16...b6?

White smashes through with 17 ♖xf7! ♔xf7 18 ♕h5+ ♔f8 19 ♖f1+ ♘f6 20 exf6 ♗xf6 21 ♗e5 ♕a7 22 ♗xf6 gxf6 23 ♖xf6+ ♔g7 24 ♖f1 and the attack is decisive. Lautier dare not take the pawn by 16...♘xe5?! as 17 ♕h5 ♘g6 (hopeless is 17...♗d6 as 18 ♘e4 ♘g6 19 ♘g5 wins quickly) 18 ♖xf7! ♔xf7 19 ♕xh7 ♘e5 20 ♕h5+ yields a winning attack.

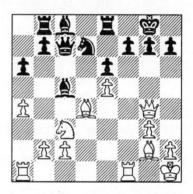

The fianchetto of the light-squared bishop is often considered to be not that testing. However, Hamdouchi uses this plan to first slow Black's queenside play, before launching an attack that is just as dangerous as in the more direct lines. Here Lautier has been unable to get his queenside going and his king is inadequately defended.

17 ♘d5!! exd5
18 ♖xf7!

The Moroccan shows no respect for Lautier's king!

18 ... ♗f8?

Weak is 18...g6 as after 19 ♗xd5 Black has no moves, but

the best defence is undoubtedly 18...♔xf7(!). It seems suicidal to allow his king to be battered by the remaining white pieces but there is a hidden resource that might have earned him a draw! Following 18...♔xf7 then play continues 19 ♗xd5+ ♔e7 (19...♔f8 is best met by 20 ♕f4+! when he should transpose with 20...♔e7! rather than 20...♘f6 21 exf6 ♕xf4 22 ♗xc5+ and wins) 20 ♕g5+ ♘f6 21 exf6+ gxf6! (losing is 21...♔d7 due to 22 ♕xg7+ ♔d8 23 ♕xc7+ ♔xc7 24 f7 ♗e6 25 ♗e5+ ♗d6 26 fxe8♘+ ♖xe8 27 ♗xd6+ ♔xd6 28 ♗xe6 ♖xe6 29 ♖d1+ ♔c6 30 ♖d2) 22 ♗xf6+ ♔d7 23 ♖d1!? (drawing is 23 ♕f5+ ♔d6 24 ♕f4+ ♔d7 25 ♕f5+ ♔d6 26 ♕f4+) 23...♕d6! 24 ♗f3 ♔c7! and White cannot take the queen because of mate in two (25 ♖xd6 ♖e1+ 26 ♔g2 ♖g1 mate). I showed Hicham my analysis, claiming that Black could draw, but next day the amiable Moroccan came up with 24 b4! (instead of 24 ♗f3?) which seems to enable White to keep an advantage. Having missed 18...♔xf7!, from here on Lautier has no chance.

19   ♗xd5   ♔h8
20   ♖af1

Look at the power of the white pieces! In fact he only has a small material deficit (two pawns for a piece) so its no surprise that the black position is indefensible.

20   ...   ♕d8
21   ♕f3!

Tripling on the f-file and avoiding any counter tactics against the queen on the exposed g4 square. The threat is 22 e6 ♘f6 23 ♖xf6! gxf6 24 ♗xf6+ winning the house.

21   ...   ♗e7

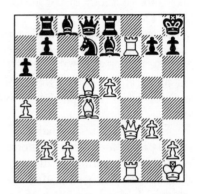

The combinations are not yet finished!

22   ♖xg7!   ♔xg7

Equally hopeless is 22...♖f8 as 23 ♕xf8+! ♕xf8 24 ♖xf8+ ♔xg7 (24...♗xf8 allows mate in one) 25 ♖g8+ ♔h6 26 ♗e3+ mates.

23   ♕f7+   ♔h6

The corner offers no salvation; 23...♔h8 24 e6+ ♘f6 25 ♖xf6! ♕xd5+ 26 ♖f3+ ♕xd4 27 ♕xe8+ ♔g7 28 ♕xe7+ and White again wins.

24   h4!

Its always nice to finish off a cascade of sacrifices with a 'quiet move' although the threat of 25 ♗e3+ can hardly be called 'quiet'! Naturally enough 24...♗xh4 25 ♗e3+ ♗g5 fails to 26 ♔g2! ♗xe3 27 ♖h1+ ♔g5 28 ♕h5 mate.

24 ... ♗g5

White could try for a flashy mate with 25 ♔g2 but there is no need, as by 'cashing in' he has a simply winning position.

25 hxg5+ ♛xg5
26 ♛xe8 ♛xg3
27 ♛e6+ ♛g6

For the record 27...♔g7 loses to 28 ♖f7+ and 27...♔g5 to 28 ♖f5+ ♔g4 29 ♖f7+ and mates.

28 ♗e3+ ♔h5

There is evidently nowhere to hide; 28...♔g7 29 ♛e7+ ♔h8 30 ♛d8+ ♔g7 31 ♛g8+, etc.

29 ♛h3+ 1-0

Lautier's recent progress has been impressive but he still loses too many one-sided games with Black.

Game Forty-One
Boris Gulko-Smbat Lputian
Glendale 1994

Boris Gulko was the celebrated victim of a human rights scandal in the 1980s that aged him prematurely, but has maintained a standard of play that was good enough to qualify for the 1994 PCA Candidates. He won the strong Bern open in February and was recently ranked a close third in the US (behind Kamsky and Kaidanov) and thirty-three worldwide (in the Intel 30th September ranking list). He has a rare positive score against Kasparov and would probably have established himself in the world top ten if his freedom hadn't been severely restricted by the Soviet authorities.

1 c4 e6
2 ♘c3 d5
3 d4 ♗e7!?

The Armenian uses a move order that forces White to show his hand. After the standard 3...♘f6 White has the option of 4 cxd5 exd5 5 ♗g5, whereas in the game if he wishes to play a type of exchange variation then he has to be content to develop his bishop on f4.

4 cxd5

After 4 ♘f3 ♘f6 Black has transposed to a typical Orthodox Queen's Gambit where White has been obliged to play the less testing move ♘f3. The most active continuation being 1 d4 d5 2 c4 e6 3 ♘c3 ♘f6 4 ♗g5.

4 ... exd5
5 ♗f4 c6
6 e3

The diagonal b1-h7 has more than passing significance; if White can establish himself with ♗f1-d3 then Black has lost control of f5, the best square for his own bishop. Control of the diagonal aids White in pursuing a number of plans such as ♖b1 intending the so-called minority attack with b2-b4-b5.

6　...　♗f5
7　g4!

A move popularized by Botvinnik that immediately challenges the bishop.

7　...　♗e6

The alternative 7...♗g6 is challenged most effectively by the aggressive 8 h4! h5 (8...♗xh4 9 ♕b3 is similar, but even more favourable than in the game as the bishop on g6 doesn't directly support the centre) 9 g5 ♗d6 10 ♘ge2 ♘e7 11 ♗xd6 ♕xd6 12 ♘f4 with ideas of taking the h-pawn with ♗f1-e2, etc.

8　h4!?

Inferior is 8 h3 h5 9 ♕f3?! ♘f6 10 ♗d3 hxg4 11 hxg4 ♖xh1 12 ♕xh1 ♘xg4! 13 ♕h8+ ♔d7 14 ♕xg7 as 14...♕b6 15 ♖b1 ♘a6 proved to be better for Black in Flear-Ubilava, Elgoibar 1994. 8 ♗d3 is the consistent positional move, taking the important b1-h7 diagonal, but with the sharp text Gulko shows that he is in aggressive mood and plays for more.

8　...　♗xh4

The books tend to consider this pawn-grab as risky and prefer 8...♘d7 9 h5 ♕b6 where White establishes a space preponderance on the kingside but Black prepares his ...c6-c5 counter in the centre.

9　♕b3　b6

Black has to be careful to avoid 9...g5 10 ♗h2 ♗xg4?! 11 ♕xb7 ♕e7 12 ♕xa8 ♕xe3+ 13 ♗e2 ♕xf2+ 14 ♔d2 and White is winning; Vaiser-Diaz, Havana

1985. The text avoids the White incursion into b7 but weakens the c6 square.

10　♘f3　♗e7
11　♘e5

For his pawn White has the better development.

11　...　♘f6
12　g5　♘fd7

The Armenian is intent on evicting the knight that is holding up the development of his queenside.

13　g6!

As is necessary in gambit play, White 'strikes while the iron is hot'.

13　...　♘xe5
14　♗xe5　♗f6!

The inferior 14...fxg6?! allows his opponent to win back the pawn and maintain the initiative with 15 ♗xg7 ♖g8 16 ♖xh7 and Black's king would in this case be a long way from a secure shelter.

15　♖xh7

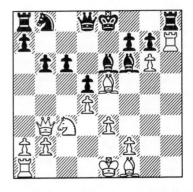

Lputian temporarily gives back the pawn, but with his next move

aims to rapidly deploy the rest of his army.

15 ... 0-0!

Not a question of 'castling into it', more giving the king an active role in tripping up the American's attack. White's heavy artillery is too distant to support the rather lonely rook on h7.

16 ♗g3

Weaker is 16 ♗d3?! as after 16...♗xe5 17 gxf7+ ♖xf7 18 dxe5 ♗f5 Black wins a pawn and White's initiative offers inadequate compensation, e.g. 19 ♗xf5 ♖xf5 20 ♖h2 ♖xe5 21 0-0-0 ♘d7 22 ♖dh1 ♔f7.

16 ... fxg6
17 ♖h2 ♔f7

Seeking a more secure shelter and defending both the extra pawn on g6 as well as the bishop on e6. The immediate 17...♘d7 could have been considered.

18 0-0-0 ♖h8?

A shame! Smbat Lputian had skilfully calmed Gulko's attacking postures but now wastes time challenging for the h-file, which has ceased to be important. Completing development by 18...♘d7 intending ...♗e7 and ...♘d7-f6 would construct a rock-solid defence.

19 ♖xh8 ♕xh8
20 e4!

The second phase commences, White again leads in development and he aims to get at Black's monarch.

20 ... ♕h5

Dangerous is 20...dxe4 21 ♗c4

♕e8 22 ♘xe4 ♗xc4 23 ♕xc4+ ♕e6 24 ♘d6+ ♔e7 25 ♕f1! as it allows the opening of too many lines near the black king.

21 ♖e1 ♘d7

Finally getting the knight into play but its rather late!

22 exd5 ♗xd5

The other recapture, 22...cxd5, is dismissed by 23 ♖xe6! ♔xe6 24 ♘xd5 when 24...♕xd5 is met by 25 ♗h3+ winning the queen and 24...♕g5+ by 25 ♗f4 etc., so Black is unable to avoid a disastrous discovered check.

23 ♘xd5 cxd5
24 ♗g2

White picks up the d5 pawn and continues the attack.

24 ... ♖c8+
25 ♔b1 ♖e8
26 ♗xd5+ ♔f8
27 ♖h1 ♕f5+
28 ♔a1

Material is equal but not the position; White threatens 29 ♗d6+ ♗e7 30 ♖h8 mate and Black is therefore obliged to (again!) centralize his king where it faces a brutal treatment at the hands of the white army.

28 ... ♔e7
29 ♕a3+ ♔d8
30 ♕d6

Threatening both 31 ♖c1 followed by 32 ♖c8+ and 33 ♕c7 mate and 31 ♕c7+ ♔e7 32 ♖e1+.

30 ... ♕c2
31 ♗c6 ♕f5
32 ♕c7+ ♔e7
33 ♗d6+ 1-0

After 33...♔f7 34 ♗xd7 wins.

1994 at a Glance

The key events of the year were:

1. Kamsky and Anand win through to the PCA Candidates final.

2. Kamsky (again!), Gelfand and Salov are the survivors in the FIDE cycle and join Karpov in the semi-finals.

3. Karpov's Linares result is hailed as the world's best ever tournament performance.

4. Judit Polgar is confirmed as the strongest-ever female player as a result of her elevated rating and remarkable victory in Madrid.

5. Other notable achievements: Leko becomes the world's youngest-ever grandmaster, and Hamdouchi the strongest-ever African player.

6. Kramnik and Kasparov share the inaugural Intel Grand Prix quick-play crown.

7. The best computers make further progress in rapid chess; even Kasparov loses on more than one occasion (Fritz 3/ Pentium in Munich and Pentium Genius in London).

8. Zsusza Polgar will play Maia Chiburdanidze for the right to challenge Xie Jun for the Women's World Championship after they finished first and second respectively in the Tilburg Candidates.

9. Kasparov's Russian team take Olympiad gold, and in the women's event Georgia outpace favourites Hungary.

10. The PCA and FIDE settle their differences in Moscow in December, where Campomanes is elected FIDE President for another term.

Index of Complete Games

Numbers refer to game numbers.